REAL~ING
~ TO ~
WRITING:
FORM AND MEANING

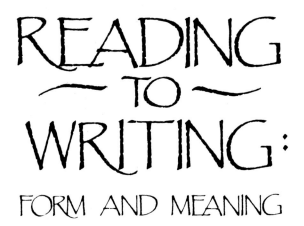

READING ~ TO ~ WRITING:

FORM AND MEANING

~JACK O'KEEFE~

RICHARD J. DALEY COLLEGE

HARCOURT BRACE JOVANOVICH, PUBLISHERS
San Diego   New York   Chicago   Austin
London   Sydney   Tokyo   Toronto

Cover credit: Lori Lohstoeter, Illustrator

ISBN: 0-15-575784-9
Library of Congress Catalog Card Number: 90-84206

Printed in the United States of America

Copyrights and acknowledgments appear on pp. 298–99, which constitute a continuation of the copyright page.

*To my wife Phyllis and our sons Jack, Kevin, and Denis
who have loved and encouraged me through it all*

PREFACE

Reading and writing are lifetime skills. Improving abilities in both areas will not only make you better students, it will also serve you long after school. Unlike most composition textbooks, *Reading to Writing: Form and Meaning* is designed to produce better readers as well as better writers. More than thirty samples of student and professional writing are provided for analysis, for discussion in class, and as both models and starting points for writing. The readings include newspaper and magazine articles, excerpts from books, a government publication, essays, and even poetry.

The text is organized like a workbook. Discussions on the reading and writing processes alternate with reading selections and lessons on grammar, mechanics, punctuation, diction, writing effective sentences, and "word demons." Several kinds of exercises are included to improve reading comprehension and to stimulate better and more writing. Readings are accompanied by exercises in prereading, prediction, vocabulary, and comprehension. Writing assignments are based on the readings. Peer writing assignments provide an opportunity to work in small groups, helping to revise and proofread one another's work. Simulation games help students become more involved in the writing process by assuming roles in a dramatic situation. These can be especially effective in teaching argument and persuasion.

Parts One and Two introduce students to the writing and reading processes, using both student and professional samples to illustrate prewriting, drafting, and revision. A chapter on writing effective sentences includes exercises on sentence variety, parallel structure, sentence fragments, sentence economy, and the run-on sentence. There is also a chapter on how to develop paragraphs using the reporter's questions of *who, what, when, where, how,* and *why.*

Parts Three and Four focus on writing a short essay, with separate chapters on the different types or modes of writing most often required in college writing—description, narration, exposition, persuasion, and argumentation. Students are provided several recent, topical articles to read on such subjects as AIDS, the use of steroids, pollution of the environment, and teenage pregnancy.

Parts Five and Six address miscellaneous problem areas for students—the correct documentation of sources; using quotations, paraphrases, and summaries in the body of the paper; writing essays for subjects other than English; preparing for content or exit essay exams; and the proper formats for job application letters and resumes.

I would like to thank Dr. Robert Coogan, Edward L. Surtz, S.J., Brother Daniel Crimmins, Dr. Barbara Kessell, Dr. James Lalley, Dr. Beverly Tinsley, Donald Murray, and Dr. Robert Wise for their guidance and inspiration, and Dr. Janice Lauer and her colleagues at the Purdue Rhetoric Seminar for renewing my interest in writing theory. Eric P. Hibbison, J. Sargent Reynolds Community College; John Roggenbeck, Henry Ford Community College; and Judith Hancock, Amarillo College, provided valuable reviews and numerous helpful suggestions. I am also indebted to my students and fellow teachers at Malcolm X College and Richard J. Daley College for their contributions and continued support. I would especially like to thank David Rodriguez, Chontella Cooks, Jacqueline Robinson, Ernesto Ayala, Debra Salvato, Marsha Grayer, Steve Espinosa, and Sandra Olea for the use of their essays.

At Harcourt Brace Jovanovich I am grateful to Stuart Miller for his patience and care, and to Jain Simmons who got me started. Christopher Nelson has been a kind, painstaking editor. Sheila Spahn has been a devoted production editor. Kay Faust has directed the art admirably. Mary Kay Yearin has been an effective production manager. Eleanor Garner has worked hard to procure a great number of permissions from different sources.

Jack O'Keefe

CONTENTS

—— PART ——
TWO

The Process at Work: Learning from Writing Models   79

—— PART ——
THREE

Types of Writing   123

READING ~ TO ~ WRITING:

FORM AND MEANING

PART
ONE

Learning and Using the Writing and Reading Processes

▲▲▲

CHAPTER

1

Getting Started

PREWRITING

For many students the hardest part of writing is getting started, overcoming what is called "writer's block." Recently, writing teachers have developed several "prewriting" techniques to help students begin the writing process. Prewriting is simply the first stage in writing. The other steps in the process are writing, in which you try to put your ideas down in readable form; revision, in which you may make important changes to what you have already written; and proofreading, in which you correct mechanical errors like spelling and punctuation. These stages often overlap, but thinking of them as distinct steps takes some of the mystery out of writing and makes it more manageable.

Brainstorming, freewriting, looping, and clustering are prewriting techniques that you can use in all your writing. In the beginning, you should try them all to see which one is best for you. Whether you like one technique or another depends on your own personal learning style; for example, clustering may appeal to someone who is visually oriented, brainstorming to a person who is more spontaneous than logical.

Brainstorming

Brainstorming is a prewriting technique in which you list as fast as possible whatever comes to mind, regardless of whether or not it makes any sense. The two rules of brainstorming are to write without stopping and to not make any corrections or scratch anything out once it is written down. When you have completed your list, circle or underline anything that *surprises* you, that you wouldn't have expected to make its way onto your paper. Then indicate any *repeaters*, marking with a check or drawing lines between things on your list that, even if worded a little differently, express the same thought or feeling. Things that surprise or repeat often make good subjects to write more about. Here is one student's brainstorming list on the topic, Why attend college?

first in my family

want to get ahead

more serious than high school

much more expensive ✓

work and go to school

cut down social life

mixed group of students - age and race

nervous ✓

don't want to screw up ✓

four classes

this teacher serious ?

is he mean ?

lots of assignments

books very expensive ✓

8:00 in morning comes fast

coffee and out

bus ride almost an hour ✓

college worth this grief ?

improve study habits

set goals for myself

make a schedule

get organized

In the list above, the student is surprised by the key question, Is college worth the grief? The ideas that repeat in the list—being nervous, worries about expenses, the long early-morning bus ride—all lead to the main point, and provide him with more possible material.

Here is a brainstorming list by another student on the same topic:

Why College?

better job   respect from others
security   for my family
my self-esteem   for myself
for my kids   improve my self-image
open field   I know I can do it
better opportunities   be someone
respect from people   read better
better life   understanding
more money   GPA up
improve skills   reading score up
learn   I'm up
never too late   I will make it
exciting people   money
new friends   more money
hate factory work   nice home

From this list she has focused on:

for my kids   learn
better opportunities   respect from others
respect from people   for my family
better life   for myself
improve skills   I know I can do it

What follows is the first draft of a paper, errors included, the student wrote from her brainstorming list. As you read, try to find how many of these ideas found their way into her paper.

Why College?

"I know I can do it!," I always tell myself these few words of wisdom whenever I feel that I am going to fail; and they've always worked for me.

You may ask yourself "Why should I go to college?," well I don't know why for you, but I sure know why I am attending college. A few of the many reasons that I am going to college is that I want to earn a degree, provide a better life for my family, and be respected by others, and to me there is no better way to fulfill my dreams, than to be in college and earn a degree.

I am attending college so I can become a Registered Nurse, specializing in Operating Room or Labor and Delivery Room Nurse, and to do this I must take many classes such as many math, science, reading, and writing classes even before I can be accepted in the nursing program. To graduate from the nursing program it takes 2 years to finish the program. I always dreamed of becoming a nurse, and now that there is a chance I am going for it.

Another reason that I am going to college is to provide a better life for my children. I have two handsome little boys Jorge 5½, and Danny 3 years old, and a understanding husband that allows and encourages me to go to school. I feel we deserve better than what we have now. I want my boys to grow up in a better neighborhood and have an example of someone, so they can also have encouragement to become an important person in life.

I also want respect from people. I am tired of people just looking at me as a plain person. I want everyone to look at me and say," Hey I am proud of you, I knew you could do it," I want everyone to look up at me with admiration. I feel a person can do whatever it is they want to do, well in my opinion, there is no excuse for not doing your best. We only make things harder on ourselves. Life is a great thing to enjoy, take advantage of the opportunities that come your way and you will see that you will meet success.

Freewriting and Looping

Another prewriting technique to help you get started is freewriting, putting down thoughts as fast as you can in rough sentence form without worrying about mechanics, grammar, spelling, or punctuation. In "focused freewriting" you write about a definite topic for ten minutes without stopping or changing anything you have written. When you are done, look it over again and pick the key point, an idea that you think you could write more about.

Here is one student's ten-minute freewriting about her first day in college:

Promotion at work, today is payday (I'm sleepy) this class seems like it's gonna be interesting, is it still cold outside, i'm hungry, I hope the bus doesnt take long, I hope this don't be a long hour. it's real quiet in here, I hope I get get home from work in time to see Johnny Carson, I have to take my dog to the vet tomorrow need a cigarrett, my spelling terribile, the sun is too bright, I think ill have burger King after school, handwriting is sloppy

In reviewing her freewriting, she picks "I'm sleepy" as the thought that keeps coming back to her. She feels she could write more about this idea.

Looping is a prewriting technique that uses one freewriting as the subject of two more freewritings, each building on the previous one. From her first freewriting, the student wrote more about "I'm sleepy" in a second freewriting:

I think I can handle working full-time and going to school full-time but it's becoming sort of hard I only have about 4 hours of sleep Mon-Thur and about 3 hours for homework on those days. This isn't normal for a person of my age I need sleep. I think when I finally do get some sleep I'll sleep for a day or two, if I have time. I'm not sure if I can really handle a promotion at work because the hours our going to kill me. I'm in the training program now 8 hrs a day. I get no sleep!

In this short paragraph, she reveals that her lack of sleep is a result of her attempt to both attend school full-time and work full-time. She realizes that there is a conflict between the demands of school and work.

With this second freewriting to guide her, the student drafted a longer freewriting, completing the "looping" process:

I'm really worried about whether or not I'll be able to pass all my courses. College is nothing like I imagined it to be financially. It's really hard trying to pay my way through school. Money is only half of it, actually attending classes in the morning, and working nights is a drag. Monday thru Thursday I only get about five hour of sleep. I feel like I am going in circles. I feel like a walking zombie whose bandages are going to unravel any second now.

Not only is school alot of pressure, so is my job. I work for a marketing research firm where all I do is conduct telephone interviews on the phone for six hours. Recently me and two other people have been selected to go through a training to become a assistant supervisors. There is three of us and only one position. From the moment I enter the door at work i'm constantly trying to make a good impression among my employers so that I will be the chosen one for position. When I leave work my mind goes back to school.

I am obsessed with becoming a nurse, it's all I think about. Being a nurse is the only reason why I am so enthused about school, because I know each day that I go to school brings me closer and closer to my goal.

There are problems here with agreement and punctuation, but the writer can work on those later. The paper is clear and to the point. The first paragraph talks about her problems with school and lack of sleep, the second about her job, and the last paragraph explains why she puts herself through this struggle: she wishes to be a nurse. Notice in the paper how sentences and phrases from her last freewriting repeat; for example, "Monday thru Thursday I only get about five hours of sleep." Looping gives her a place to begin, a process on which to build further writing.

Clustering

Clustering, sometimes called mapping or webbing, is a prewriting technique that provides a visual stimulus for writing. Start by writing down a phrase or an idea in the middle of a piece of paper and draw a "bubble" around it as in the student example below, "first day of school jitters." Then draw lines to other words or phrases—also indicated by bubbles— that relate to the original phrase, for example, "goal." Under "goal" a new cluster of words pops into the writer's mind, such as "nurse," leading her to think about "qualifications" for that career like "school" and "clinical experience" in hospitals.

A different cluster of words springs from the student's normal "fear of failure": she has "been away from school so long" and is "older than most." The student is also intimidated by a "teacher" who is "all business." She also realizes that school is a "new start," leading her to think of personal "responsibilities," such as "helping with the income" of the family, including the children's "private school tuition" that needs to be paid. By going to college, the student knows, too, that she provides the "kids" an "example of the importance of school."

Writing Practice

1. Brainstorm for ten minutes about how you are doing and feeling in school right now. List as fast as you can whatever comes to mind. Remember the two rules of brainstorming: write without stopping and don't make corrections or scratch anything out. Once you have completed your list, go back over it and indicate any surprises or repeaters.

2. Freewrite for ten minutes about how you are doing and feeling in school.

3. Using the freewriting in exercise 2 above, try looping. Pick something from your first freewriting and write about it two more times.

4. Now try clustering ideas about how you are doing and feeling in school. Use lines and bubbles to connect related ideas.

5. Write a longer paper about the beginning of the school year, using one of the exercises above as your prewriting.

JOURNAL WRITING

One of the most organized and systematic ways to practice writing is to write every day in a journal. Try to set aside a time and a place for your journal work. Put down the date and then either brainstorm or freewrite as quickly as you can for ten minutes each day, not worrying about grammar, mechanics, punctuation, or spelling. Some days your work will come easily; at other times you will feel blocked. Just keep writing. The only people who will look at your journal are you and your teacher, so this kind of writing gives you the chance to take some risks with what you say and how you say it.

A journal is not a diary. Concentrate your thoughts and feelings on important people and events in your life. Some important topics for you might be:

▲ problems at school
▲ success at school
▲ people important to you
▲ events important to you
▲ your goals—educational, career, and life
▲ important decisions you have made
▲ gains or losses in your life
▲ your personal heroes

When writing about events in your life, use the reporter's questions of *who, what, where, when, how,* and/or *why.* Answering these questions will provide you with factual information and give you a pattern to use. For example, for each journal entry tell *who* was involved, *what* happened, *where* it took place, *when* it happened, and *how* and/or *why* it happened. Besides providing a format for you to practice your writing skills every day, a journal can also be a source of information for both future essays and questions you have about the work you're doing in school right now.

SUBJECT, PURPOSE, AUDIENCE, AND THESIS

Every piece of writing has a purpose. Many things you write—a shopping list, a reminder on the refrigerator, lecture notes—are written for yourself, to remember or perhaps learn more about something. You are the audience for such writing. Other kinds of writing, however, have different purposes and different audiences that will determine what you say and how you say it.

The purpose of writing is linked with the concept of audience—for whom you are writing. The type of audience will influence both the purpose and subject of your writing. Letters complaining about a company's faulty product or correspondence to a boyfriend or girlfriend have obvious audiences that guide the message and form of your writing. The purpose of writing may change; for example, journal writing originally written for yourself may some day form the contents of a paper for the more public audience of your teacher and classmates. It is this audience you must analyze to see how you can best communicate with them.

For what purpose are you writing? Personal writing helps you to *remember*, to *learn more* about your thoughts and feelings. You may also write to *explain*, to *inform*, or to *persuade* your teacher and classmates. Often you write for a combination of purposes, for example, to inform and to *entertain*—as in a humorous letter to a friend about the adventures of college life. Or you might explain and persuade in an essay about the harmful effects of steroids. To help clarify the subject and purpose of your writing, you must ask who makes up the audience for every writing assignment. Different audiences will need to know different things and have them said in different ways. Here are the kinds of questions you should ask yourself about your intended audience:

1. What is the age, sex, and economic and racial background of your audience? Perhaps they are a mixed group of young and old, male and female, black and white.

2. What do they know about the subject? Will they be sympathetic or not?

3. How can you frame your message and writing to this group? How can you best get and hold their attention?

Answers to these questions will sharpen your purpose and focus in writing.

For everything you write, then, you must consider the *subject*—what the writing is about; the *purpose*—what you are trying to do in the paper;

and the *audience*—how they will respond to what you say. As you gather more information about your subject and your audience, you can narrow your thoughts to a central *thesis*, or *main idea*. It is this idea you wish to leave with your audience. These examples illustrate how the writer progresses from subject to thesis:

Subject	Purpose	Thesis
first week in college	to explain your feelings	School is hell.
steroids	to inform and warn	Steroids are killers.
boxing	to persuade	Boxing should be banned.

Writing for a specific audience helps form and narrow your purpose and thesis. In the above example, "first week in college," the student may be writing to his teacher and classmates or to a close personal friend. But the writer might not say the same things in a letter to his parents, who have invested thousands of dollars in his college career. The two letters will differ in their purpose and thesis because they are written for two different audiences. The writer may wish to inform his friend that "school is hell" to get some sympathy. For his parents, the writer might want to give them assurances that all is well.

In every piece of writing, the subject, purpose, audience, and thesis are so tightly linked that a change in one affects the others. For example, a change in your audience will affect what you say and your reasons for saying it. Analysis of your audience will define further why you are writing, how much your audience needs to know, and what you are going to tell them. So for every writing assignment, remember to consider your subject, purpose, audience, and thesis.

Writing Practice

1. Write a letter about troubles in the first week of school to a friend of yours who chose not to attend college. Then write a reassuring letter about the first week in college to your parents, anxious for your success.

2. You have placed an advertisement in the paper to sell your used car. A potential buyer responds by asking you for a written description of the features and condition of the car before making a long trip over to see it. Write a letter back encouraging the prospective buyer. Then write a letter to a friend away at school telling what the car is really like.

3. During a visit to the shopping mall, unobserved, you see the boyfriend/girlfriend of your best friend (now away at school) emotionally involved with someone else. Write a letter to your friend about your discovery. Then write a letter about the same incident to a mutual friend.

IMPROVING YOUR READING

Have you ever caught yourself staring at a page of a book you have been reading for a few minutes, only to realize you don't remember anything you've just read? One way to help solve this problem is to become an active reader, keeping yourself awake and alert while you read. There are several ways to do this. One is to take notes with a pencil while you read, underlining key words or ideas. Another is to make small checks in the margin when you find your attention wandering. Reading with a pencil in hand to underline, mark sentences, or make checks will help you keep your interest.

The keen, alert reader uses all the cues or hints in the reading material to help derive meaning; this technique is called "prereading." The title or headline, and photos or illustrations, especially those with captions or explanations, are aids for your reading. Always look at all these hints before reading the text. Like prewriting, prereading warms you up and prepares you for more reading.

Reading as a Process

Like writing, reading is a process with complex and interrelated steps. You can become a better reader if you have a strategy or plan for reading and consciously involve yourself in this process. Here is a three-step strategy that can help you become a better reader:

1. *Prequest.* Predict what question the teacher would ask you to summarize the main idea of a paragraph.
2. *Clarify.* Stop to clarify the meaning of any difficult words or sentences.
3. *Prenext.* Predict what the next paragraph will say.

Applying this three-step strategy to your reading will at first be slow and tiresome because it is so conscious and analytic. Once you have mastered the three steps, however, reading in this way will become faster and more natural.

Reading: "Study Calls Salaries a Matter of Degrees"

Now try to read a short, informative article using the three-step strategy. First look at the title of the article to predict what the article says:

Study calls salaries a matter of degrees

How are salaries a "matter of degrees"? Write down your answer on a piece of paper.

For the first few paragraphs, we'll show you how a student would predict the question for the main idea, clarify meaning, and predict what comes next. Then you can do the rest. Once again, keep in mind that the act of predicting is more important than what you predict. Just exercising the skill makes you a better reader.

Paragraph 1

WASHINGTON (AP)—School pays handsomely, a new government report shows.

1. *Prequest*—What does the study show? *(That the more schooling you have, the more you'll earn.)*
2. *Clarify*—There is nothing to clarify.
3. *Prenext*—The study may show the details of how more schooling pays off.

Paragraph 2

Professionals earn more than five times as much as people who didn't finish high school and double the income of those who earned only a bachelor's degree.

(Our prediction was accurate; the next paragraph tells how more schooling helps people earn more.)

1. *Prequest*—According to the study, what group makes the most money? *(Professionals.)*
2. *Clarify*—What is a "professional"? *(A person with specialized schooling and training, like a doctor or lawyer.)*
3. *Prenext*—The article will go on to compare professionals with those who don't hold degrees.

Paragraph 3

Only about 1 American in 5 has a college degree, but those people earn far and away more money than the others, the Census Bureau reported Thursday.

(Our prediction is pretty close: people with degrees earn more than those without them.)

1. *Prequest*—Who makes the most money? *(Degree holders.)*
2. *Clarify*—There is nothing to clarify.
3. *Prenext*—The author will give exact salary figures for different jobs.

For each of the remaining paragraphs of the article, (a) predict the main idea question, (b) clarify the meaning of any difficult words or sentences, and (c) predict what the next paragraph will say.

Study calls salaries a matter of degrees

1   WASHINGTON (AP)—School pays handsomely, a new government report shows.

2   Professionals earn more than five times as much as people who didn't finish high school and double the income of those who earned only a bachelor's degree.

3   Only about 1 American in 5 has a college degree, but those people earn far and away more money than the others, the Census Bureau reported Thursday.

4   Professionals, such as doctors and lawyers, are the nation's leading money earners, averaging $3,871 a month, the bureau said in its study: "What's It Worth? Educational Background and Economic Status: Spring 1984."

5   Youngsters considering dropping out of high school may want to compare the professionals' income with the average received by people who haven't finished high school: $693 a month.

6   "There's a hard lesson shown just in the listing of degrees, irrespective of field. There's a clear relationship: that economic rewards do accrue at each progressive level" of education, Robert Kominski of the Census Bureau said in an interview.

7   Following professionals at $3,871 a month, the study said, were people who had received doctorates—they averaged $3,265 a month over the four-month study period.

8   Holders of Ph.D. degrees, while having extensive professional training, are scattered over a wide variety of fields, and thus on average earn less than professionals, who are concentrated in the high-paying areas of law and medicine, Kominski said.

9   At the next step down, people who have achieved a master's degree averaged $2,288 a month, the study found. Holders of a bachelor's degree averaged $1,841, followed by those with an associate's degree at $1,346.

10   Close behind were people who received vocational training, who had average monthly earnings of $1,219. People who attended college but left without a degree averaged $1,169, and high school graduates managed $1,045 a month.

11   Well back at $693 were those who dropped out without finishing high school.

12   Within each degree category, of course, many people earned more and others less than the average, Kominski said, and the field of study the student pursued in college is a major factor.

13   For example, in addition to law and medicine, engineering and business proved to be lucrative fields, he found, while at the low end of the scale were such studies as theology, liberal arts and home economics.

Reading for Meaning

Now that you have read and analyzed the article, go back to your prediction about the title. Was the prediction on target? Recall that a prediction's accuracy isn't the most important thing: predicting is valuable in itself by making you an active reader. Refer to the article to answer the following questions on meaning.

1. What is the main point of the article?

2. How does the author support his thesis or main idea?

3. What occupations are the most financially rewarding?

4. What percentage of Americans has a college degree?

5. From what year was the information on salaries drawn?

6. What effect does your field of study in college have on your future earning power?

7. What careers does the article refer to as "professional"?

8. What data in the article would support the choice of attending a community college instead of going to work right after high school?

9. According to the article, what college majors are the least financially beneficial?

10. What important aspects of career choice does the article *not* touch on?

Writing from Reading

For each of the following assignments, brainstorm for ten minutes, write a rough draft, and then write a final draft. Remember to consider your *subject*—what you are writing about; your *purpose*—what you are trying to achieve in your writing; and your *audience*—for whom you are writing.

1. Does this article have any personal meaning for you? Explain your answer.

2. Were you surprised by any of the information in the article?

3. Pretend that you are a parent with high-school children and that you have just read the article. Explain the advice you would give your children. (Note how in this writing, the audience and purpose change. You have to consider a way to have the subject make sense to them.)

4. *Peer reading assignment.* Do any of the assignments above, sharing your work with one or more readers at each stage of the writing process—prewriting, first draft, and final draft.

VOCABULARY STUDY

As you make your way through college, you will often encounter advanced or unfamiliar vocabulary words that can make reading difficult. Current research on reading suggests that you should not stop at each new word, interrupting the reading process to consult a dictionary. Instead, as you read, underline or circle the word and try to infer the meaning from the context; look up the new word only after finishing the reading. In this way, you do not erect a mental roadblock to understanding the overall meaning of what you are reading. Of course, if the reading is thick with technical or unfamiliar words, you are going to have to slow down and almost translate what you are reading.

What follows is a short lesson in how to improve your vocabulary. We will also periodically stop and work on difficult vocabulary words as they appear in readings throughout the textbook.

Vocabulary Cards

There are many ways to learn new words. One is to use vocabulary cards—homemade flash cards. On one side write the spelling, part of speech, pronunciation, and the sentence the word came from; on the other side, write the meaning of the word and a sample sentence of your own. For example, the subtitle of Frank Deford's article "Let's Count Boxing Out" (see pp. 240–41) asks, "What's sporting about men *pummeling* each other?" If the student didn't know the meaning of "pummel," he or she would look it up in a dictionary and find the meaning "pound, beat." The student would then write a vocabulary card like that below:

PUMMEL V. "What's sporting about men pummeling each other?"	"POUND, BEAT" There are days when I would like to pummel my brother.
SIDE 1	**SIDE 2**

When you have odd moments to spare, like time between classes, you can shuffle your cards and see if you have mastered the words' meanings. This can be a slow, painful process, but it produces results when you recognize the new word in your reading or use it yourself in your writing.

Etymology

Another way to learn new words is to study their etymology—how words are formed from prefixes, word roots, and suffixes. Consider the words "prescription," a doctor's formula for medicine, and "antipathy," hatred or dislike:

pre-
(prefix meaning "before")

script
(Latin root meaning "writing")

-tion
(suffix ending for a noun)

anti-
(prefix meaning "against")

path
(Greek root meaning "feeling")

-y
(suffix ending for a noun)

Because Latin and Greek roots make up over eighty-five percent of English words, memorizing key prefixes and suffixes can help you acquire new words. The list below has some commonly used prefixes, with their English meanings, and sample English words formed from them.

Prefix	Meaning	Sample Word
ante-, anti-	before	anteroom, antecedent
anti-	against	antipathy, antidote
auto-	self	autobiography, automaton
bene-	good	benign, benefactor
mal-	bad, evil	malignant, malefactor
dis-	not	distasteful
un-	not	unauthorized
in-	not	incongruous
macro-	large	macrocosm
micro-	small	microcosm, microscope
pre-	before	prenatal, premature
post-	after	postnatal

Prefixes about Direction

Prefix	Meaning	Sample Word
ad-	to, towards	adherent, advocate
circum-	around	circumnavigate, circumvent
contra-	against	contravene, contraband

continued

continued

Prefix	Meaning	Sample Word
co-, com-, con-, col-, cor-	with	commiserate, consensual, collaborate, corroborate
de-	down, off	denigrate, dethrone
e-, ex-	out, former	exonerate, exude
extra-	beyond	extracurricular, extraterrestrial
pro-	forward	prohibitive, prolix
re-	again	regress, repose
retro-	backwards	retroactive, retrogress
sub-	under	subterranean
trans-	across	transverse, transpose

Prefixes about Numbers

Prefix	Meaning	Sample Word
mono-	one	monogamy, mononucleosis
bi-	two	bilateral
tri-	three	trident

Vocabulary Practice

There are nearly fifty sample words in the three lists above for you to learn. Some you can figure out from the knowledge of the prefix. For those whose meanings you can't deduce, look them up in the dictionary and write vocabulary cards for them.

Context

A third way of learning new words is from the context—that is, other surrounding words and phrases. Sometimes you can guess the meaning of new words from other synonymous words, and at other times you can learn the meaning from the "mood" of the piece. To explain how to use context, let's look at some sample paragraphs from Deford's article cited earlier.

From the title of the article, "Let's Count Boxing Out," we can deduce that Deford is against boxing; he wants to "count it out." The subtitle reinforces this view—"What's sporting about men pummeling each other?" To Deford, there is nothing "sporting" about boxing; it is too brutal. Here is Deford's first paragraph:

> Now that the Super Bowl is behind us, we can turn our attention to the bout between Sugar Ray Leonard and Marvin Hagler, Fight of the Century for this year. With luck, it will also be the last boxing extravaganza to hinder the lurching progress of mankind.

Deford is being sarcastic when he describes the Hagler–Leonard bout as the "Fight of the Century for this year." In the next sentence he calls it "the last boxing *extravaganza*." If we don't know what "extravaganza" means, we see that it has the Latin prefix "extra," meaning "beyond." Also, "Fight of the Century" from the previous sentence is a phrase that is synonymous with it. So, we can reason that "extravaganza" means something "beyond the ordinary, spectacular." Deford hopes that the Hagler–Leonard fight will be the last one "to hinder the *lurching* progress of mankind." It is hard to figure out what "lurching" means from the context, so we may simply have to look it up in the dictionary when we finish reading.

Deford's next paragraph is even more complex, because there are so many difficult vocabulary words close to each other:

> It says a great deal about the enfeebled state of boxing that no fight of broad interest can be concocted with existing pugilists. This one is being forced on us only by bringing back the fetching Mr. Leonard from retirement and then tantalizing our most sordid instincts with the gruesome proposition that he might come away from the proceedings no longer able to make out light and form.

The phrase "existing *pugilists*" may be hard, but we may be able to infer from "the enfeebled state of boxing" and from "no fight of broad interest" that "existing *pugilists*" may mean "present-day boxers." "Pugilist," then, is a synonym for "boxer."

The words "*fetching* Mr. Leonard" use "fetch" in a meaning other than "to get or procure." But from the following phrase, "tantalizing our . . . interests," we may be able to assign the meaning "tempting" or "attractive" to "fetching," that is, the "attractive Mr. Leonard."

"*Tantalizing* our most *sordid* instincts" might be able to be better understood by the following phrase, "gruesome proposition," with "gruesome" a synonym for "sordid"—"base" or "terrible." From "proposition," we might be able to infer that "tantalizing" is "tempting" or "teasing." So "*tantalizing* our most *sordid* instincts" means "tempting our basest instincts."

Deford's last phrase in this sentence, that Leonard might come away from the fight "no longer able to make out light and form," is a roundabout way of saying that he might be "blinded"; he might lose his sight as a result of the match. The possibility of Leonard's blindness also explains the "*gruesome* proposition" and our "*sordid* instincts," to be interested in a fight because one of the fighters may be blinded.

In this complex paragraph we see that very often the "mood" is reinforced by synonyms; the words describe the "attractive violence" of professional boxing. Many of the words in the paragraph are synonyms for "attractive," such as "fetching" and "tantalizing." Other words are synonyms for or refer to violence, such as "gruesome," "sordid," and being "blinded."

Punctuation

Finally, punctuation—commas, dashes, and parentheses—often reveals the meanings of new words. Consider these sentences:

1. The art of pugilism, or boxing, is under attack in Deford's article. *(Commas signal that boxing is a synonym for pugilism.)*

2. The Scholastic Aptitude Test (SAT) uses antonyms, words that mean the opposite, to measure students' vocabulary skills. *(The parentheses around "SAT" indicate the acronym, and the commas after "antonyms" frame the definition.)*

3. One of the hardest sections of the SAT is that on analogies—words comparing relationships. *(The dash is the sign for a definition of "analogies.")*

CHAPTER
2

Getting Organized

PLANNING

While clustering is a prewriting technique used to stimulate the writing
process, it can also be helpful in planning a paper. Refer to the example on
page 8. By mapping words and ideas, the student has framed three possible directions for further writing, each of which can be part of a tentative
outline for a paper stemming from "first day of school jitters":

```
New start for me
 Responsibilities
  Kids
    Example of importance of school
  Help with income
    Private school tuition

Fear of failing
 Been away from school so long
 Older than most
 Teacher all business

Goal
 Nurse
  Qualifications
   School
   Clinical experience
```

By revising some words and adding others, the student can convert this
rough outline into a formal outline. "First day jitters" can be phrased a little differently into the title "Returning to School: Worries and Possibilities."

The paper can use the classical outline format—Roman numerals, Uppercase (capital) letters, Arabic numbers, and Lowercase letters—as in the sample below:

```
Returning to School: Worries and Possibilities

   I. School a new beginning
      A. Responsibilities
         1. Kids
            a. Private school tuition
            b. Supervision when spouse working
         2. Help with income
      B. Serve as an example to my kids
         1. Importance of education
         2. Need to strive for goals
  II. Fear of failure
      A. Away from school so long
      B. Older than most students
      C. Demands of business-like teacher
 III. Goal to be a nurse
      A. Qualifications needed
         1. Finish school
         2. Pass nursing boards
      B. Opportunities
```

CLUSTERING VERSUS OUTLINING

For some students, a clustering map alone is sufficient to plan a paper. For others, an outline is more useful. Which is best for you? Each of these strategies can help form your writing. Experiment with both techniques for a while in doing your papers to see which feels more comfortable. If your learning style is visual and intuitive, you may prefer the pictorial, informal structure of clustering. For the student with a more cognitive, sequential learning style, the outline is probably better. The important point is that after prewriting, you need *some plan* for the actual writing. Both mapping and outlining give you a place to begin.

Narrowing Focus and Changing Plans

Using either the map or outline above, the student again considers the *subject*—what she is writing; the *purpose*—why she is writing; and the *audience*—for whom she is writing. The subject seems clear: the first days of college. The purpose is to describe and inform about her thoughts and feelings. The audience is made up of her teacher and classmates who, because they are in the same situation, should sympathize and understand what she is going through—beginning college and working toward a long-term goal.

As the student thinks about these aspects of writing, a narrower focus becomes clear: "The difficulties of college are the first hurdle in my goal to become a nurse." This thought is the student's tentative thesis or main idea. But what about the goal? Why does the student want *that* goal? The answer is in the prewriting and outline—to help her family. So she revises the thesis: "College will help me become a nurse, so that I can support my family." The fears and difficulties of the first few days of college still remain, but they are secondary to the writer's goal.

With this revised thesis, she reconsiders the original outline and changes it:

```
Returning to School: Worries about Possibilities

   I. Problems of college
      A. Feelings of nervousness and insecurity
      B. Expense of books and tuition
  II. Rewards of going to college
      A. Fulfill my prerequisites for degree
      B. Qualify for the nursing program
      C. Get my R.N. degree and pass the state boards
 III. Overall goal
      A. Help my family
         1. Add to family income
         2. Give my kids a good example
      B. Help myself
         1. Raise my self-esteem
         2. Gain fulfillment in my career
```

Writing Practice

1. Make a clustering map and an outline for an essay titled, "Why Go to College?"
2. Revise either your clustering map or outline for a *final* plan for writing the essay.
3. *Journal writing.* Now that you've written about why you are going to college and read about the topic, use your journal to explain the reasons to yourself. Also, are there any reasons why you *shouldn't* go to college? Those reasons are important, so write about those as well.

TIME

In his excellent book on writing, *Write to Learn*, Donald M. Murray counsels writers to use scraps of time, those "in between" moments like waiting for someone or watching television. He points out that much of the best writing comes from such snatched moments. Especially with difficult writing, you can do some of it, stop, and then return to it. This allows your mind to continue to work on your writing so that when you go back to it you have new ideas to get started on again right away. Of course, there are other ways that work, too. Murray recalls the story of the great Southern writer Flannery O'Connor, who tried to write from 9 until 12 every day. She reasoned that if an idea came to her about writing during that time, she was there to receive it.

In your own writing you should try to make use of both kinds of time—those snatched moments when you scribble in a notebook and regularly scheduled blocks of time set aside to do the bulk of your writing. The important thing is to write, not just think about writing. One way to help you find snatched moments of time to write is to make a daily, or even weekly schedule for yourself, for example:

Monday

7:00   Get up, have breakfast, leave for school
8:00   Go to library and study before class
9:00   Math class
10:00 Biology
12:00 Lunch
1:00   English class
2:00   Return home, change for work
3:00   Work
6:30   Home for supper
8:00   TV, listen to tapes
9:00   Study
10:30 TV
11:30 Bed

This is a pretty busy day. Is there any time that you could use for writing, like the twenty minutes after lunch and before English class? Or what about the few minutes you have before supper? These moments could be used for prewriting on your English essay or biology term paper. If you can chip away at long writing assignments by using short blocks of time, you won't have all that panic the night before the assignment is due. Again, by writing in short bursts, you allow ideas to percolate inside your head before it is time to sit down to write.

Once you have written even a preliminary draft, you can benefit from letting some time pass before you pick it up again. You will be fresher and perhaps get a new look at what you've done. Another help can be a second reader—perhaps a family member or a friend—to whom you read the paper out loud. See if the paper makes sense to your reader. Then have the person read it silently. This gives you another pair of eyes and ears for your audience.

For proofreading, a final but necessary step in the writing process, you can try one of two techniques. The first is to begin at the end of your paper and read it from end to beginning. When you read from right to left (the opposite of how we normally read), you see words and phrases in isolation. This is especially good for typographical and spelling errors. Another proofreading technique is to cut a hole the size of a written word in the center of an index card. This allows you to see only one word at a time as you move it along the page. Remember that when we write or type, the mind is always much faster than the mechanics of typing or writing a word, and we often presume something is down on paper because we *thought* it.

Reading: "Benefit of B.A. Is Greater Than Ever"

The following article by Gary Putka is, like the first article you read, about college. First read the title and subtitle, and look at the two illustrations that accompanied the article:

Benefit of B.A. Is Greater Than Ever
Latest Data Show College Degree Greatly Increases Earnings Power

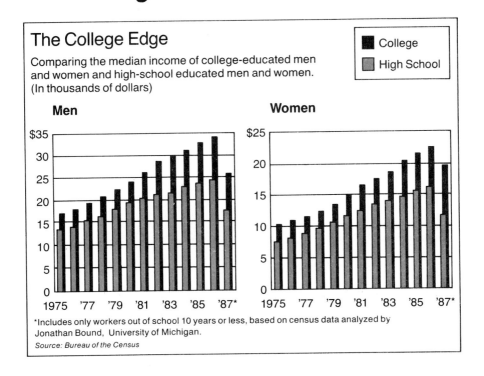

The College Edge

Comparing the median income of college-educated men and women and high-school educated men and women. (In thousands of dollars)

■ College
▨ High School

Men

Women

*Includes only workers out of school 10 years or less, based on census data analyzed by Jonathan Bound, University of Michigan.

Source: Bureau of the Census

High Cost of College
Average annual price of four-year colleges

| | TUITION AND FEES | |
	PUBLIC	PRIVATE
1977-78	$ 621	$2,476
1978-79	651	2,647
1979-80	680	2,923
1980-81	706	3,279
1981-82	819	3,709
1982-83	979	4,021
1983-84	1,105	4,627
1984-85	1,126	5,016
1985-86	1,242	5,418
1986-87	1,337	5,793
1987-88*	1,359	7,110
1988-89*	1,566	7,693

NOTE: Figures are as reported in year of survey
*Weighted averages; all others unweighted

Source: College Board

On a piece of paper write down what you think the article will say. Next read the first two and last two paragraphs:

There may be something rising faster than the price of going to college, after all. The price of not going.

• • •

As for the future?

Higher tuitions still, say the economists who study higher education, until quality, or at least the economic value of higher education, is perceived to decline. "Colleges will act like businessmen on a board," says Mr. Morrell of Radcliffe. "They price themselves according to what the value of the good is perceived to be, and they'll continue to do that until the market says it won't accept it."

What can you predict further about the content of the article? Write down your answer.

Now read the entire article, using the three-step strategy outlined in Chapter 1 as you make your way through it. As you read, note the reasons the writer gives for the increased importance of a college education.

Benefit of B.A. Is Greater Than Ever

Latest Data Show College Degree Greatly Increases Earnings Power

By GARY PUTKA
Staff Reporter of THE WALL STREET JOURNAL

There may be something rising faster than the price of going to college, after all.

The price of not going.

In a ritual well known to strapped parents, the College Board recently released its annual survey showing tuitions rising faster than inflation. As is customary, the big admissions group gave no explanation for the 7% increase for 1988–89, the eighth year in a row that the rise in college tuition has outpaced inflation.

Pressed by Congress and others for the reasons, colleges have in the past blamed the need for more scholarships and higher faculty salaries. But a growing body of research suggests a more markets-like answer: College costs more because the product is worth more.

Measured in terms of income, returns on a bachelor's degree ''have been exploding in the '80s,'' says Finis Welch, an economics professor at the University of California at Los Angeles who specializes in the labor market. Mr. Welch and other analysts, using census data, see a dramatic rise in the amount of income gained by going to college over a time period roughly coinciding with the big tuition increases.

Salary Gap

Male college graduates in the work force made 39.2% more than high school graduates in 1986, the latest year of Census Bureau reports, compared with 23.8% in 1979. For women, the difference rose to 40.5% from 27.9%.

More recent data, derived by University of Michigan economist Jonathan Bound from computer tapes of the Census Bureau's monthly surveys, indicate that the differences were more pronounced in 1987. Mr. Bound's figures show that the gap last year was 70% for women in their first 10 working years and 46% for males of that experience. Economists caution that when data for all workers is reported by the Census Bureau, the unusually large gap for women will probably shrink, though it still will be above the 1986 figure.

Moreover, Mr. Bound says the figures don't reflect another benefit of college, namely that the college educated are less likely to be unemployed than high school graduates. And Mr. Welch's research shows that the gap between more-seasoned workers is widening even faster, peaking at about 20 years' experience and remaining steady afterward.

continued

continued

No one is sure what's behind the growing income gap, but some economists point to a drop in high-paying factory jobs among high school graduates. Another reason may be the growing importance of high-tech employment demanding more education. Also, while the number of new college graduates has edged up only about 5% in the past 10 years to about 980,000 a year, the work force has expanded much faster. This has given a sheepskin a rarity value unimagined in the 1970s, when the well-educated flooded the labor market and the cabbie with a doctorate drove his way into national folklore.

"It's rather remarkable," says Richard Freeman, an economist whose 1976 book, "The Overeducated American," presented evidence on the decline of a diploma's value. Now director of labor studies at the National Bureau for Economic Research in Boston, Mr. Freeman says he had expected college's value to make a comeback, "but no one anticipated the magnitude" of the gains for college graduates.

Census data show that the median income of the college-educated man in 1986 was $34,391 versus $24,701 for those without college. That means that the college "payback time"—the number of years it takes a worker to recoup four years of tuition and lost earnings—has shrunk despite the soaring tuitions. Using tuition figures for public colleges, which educate about 77% of all students, the payback time is down to about 11 years, from about 17 in 1979, before the big tuition mark-ups.

Economists don't suggest that high school seniors are delving through census data and punching calculators before deciding whether or not to attend college. But they do say students and parents know what's going on around them—and act accordingly.

"People see some of the kind of job creation that's going on, and they realize without a college education they're up a tree," says Louis Morrell, treasurer of Radcliffe College, Cambridge, Mass. "People want it and they're willing to pay for it."

Relatively stable annual enrollment of about 12 million students in the 1980s wouldn't seem to support the idea of more clamoring for college. But enrollment has held steady in the face of a 16% decline in the number of high school graduates since 1977. More college freshmen than ever say they're there to make more money, and according to the most recent Gallup survey on the subject, 64% of Americans rate a college education as "very important" in getting ahead, up from 36% in 1978.

"Costs have escalated at the very moment in history when more people believe that (college) is worth it," says Terry Hartle, education aide to Sen. Edward Kennedy of Massachusetts. "I don't think it's unrelated."

Market Forces

The figures tend to support the economic value of college. But they also suggest that prices in higher education are more subject to market forces than universities have generally acknowledged. Richard Rosser, president of the National Association of Independent Colleges and Universities, says many colleges struggle to hold the line on costs without sacrificing quality. And he adds that tuitions cover only a portion of total costs, with the balance coming from governments, private donations and investment earnings. "Colleges agonize over tuition decisions," he says. "What they're doing is simply covering the real cost of running our universities."

With soaring applications, officials of Ivy League and other top private colleges have long contended that they could raise tuitions by more than they have, and still retain enrollments. They say they have resisted doing so because of concern about the ability of some people to pay.

As for the future?

Higher tuitions still, say the economists who study higher education, until quality, or at least the economic value of higher education, is perceived to decline. "Colleges will act like businessmen on a board," says Mr. Morrell of Radcliffe. "They price themselves according to what the value of the good is perceived to be, and they'll continue to do that until the market says it won't accept it."

Reading for Meaning

1. What is the thesis of the article?
2. What proofs or reasons does the author give to support his thesis?
3. What are the reasons for the growing gap between college graduates and nongraduates?
4. At what level of experience does the difference between graduates and nongraduates peak?
5. According to the article, what was the difference between the median salaries of college graduates and nongraduates in 1986?
6. What is the "payback time" for college costs and lost salaries for college graduates?
7. What has happened to college enrollment despite the 16 percent decline of high-school graduate applicants since 1977?
8. What sources of income do colleges rely on besides tuition?
9. What is the reason colleges give for not raising tuitions even more?
10. According to the article, when will colleges stop raising tuitions?
11. What does the article imply about the reasons for the rise in tuitions?

Vocabulary in Context

Write down the definition of each of the italicized words below taken from the article. Try to guess the meaning from the context. Use a dictionary only if you have to.

1. "... differences were more *pronounced* ..."
2. "... —the number of years it takes a worker to *recoup* four years' tuition and lost earnings— ..."
3. "Costs have *escalated* ..."

4. "... more *clamoring* for college."
5. "This has given a *sheepskin* a rarity value ..."

Writing from Reading

For each of the following assignments, do at least ten minutes of prewriting, write a rough draft, and then write a final draft. Remember to consider your *subject*—what you are writing about; your *purpose*—what you are trying to achieve in your writing; and your *audience*—for whom you are writing.

1. Explain what is meant by "market forces" controlling the cost of higher education.
2. Explain some of the reasons for the increase in the salary gap between high-school and college graduates.
3. Discuss how this article might affect your views about staying in college.
4. What projections does the article make for the future about college tuition?
5. Pretend you are a high-school counselor advising seniors about their future. What would you say in a talk to them? (In this assignment, notice how the purpose and audience for your writing have changed: what are high-school seniors like and how can you get your message to them?)

SENTENCE COMBINING

There is nothing worse for a reader than having to read boring writing. Adding variety to your sentences will greatly improve your writing style and make it more enjoyable for your readers. We will now turn to sentence combining, a technique used by writers to vary the length and types of their sentences.

Consider these simple sentences:

The class was over. The students filed out of the building. They headed for home.

Now read this revision, combining the three simple sentences into one complex one:

Class over, the students filed out of the building and headed for home.

This is definitely an improvement. This longer sentence has a phrase before the subject and a compound (more than one) verb, communicating the same actions as the original sentences but without interruption.

The following article illustrates how sentence combining can improve variety and clarity in your writing:

This Should Keep the Table Talk Lively at Thanksgiving Dinner

By Jerry E. Bishop
Staff Reporter of The Wall Street Journal

Everyone knows what to do with a bird's wishbone. But what does the *bird* do with it?

For scientists who've longed for an answer to that question while tugging at the wishbone—or pullie bone, as it's also called—after Sunday dinner, their wish may have finally come true. Two Harvard University paleontologists and a Northern Arizona University physiologist say they have figured out the secret of the wishbone.

Flying in a Wind Tunnel

To find the answer, the three scientists put some starlings in a wind tunnel and took X-ray movies of the birds' skeletons as they flew in winds ranging from 20 to 40 miles per hour. The movies show that the furcula, as the wishbone is known technically, acts like a spring when a bird is flying, report Farish Jenkens and Kenneth Dial of Harvard and Ted Goslow of Northern Arizona University in the current issue of the journal Science.

When the birds are at rest, the two tips of the wishbone are about half an inch apart, the researchers say. But when the wings are stroking downward during flight the tips spread out until they are about three-quarters of an inch apart at the end of the downstroke. On the upstroke of the wings, the tips spring back to their original position.

The scientists also found that the breastbone, or sternum, located just behind the wishbone's junction, moves up and down during flight.

What good is all this to the bird? The scientists speculate that these moving bones push air through the bird's body during flight. They base their theory on the air sacs that birds have scattered through their bodies, including some between the prongs of the wishbone and others near the breastbone. It's possible, the scientists say, that the moving bones alternately deflate and expand the air sacs, forcing air from one sac to another during flight.

On to the Next Mystery

Starlings, for example, only inhale and exhale three times a second, while their wings flap 12 to 16 times a second. So, the scientists theorize, the springy wishbone and moving breastbone may be a way of moving air about the body between breaths.

Now, if they could only figure out what the appendix is for.

Look again at the first sentence of the second paragraph:

For scientists who've longed for an answer to that question [how birds use the wishbone] while tugging at the wishbone—or pullie bone, as it's also called—after Sunday dinner, their wish may finally have come true.

Now consider three sentences that say the same thing, but in a dull and clumsy way:

Scientists have longed to know what the wishbone is for. They have been tugging at it. Their wish may finally have come true.

The sentence from the article combines all the ideas of the three short sentences into one longer sentence with subordinate word groups placed before the subject.

Here is another example from the same piece, set side by side with another version broken down into simple sentences:

Simple Sentences	Combined Sentences
To find the answer, the three scientists put some starlings in a wind tunnel. They took X-ray movies of the birds' skeletons. The birds flew in winds ranging from 20 to 40 miles per hour. The wishbone is known technically as the furcula. The movies show that the furcula acts like a spring when a bird is flying.	To find the answer, the three scientists put some starlings in a wind tunnel and took X-ray movies of the birds' skeletons as they flew in winds ranging from 20 to 40 miles per hour. The movies show that the furcula, as the wishbone is known technically, acts like a spring when a bird is flying. . . .

Notice how the sentences in the more complex version from the article combine the five simple sentences into two longer sentences that use a compound verb and subordinate word groups to achieve variety and fluency.

Let's now study some specific ways to combine sentences, giving them variety and clarity.

Method 1

A comma and a conjunction (usually "and," "or," "nor," "for," "but," "yet") can be used to join shorter sentences into longer ones. "And" adds ideas; "or" and "nor" express choice; "for" means "because"; "but" and "yet" show contrast.

Simple Sentences	Combined Sentences
Fall comes on quickly in the Midwest after summer. It brings darkness in the late afternoon.	Fall comes quickly in the Midwest after summer, and it brings darkness in the late afternoon.
Hector is a perfect angel around the house. He's a little devil at school.	Hector is a perfect angel around the house, but he's a little devil at school.

Writing Practice

Now you try it. Combine the following shorter sentences into longer, more effective ones by using a comma and a conjunction.

1. The game was over. The fans went home.
2. The day had been a long one. The whole family was tired.

3. Tim studied as hard as he could. He failed the test.

4. All of his friends were invited. None of them came.

5. Juan arrived too late for the interview. His car had broken down.

6. Phyllis was deeply in love with Tom. He did not love her.

7. The Eastern campaign had been a failure for Hitler. He refused to admit defeat at Stalingrad and sacrificed 300,000 men.

8. Hitler opened a second front in the war. This strategy doomed his efforts.

9. At Yalta Roosevelt tried to appease Stalin. The cost in lost freedom for Eastern Europe was terrible.

10. Under Communist control Poland lost her freedom. Other Russian-dominated nations soon followed.

Method 2

Use a semicolon between ideas to form longer sentences.

Simple Sentences	Combined Sentences
Henry doesn't possess a tuxedo. He wisely maintains it's more sensible to rent one.	Henry doesn't possess a tuxedo; he wisely maintains that it's more sensible to rent one.
Churchill begged America to enter the war. Finally we did.	Churchill begged America to enter the war; finally we did.

Writing Practice

Use semicolons to combine the following shorter sentences.

1. The beautiful German city of Dresden was firebombed. No one wanted to accept blame later.

2. The book *900 Days* recounts the German siege of Leningrad. It details the horrors of the prolonged conflict.

3. Hitler committed suicide at the end of the war. He could not face the thought of losing to his enemies.

4. Many notorious Nazis escaped capture. Some fled to South America.

5. General Patton claimed we should have fought the Russians right after we defeated Germany. Many historians believe he was correct.

Method 3

Combine ideas with a semicolon and the conjunctive adverbs "however," "nevertheless," "moreover," "consequently," and "therefore." Conjunctive adverbs help show a logical relationship between ideas; for example, "however" and "nevertheless" show contrast. "Moreover" functions like "and"—to add to or join ideas. "Consequently" and "therefore" indicate a result or effect.

Simple Sentences	Combined Sentences
Montez had endured a bad week. Payday arrived to save him.	Montez had endured a bad week; however, payday arrived to save him.
Mary got "A's" in all her classes. She was elected to the National Honor Society.	Mary got all "A's" in her classes; moreover, she was elected to the National Honor Society.
The drought had lasted most of the summer. The fall crop was stunted.	The drought had lasted most of the summer; therefore, the fall crop was stunted.

Writing Practice

Choose one of the five conjunctive adverbs listed above to combine the following sentences. Remember to use a semicolon before and a comma after the conjunctive adverbs.

1. John F. Kennedy's assassination remains a mystery even after more than twenty-five years. Some feel we will never have all the answers.
2. Governor Wallace felt blacks shouldn't be allowed to attend the University of Alabama. The Kennedy administration enforced the desegregation laws, and blacks were permitted to enroll there.
3. Samuel felt ill. He wouldn't consult a doctor for his problems.
4. The nations of Europe had been devastated by World War II. They would need America's help to rebuild.
5. Many ills combined to cause the Civil War. High emotions aggravated the situation.
6. The sixties were a time of radical change for America. The nation survived and was strengthened.
7. The Civil Rights movement in America led to great unrest. Progress came slowly and painfully.
8. Snow and sleet crashed down on the city. This was followed by a howling wind off the lake.
9. Venice has been decimated by the loss of its middle-class workers. Much of the vibrancy of the city has been lost to boutiques and other tourist traps.
10. At the end of World War II, the Poles were encouraged by the Russians to begin an uprising against their Nazi oppressors. The Soviet forces merely watched from outside Warsaw as the Poles were slaughtered.

CHAPTER
3

Drafting and Revising

REARRANGING FOR IMPACT

Now that you have made a plan for the essay "Why Go to College?" in Chapter 2, reexamine it again in the light of subject, purpose, and audience.

Subject. This is clear—explain the reasons you have for going to college. You have done prewriting, planned, and read about this topic. Is there anything else you wish to say? Because *personal* examples and accounts ring true in an essay, think of the most personal reasons you have for going to college.

Purpose. You want to inform your audience of teacher and peers *why* you are in college. You might also want to *persuade* some of the wavering students in your class (maybe including yourself) that all the effort and money expended on college is really worth it.

Audience. Your teacher and classmates are familiar with the topic because, like you, they are testing themselves and college. The students are all freshmen; both male and female; black, white, and Hispanic; and all are between the ages of 18 and 21. Most are probably from middle-class ethnic neighborhoods who must work to support themselves in school.

Here is one student's first plan for writing his essay. Just beginning college, he hopes to major in engineering.

Why Go to College?

```
  III. I will meet new people in college.
   IV. I will learn about others in college.
    V. I will learn about myself in college.
   VI. I will experience new challenges in college.
  VII. College will cause me to have a new lifestyle.
```

After further consideration of subject, purpose, and audience, he decides to make his essay more personal and to focus on one aspect of college in his thesis: "In college there's more to learn than just what's in books." Rejecting the ideas of college as a place only to acquire academic skills, learn to improve, and create a new lifestyle, he instead narrows his thesis on the more personal learning aspects of college.

NATURAL ORDER VERSUS COMMON STRUCTURES

The organization of the plan for your essay will often suggest itself from the information; that is, the essay will grow organically, from the very nature of the subject. In the case of the plan for "Why Go to College?", what natural order might suggest itself from the reasons you have for going to college? One might be from *least important reason to most important reason*. This pattern represents a natural way of thinking about priorities and reasons. It is often found in papers used to argue or to persuade. In narrative writing or storytelling, a natural order would be chronological—from beginning to end in time—or the flashback order in which the story might begin at the climax and work backward. Descriptive writing about a place or a person can move from least prominent features to most prominent, or by directions—bottom to top, top to bottom, right to left, and so on.

Common structures are those used in certain modes or types of writing, like cause-and-effect papers or problem-and-solution papers. The *causes* for a student to wish to attend college might be, for example, the lack of good job prospects, uncertainty about the future, the need to discover one's own strengths and skills, and the availability of financial aid for college. The *effect* would be the desire to attend college. In a problem/solution paper, the student's *problem* might be, for example, a lack of job skills, poor prospects for jobs, and the need to acquire academic and job skills. The *solution* would be to attend college and acquire the skills needed.

Our student who wants to be an engineer has settled on this thesis and brief outline:

```
    In college there's more to learn than just what's in the
books.

1. You will learn about new people you meet.
2. You will learn to handle new challenges.
3. You will learn more about yourself.
```

For him the most important thing to learn from college is about himself. While this outline seems skimpy and bald, the essay developed from it is clear and more detailed:

Some people attend college to prepare for their first career choice. Others attend to learn a new trade or to improve in their current one. Whatever the reason you attend, I'm sure that most prospective students think that all of their learning will be from the classroom. Well, I'd like to let you in on a little secret. There's more to learn in college than just what's in the books.

First off, you're going to learn about all of these new people that you're going to meet. These range from ones in your class to those in the halls, the frequent library users and even your teachers. All of these characters are part of your new environment, and you are going to want to know how to be in balance with them. One way is by learning how they react to you and their other surroundings.

Another thing that the textbook doesn't tell you is how to handle your new challenges. The pressures of meeting deadlines of various assignments and studying for exams do not correspond to those of your previous job or your responsibilities at home. Juggling school with a job, a social life and other activities (whether they are necessary or not) only compounds the challenge. Your priorities will have to change if you intend to succeed in school. Realizing what's more important to you and dealing with these new demands is part of the learning process.

Moreover, you're going to learn about something that may very well outweigh any of these extra lessons. You are going to learn more about yourself. You are sure to have to come up with some new methods to handle all of these challenges. If you don't stand back every so often and see what you've done and how you've done it, you're going to be missing out on some good stuff. Doesn't it make sense to apply these ways of succeeding in school to remaining successful for the rest of your life?

Hopefully, you're now aware that for any reason that you go to college, you're going to learn more than just what's in the books. I say hopefully because I feel that this hidden education is also of value. You may later find that in some respects it is even more valuable.

Writing Practice

1. Below is a list of reasons for going to college, but in no order or pattern. Put the list in any order you think appropriate—natural, cause-and-effect, or problem/solution. Note that there may be *many* correct ways of organizing the list.

Reasons for Going to College

Grant
Need job skills
Financial aid
    available
Poor job prospects
Have to commute to
    suburbs even for
    minimum-wage
    jobs

Unsure about my
    future
Join the armed
    forces?
Weak in math
Personable with
    people
C high-school
    student

Borrow money from
    parents
Cashier at
    McDonald's
Stock work at Toys R
    Us
Discover my own
    interests and skills
Bank loan

2. Using your revised plan, write an essay titled, "Why Go to College?"

3. Use the checklist below to give advice and to help improve one of your classmates' essays, making your marks right on his or her paper. You should talk with the student as you fill out the checklist as well as read the paper.

Essay Checklist for "Why Go to College?"

a. What type of prewriting does the writer use? Explain.
b. Explain how the writer analyzes the three aspects of writing—subject, purpose, and audience.
c. Does the writer use an outline or clustering map?
d. How is the plan, whether outline or clustering map, organized?
e. What is the writer's thesis?
f. List the reasons the writer uses to support his or her thesis.
g. Are the reasons explained clearly and logically? Explain.
h. What is the best sentence or idea in the paper?
i. List any personal examples used in the paper.
j. Correct any errors in spelling or sentence structure.

4. *Journal writing.* Write about the experience of giving and receiving peer advice on writing. What do you like and dislike about it? How does it help or hurt? Be honest about your thoughts and feelings.

Reading: "Wy Cant This Man Git Himself a Job?"

In the following article by columnist Mike Royko, evidence for an argument is presented neither explicitly nor openly, but nevertheless builds slowly until it is overwhelming. Use your prereading techniques to look over the title, and the first two and last two paragraphs:

Wy cant this man git himself a job?

It has to be frustrating and discouraging. A young man spends eight years in elementary school, four years in high school and four more years going to college and getting a degree.

Sixteen years of cracking the books. But when he finally jumps into the job market, looking for the payoff, the doors slam in his face.

• • •

As I said, I'm not sure what the young man's problem is or what to tell him.

Do you think it might have something to do with the kind of ties he wears to interviews?

Write down why you think Royko uses the oddly spelled title.

Now read the entire piece. You may find that your prereading fooled you about its content, which only a complete reading can reveal.

Wy cant this man git himself a job?

Mike Royko

It has to be frustrating and discouraging. A young man spends eight years in elementary school, four years in high school and four more years going to college and getting a degree.

Sixteen years of cracking the books. But when he finally jumps into the job market, looking for the payoff, the doors slam in his face.

That's the problem a Chicagoan recently wrote me about. He says he just doesn't understand why he can't find a job in his chosen field.

He believes that he's been conned by the part of the American dream that promises success through formal education. And he wants to know why it has turned out this way.

It's been many years since I've done any job hunting, so I'm not equipped to give him advice.

But I thought that if I printed his letter, someone out there—maybe a personnel director or a job counselor—might offer suggestions, which I'll gladly pass along to him.

Here's what the college graduate wrote—exactly as he wrote it:

"I was wondering can you write an article to the related situation: A college graduate who has earned a degree in Computer Information System, trying to seek employment in the computer-business industry.

"On Sundays I grab the newspaper jobs section, and follow up by mailing ten

continued

continued

to fifteen resumes to different companys inside as well as outside the states, then riding into the city twice a week to various coporations to fill out applications, knowing that it will be place on file and half of the time they are not even look at.

"It all seem easy when you are young. First they tell you that you need to go to school to get a education [hopeful a position] so you can get a job.

"But when you are finish with school then they tell you, I'm sorry we are looking for someone with three to five years of experience, and right there, Bang, you fell it and everywhere you go. It's crazy but it seem funny when you know that they are hiring.

"If you tell them how can you get experience when no one is hiring, they look at you an say I don't know.

"A few weeks ago when I was applying for this job, I over heard this receptionist argue at her daughter about missing so many days, because she like to stay out late with her friend, when the receptionist switch to the next line and told her boss the young lady won't be in due to a fever.

"How would you fell after applying for a position, when after waiting several weeks you see the same ad for the same position.

"The government have this set-up call the Job Service, which is to help individual find jobs when ninety percent of the people who goes there are still unemployed.

"The though of going back to school to receive a masters degree was in mind, but we know when the employer see that you have obtain your MBA right after your bachelor, he will say to himself, ahh, a lot of book sense but no experience, if I hire him I will have to pay him more then a person with one degree or no degree. It also cost money to go back to school, most people have a hard time getting through undergrad with the help of odd jobs an loans. It's hard paying the bank back when you are not working.

"Well, I guess that's life after college, maybe you haven't experienced this, but I though that I should share this with you and to the others who are having such a hard time. I hope to hear some type of response good or bad to add to my collection of dear John Letter."

As I said, I'm not sure what the young man's problem is or what to tell him.

Do you think it might have something to do with the kind of ties he wears to interviews?

Reading for Meaning

1. What is Royko arguing for or against in this column? What is his evidence?

2. What spurious, or phony, reason does Royko give for reprinting the job applicant's letter?

3. How do Royko's last two short paragraphs function in the piece?

Writing from Reading

1. Rewrite the young man's letter, making as many corrections as you can.

2. Assume the role of the young man and write an angry letter to Mike Royko protesting his use of your original letter. Write in your own style or mimic the style and mistakes of the young man.

3. *Simulation game.* Imagine an employer that feels bad for the young man ridiculed in Royko's article. He calls Royko to arrange for an interview with the young man, his college English teacher, and Royko. Assume one of the roles above for yourself and then brainstorm or freewrite about what you might say in the interview. Then organize your thoughts into four or five paragraphs.

SENTENCE COMBINING (CONTINUED)

Method 4

Another method of combining sentences is to omit repeated subjects and to use a series of verbs.

Simple Sentences	Combined Sentences
The dawn rose suddenly. It jumped from behind the mountain. It shimmered on the lake.	The dawn rose suddenly, jumped from behind the mountain, and shimmered on the lake.
The boa constrictor raised its head. It uncoiled slowly. It advanced stealthily on the unsuspecting rat. It struck savagely.	The boa constrictor raised its head, uncoiled slowly, advanced stealthily on the unsuspecting rat, and struck savagely.

Writing Practice

Revise the following sentences by omitting repeated subjects and using a series of verbs.

1. The killer crawled to the window. He stood slowly. He groped for his .45. He aimed at the fat man.
2. The husky youth looked over the crowd. He selected the old lady. He bumped into her. He bolted with her purse.
3. The President approached the podium. He stood tall before the microphone. He blinked into the lights.
4. The explosion shattered the sky. It left a trail of smoke. It released the dead parachutist.
5. Primary jungle was damp. It was dark. It was forbidding.

Method 5

Two ideas can often be combined into a subordinate word group and a main idea if there is a special relationship between them; for example, cause and effect, time, or concession (yielding or giving into). The subordinate conjunction "because" signifies cause and effect; "unless," "although," and "if" introduce "conditional" clauses; and "since," "after," and "until" suggest a time relationship.

Simple Sentences	Combined Sentences
It snowed for ten hours straight. We couldn't get to school.	Because it snowed for ten hours straight, we couldn't get to school.
The police arrived at the scene of the shooting. They found the bullet-riddled corpse of Big Tuna.	When the police arrived at the scene of the shooting, they found the bullet-riddled corpse of Big Tuna.
Roosevelt was crippled by polio. He was a great president.	Although Roosevelt was crippled by polio, he was a great president.

Writing Practice

Combine each of the following main clauses by using one of the subordinating conjunctions listed above.

1. Jim sailed easily through all the nursing courses. He came to microbiology.
2. The senators all vote against him. The new President will be stymied.
3. Tony drank too much. His wife left him.
4. The summer had been a time of great drought. People were worried about the "greenhouse effect."
5. World War II was over. Europe needed the Marshall Plan to get back on its feet.
6. The incumbent stumped hard the last few weeks of the campaign. The challenger still beat him easily.
7. The Russians can be trusted. There may be a new era of peace for the world.
8. The poor have much less medical care than the affluent. AIDS is increasing much more rapidly among minorities.
9. You read all the books. You will pass the class.
10. All the problems are solved. You may go home.

WORD DEMONS

Some words frequently confuse students. This is a short lesson on how to overcome problems with some of these difficult words. The first group of words we will look at are called homophones, words that are pronounced alike, but have different spellings and meanings.

1. Their, They're, There

"Their" refers to possessing or owning something, as in "*their* books," "*their* vouchers": "*Their* car has been stolen."

   "They're" is a contraction or combination of the two words "they are." The apostrophe goes where the letter "a" is missing from the word "are." "*They're* going to the game" means "They are going to the game." A simple test for the correct use of "they're" is to try out "they are"; for example, "They're sick" means "They are sick."

"There" very often indicates place: "The car is over *there*" and "Put the book *there*." Another use of the word "there" is simply to begin a sentence: "*There* will be much trouble over this matter" and "*There* are many serious problems with this issue."

If you are unsure which of these three words to use, try the process of elimination. See if the word shows ownership—"their car"—or if it should be broken down into two words—"They're sick," meaning "They are sick." If neither of these meanings works, use "there."

Exercises

Complete the following sentences with "their," "they're," or "their."

a. The gun was found in _____ house.

b. _____ going to find the murderer.

c. _____ will be a lot of students failing.

d. Only _____ faith can save them.

e. Many students have gone _____ to purchase books.

f. _____ is no pleasing some people.

g. _____ too sick to make the trip.

h. _____ will be hell to pay.

i. If only _____ telling the truth, we would know the answer.

j. _____ too tired out to care.

2. Too, To

Two other homophones that often cause problems are "too" and "to." Part of the confusion with these words is that "too" has two separate and unrelated meanings. "Too" means "very" or "excessively," as in "*too* hot" and "*too* crowded." The other meaning of "too" is "also," as in "I, *also*, will go" or "I bought the meat *also*."

The other word, "to," is usually part of a prepositional phrase like "*to* the store" or "*to* school"; it may also be part of an infinitive phrase—"to" plus a verb—as in "*to* talk" or "*to* run." In any case, "to" never means "very" or "too much" as in "*too* hot," or "also" as in "I, too."

Exercises

Complete the following sentences with either "to" or "too."

a. It is _____ hot.

b. There is _____ much food.

c. Jim will go, _____ .

d. Don will go _____ his grandmother's house.

e. Pete lives _____ eat.

f. After the game, Baines was _____ angry to go home.

g. "_____ hot," he said. "It's _____ damned hot for food."

h. In the end, Sara gave up and went _____.

i. _____ dream relaxes some people.

j. Cheryl seems _____ concerned with herself lately.

3. Its, It's

Another troublesome pair of words is "its" and "it's." Perhaps the simplest way to tell them apart is that "it's" can only mean "it is," with the apostrophe replacing the "i" of "is" in "it is," as in *"It's* raining" or *"It's* cold outside."

The other word, "its," can never mean "it is"; instead, "its" shows ownership or possession, as in "The cat lost *its* collar" or "The army lost *its* leader." If you still aren't sure which word to use, try the "it is" test: if "it is" ("it's") doesn't make sense, then use "its."

Exercises

Complete the following sentences with either "its" or "it's."

a. _____ raining too hard to go out now.

b. After a long battle, the city lost _____ court case.

c. The lion lost _____ claw.

d. _____ hard to study if the kids are loud.

e. _____ a long battle to win your diploma.

f. After the car lost _____ original paint job, it was never the same again.

g. _____ a hot day.

h. _____ too much to do in one day.

i. _____ a thrill to get an A in that class.

CHAPTER

4

Finishing and Polishing

REVISING FOR STYLE: THE SENTENCE

Sentences should be clear and forceful. The key to writing sentences is to use variety: make some short, some of medium length, and some long. There are three basic sentence patterns in English, as illustrated in Yumiko Ono's article in the *Wall Street Journal*, "Pampered Pooches Can Lap Up the Life Of Luxury in Japan" (see pp. 63–65):

1. *Cumulative*—begins with a base sentence of subject and verb, followed by added information set off by commas, for example:

   Sentence base.

   Information added after the comma.

   { Hotel owner Keiko Akutsu began offering pet lodging and meals last year, after she took a trip to Europe and was impressed by the welcome many hotels there extended to animals.

2. *Periodic*—a sentence base by itself, for example:

   Her hotel's revenues have nearly doubled.

   It can also be a sentence base *preceded* by added information that requires reading all the way to the period to understand the sentence, for example:

   After the prized pet eventually passes away, a funeral service will cremate the pet right outside the owner's door.

3. A variation of the cumulative sentence which combines information added both *before* and *after* the sentence base, for example:

Information before base.	{ Seeking attention, he strolls over to the bar
Sentence base.	{ and urinates on the carpet, making Mrs.
Information after sentence base.	{ Akutsu rush over with a can of deodorant
	{ spray.

For a sense of how these sentence patterns are distributed in one paragraph, study this excerpt from the same article:

Sentence base (periodic sentence).	{ Chuji and Mary rub noses, and their owners coo in delight. Shingo, a two-pound
Information added to beginning of base (periodic sentence).	{ Chihuahua wrapped in a red-kilted vest, is jealous. Seeking attention, he strolls over to
Information added to beginning and end of base (cumulative sentence).	{ the bar and urinates on the carpet, making Mrs. Akutsu rush over with a can of deodor-
Information added to beginning of base (periodic sentence).	{ ant spray. His owner, a middle-aged woman in pink pajamas, gives him a little slap, then cuddles him tightly.

Let's examine another paragraph. This is from an essay by David Blankenhorn called "Values, Opportunities, and Unwed Parenthood" (see pp. 220–22). See how he varies the types of sentences he uses:

Cumulative sentence.	{ A serious effort to combat unwed parenthood must include an employment strategy, especially for poor and minority youth, for whom joblessness and unwed parent-
Periodic sentence.	{ hood are closely intertwined. One place to start is the welfare system. Welfare pay-
Combined.	{ ments, whenever possible, should be replaced with guaranteed jobs, including child
Periodic sentence.	{ care. Initially, such a program would be more costly than the current system, but in the long run it would offer recipients a genuine ladder out of poverty. Moreover, it would
Cumulative sentence.	{ curtail the subsidies for unwed parenthood that plague the current system, replacing them with the same incentives for family formation that operate in the larger society.

Writing Practice

1. The following sentences are adapted from George Vecsey's *New York Times* article "Cantaloupe for the N.F.L." (see pp. 214–16). Revise the sentences below according to the directions and then compare your revisions to the original sentences taken from the article.
   a. Pedro Delgado of Spain kept the maillot jaune, the yellow jersey of the Tour de France champion. He kept it only because he tested positive for a drug. The drug will not become illegal until next week.

Make this a cumulative sentence by putting commas after "champion" and "drug," and omitting "he" and other unnecessary words. Original sentence: "Pedro Delgado of Spain kept the maillot jaune, the yellow jersey of the Tour de France champion, only because he tested positive for a drug that will not become illegal until next week."

    b. Many athletes are tempted to play with pain. They do not know if they can really trust the team doctor. The doctor is paid by management. *Make into a cumulative sentence by putting a comma after "pain," omitting "They," changing "know" into "knowing," inserting a comma after "doctor," and adding "who."*
    Original sentence: "Many athletes are tempted to play with pain, not knowing if they can really trust the team doctor, who is paid by management."

2. Take five sentences from one of your essays and try to rewrite them as cumulative sentences. Remember that the pattern is: *sentence base, added information, added information*—for example, "The youth rides quickly over the ridge, his saddle sweating with the morning dew, his horse chafing for action."

3. *Absolutes* are participial phrases ending in "-ing" or "-ed" with a noun or pronoun describing the whole sentence. In the example from exercise 2, "his saddle sweating with the morning dew" and "his horse chafing for action" are absolutes. Absolutes compress the number of necessary words and add variety to sentence structure. Replace the absolutes in the following sentences with those of your own.

EXAMPLE Sweating out how she would react to him, Paul knocked timidly on Mary's door.

ANSWER *Wondering how she would greet him,* Paul knocked timidly on Mary's door.

    a. A teacher beaten down by years of drudgery, Miss Marple quit.
    b. The Yankees beat the Red Sox, returning to an old habit for the team from New York.
    c. His heart racing wildly, he wondered how the police got on to him so quickly.
    d. Mary emerged triumphant from the meeting, her boss appointing her to the new marketing position.

SENTENCE VARIETY

Good writing demands not only correctness, but variety. Every sentence should not be the same length, nor should it be written in the same pattern of *subject–verb*. You must judge when your sentence pattern has become so boring and repetitive that you have to work at revising *some* of your sentences. To achieve variety, you can use sentence combining and other techniques to change the beginnings of your sentences. Instead of always beginning your sentence with the subject, you can use any of these four types of openings:

1. "-ed" words (participles)—words that are part verb and part adjective that modify a noun or pronoun—or participial phrases placed in front of the subject.

    NOT   The horse was drugged and sick. He ran poorly.

    BUT   *Drugged and sick,* the horse ran poorly.

    The "-ed" word "drugged" and the adjective "sick" are placed in front of the subject, "horse." Note, too, that here the "-ed" phrase "Drugged and sick" is the cause, and the last part of the sentence the effect—"the horse ran poorly."

    NOT   The new teacher was flustered and embarrassed by the large class of wise-cracking sophomores. He endured a day of hell.

    BUT   *Flustered and embarrassed by the large class of wise-cracking sophomores,* the new teacher endured a day of hell.

    The "-ed" words "flustered" and "embarrassed" and the following prepositional phrase, "by the large class of wise-cracking sophomores," are placed in front of the subject, "teacher." Again, the relationship between the "-ed" phrase and the rest of the sentence is cause and effect (*because* the teacher was flustered and embarrassed by the large class of wise-cracking sophomores, he endured a day of hell).

2. "-ing" words or phrases (also participles or participial phrases) placed in front of the subject.

    NOT   She was running for the bus. She tripped and fell.

    BUT   *Running for the bus,* she tripped and fell.

    "Running for the bus" is an "-ing" phrase placed in front of the subject, "she."

    NOT   Jim dominated the class discussion. The rest of the students had little chance to talk.

    BUT   *Dominating the class discussion,* Jim left the rest of the students little chance to talk.

    The "-ing" phrase "dominating the class discussion" is positioned in front of the subject, "Jim."

3. "to" infinitive phrase—"to" and a verb—put in front of the subject.

    NOT   You must concentrate fully on the reading section of the SAT to score well.

    BUT   *To score well on the reading section of the SAT,* you must concentrate fully.

To add variety to the sentence, place the "to" phrase—"to score well on the reading section of the SAT"—before the subject, "you."

NOT It costs $15 and up to get even a mediocre seat at an NFL football game.

BUT *To get even a mediocre seat at an NFL football game,* it costs $15 and up.

Again, for the sake of variety, place the "to" phrase "to . . . game" before the subject "it."

4. A prepositional phrase placed before the subject.

NOT They got up early for the long, cross-country drive.

BUT *For the long cross-country drive,* they got up early.

In the revised sentence, put the prepositional phrase "for . . . drive" in front of the subject.

NOT He yelled at the top of his voice for help.

BUT *At the top of his voice,* he yelled for help.

Again, in the revised sentence, put the prepositional phrase in front of the subject "he."

Writing Practice

1. Revise the following sentences using "-ed" words and phrases. As you work through each sentence, note that the pattern is cause and effect.
   a. The young mother was badgered by her three children into buying them ice cream.
   b. His new Porsche was battered and scratched in the collision. It looked old.
   c. The rookie NFL quarterback was crushed by the veteran defensive line. He wished he was still in college.
   d. His first visit to New York City was marred by frequent encounters with beggars and street people. He began to yearn for Oklahoma.
   e. The losers were demoralized and sullen. They limped to the locker room.

2. Use "-ing" words and phrases to revise the sentences below.
   a. The FBI director was twisting slowly in the wind. He was a victim of Nixon's Watergate scandal.
   b. The horse was jumping over the last hurdle when disaster struck.
   c. The boa constrictor was slithering noiselessly towards his prey. He was ready for the kill.
   d. She was skating flawlessly across the ice. She won the gold medal.
   e. The Russian trawler was steaming towards the trapped whales and later rescued them.

3. Read the following paragraph, taken from a student essay, and copy it, revising one sentence with an "-ed" phrase and another with an "-ing" phrase. Remember that every sentence cannot begin with an "-ed" or "ing" phrase; sentence variety means that *some* sentences can use material added before the subject.

> College teaches students how to discipline themselves. Unlike high school and grade school, students are not under the watchful eye of a teacher. Students must learn to schedule their time so that they can complete all their homework and studies punctually, as they are given assignments and expected to finish them without further guidance. Students who can comply with these requirements will discover that they have learned self-discipline.

4. Revise the sentences below using "to" infinitive phrases.
   a. The students had to have a school I.D. to get into the dance.
   b. You have to work very hard to get an A in Biology III.
   c. Many old people get flu shots before winter sets in to avoid respiratory problems.
   d. Many young athletes foolishly use steroids to bulk themselves up.
   e. Lincoln did everything he could to avoid the Civil War.

5. Place prepositional phrases before the subject in each of the following sentences.
   a. He scrambled down the hill and into the forest.
   b. She stayed working in the library until midnight.
   c. The speaker resumed his talk after the disruption by the demonstrators.
   d. Tempers flared in the heat of the quarrel.
   e. The revelers crawled back to their rooms after the party.

6. Copy the following paragraph from a student essay and add variety by using a "to" infinitive phrase at the beginning of one sentence and a prepositional phrase at the beginning of another. There are different ways to achieve variety in this example.

> Some people attend college to prepare for their first career choice. Others attend to learn a new trade or to improve in their current one. Whatever the reason they attend, most prospective students think that all of their learning will be in the classroom. Well, I'd like to let you in on a little secret. There's more to learn in college than just what's in the books.

7. Revise the following sentences using any of the techniques we studied in this chapter.
   a. Outside, the people are rushing by in their usual hurry to get from one place to another.
   b. He turns into the alleyway and disappears out of sight.

   c. I wash down the last of my cardboard muffin with some of this ferocious dirt coffee and head for my car.

8. Try to add some sentence variety to one of your own essays that has
already been corrected by revising some of the sentence beginnings in
the four ways we have studied: "-ed" words and phrases; "-ing" words
and phrases; "to" infinitive phrases; and prepositional phrases.

PARALLEL STRUCTURE

To be readable, sentences must not only be clear and correct, they must
also have style. One of the most effective elements of style is parallel
structure, in which words are written in a similar grammatical order—as
in Julius Caesar's description of his victories, "I came, I saw, I conquered."
This sentence repeats the pronoun "I," puts all three verbs in the past
tense, and ends the climactic pattern with "conquered." The purpose of
the emphasis on "I," the role of Caesar, is intentional: the three simple
verbs make the conquests seem easy for Caesar.

   Consider President John F. Kennedy's famous line from his inaugural
address, "Ask not what your country can do for you, but what you can do
for your country." By inverting the words "country" and "you," and by
repeating the verb "can do," the speaker achieves force and power. Lincoln's Gettysburg Address also uses powerful parallel structure—"that
government of the people, by the people, and for the people, shall not per-
ish from this earth." The three prepositional phrases emphasize the relationship between the government *and the people*.

   Although parallel structure is effective in speech-making, it is also a
powerful tool for the writer. In the government-issued pamphlet *Understanding AIDS* (see pp. 191–97), important ideas are repeated in parallel
structure—for example, "You won't get AIDS from *saliva, sweat, tears,
urine* or a *bowel movement*"; and "People who have died of AIDS in the
U.S. have been *male* and *female, rich* and *poor, white, black, Hispanic,
Asian,* and *American Indian*." Very often parallel structure is used for contrast, as in the example above from Kennedy's speech and in these sentences from the AIDS pamphlet: "If you know someone well enough to
have sex, then you should be able to talk about AIDS. If someone is unwilling to talk, you shouldn't have sex." Another reason for using parallel
structure is to make *directions* clear and simple: "To throw a good curveball, *snap your wrist* down and across your chest, *spin the ball* off of your
first two fingers, and then *curl your hand* against your chest on the follow-
through."

   Parallel structure should be used for emphasis; overused, it becomes
monotonous and boring to the reader. What follows is a paragraph from
William Least Heat Moon's *Blue Highways*, which should give you a sense
of the proper distribution of parallelisms:

She longed for the true journey *of an Odysseus or Ishmael or Gulliver or even a Dorothy of Kansas*, wherein passage through *space* and *time* becomes only a metaphor of a movement through the interior of being. A true journey, no matter how long the travel takes, has no end. What's more, as John Le Carré, in speaking of the journey of death, said, "Nothing ever bridged the gulf between *the man who went* and *the man who stayed behind.*

Writing Practice

1. The passage that follows is from Charles Dickens' *A Tale of Two Cities.* Write down the correct words to make each part of the sentence parallel.

   a. "It was the best of times, it was the worst _____,

   b. it was the age of wisdom, it was _____ of foolishness,

   c. it was the epoch of belief, it was _____ of incredulity,

   d. it was the season of Light, it was _____ of Darkness,

   e. it was the spring of hope, it was the _____ of despair."

2. Correct each of the sentences below to make them parallel. Some may have several correct answers.

   EXAMPLE   He desired fame, wealth, and to be happy.

   ANSWER   He desired fame, wealth, and *happiness.*

   a. Joe Louis danced around the ring, jabbed with his left hand, and finally flattens Schmeling with a thunderous right.

   b. One Japanese tidal wave flattened several towns in 1896, also killed 27,000 people.

   c. He parked the tractor behind the shed, have tied the dogs to an oak tree, and put the cows out to pasture.

   d. The film showed real occurrences: a train approaching the station, people leaving a factory, workers to destroy a wall.

   e. A stream can provide boating adventures if it has a swift current, if it has close banks, and plenty of twists and turns.

   f. There was a striking contrast between the rich and those who had nothing.

   g. Many people find jogging lonely and it is boring.

   h. The circus immerses you in sights, sounds, and it has smells.

   i. The veteran teacher loved to kid with the freshmen, bully the sophomores, criticize the juniors, and he fought with the seniors.

   j. All men seek life, liberty, and pursuing happiness.

3. Use words of your own to make each of the following sentences parallel.

   a. The car was dented, broken, and _____.

   b. Babe Ruth was undisciplined and overweight, yet he could run, _____, and _____ like no other player before or since.

   c. There are many types of crime: murder, _____, and _____.

    d. The truck ran out of control, _____, and finally smashed into the abutment.

    e. When he came into the store, he looked around, picked out what he wanted, _____, and _____.

    f. Lincoln wanted to preserve the Union and _____.

    g. Truman was a man who spoke his mind and _____.

    h. If the symptoms worsen, call the doctor. If they stay the same, keep giving him aspirin. _____, let him go back to school.

    i. In a nation that loves movie stars and _____ athletes, the ordinary hero is often forgotten.

4. List in parallel structure the homework assignments you have.

5. Using parallel structure, write a few sentences explaining how you study.

SENTENCE ECONOMY

The fewer words you use, the better your writing will be. This principle of clear and forceful writing, or sentence economy, is something you probably never practiced in high school where, to impress your teacher, you tried to "pad" your papers to make them longer. We will now look at three original sentences from a student's rough draft and then see how she revised them for her final draft, shortening them to get rid of wordiness and making them clearer.

1. Original sentence:

```
Though consciously I do not recall this blessed event, for
I was only three years old, what I have always felt for
him tells me the story is true.
```

This sentence is unclear. "Blessed event" is a cliché, or overused phrase, for the "birth of a baby." But since we are not sure if that is what she means here, she revised the sentence:

```
Because I was only three years old when my parents brought
Michael home, I could not really recall our first meeting—
but the love I have always had for him tells me the story
is true.
```

In this version, she tells us that Michael was brought home (the blessed event), and she is more specific than in her original sentence—"what I have always felt for him"—by telling us what that feeling is: "the love I have always had for him." Can you think of a way to make the first part of her revised sentence even more clear? She could have said, for example, "when my parents (first) brought (baby) Michael home (from the hospital)."

2. Original sentence:

> Many of the characteristics we share are ones that bind us
> by blood, but the ones we share in spirit have given us
> the treasure of friendship.

Here the student wants to point out that she and Michael have more than blood ties in common. She explains this extra dimension of their relationship in her revised sentence:

> We are bound not only by ties of blood, but also of
> spirit—which has given us the additional treasure of
> friendship.

Not only is Michael her relative, he is also her friend.

3. Original sentence:

> Through the years of our transition from children to
> adults, our relationship made the journey, adhering to
> each of our lives a permanence of love and trust unyield-
> ing to time.

The writer's reference to "journey" here is awkward and unclear, as is the idea of "love and trust *adhering*." Her revised sentence is shorter and simpler:

> As we matured to adulthood, our relationship grew also,
> deepening in love and trust.

Sentence revision at this level can be hard work. It really helps to occasionally put your paper away for a time, and look at it again later for a fresher look. Sharing your writing with another trusted reader who can suggest ways to make it more concise always helps.

Writing Practice

1. The sentences below are too wordy; they contain redundant, or unnecessary, words and phrases. Rewrite each sentence, using as few words as possible while retaining the meaning.

EXAMPLE It was the custom and practice of the old chiefs to teach their young to survive many and countless difficulties.

ANSWER The old chiefs always taught their young to endure all difficulties.

    a. Jim was an early pioneer in the Civil Rights movement.
    b. Many factors tend toward influencing the collapse and fall of the economy.
    c. The Romans built and constructed miles of strong, durable roads.
    d. Freedom of speech is a basic, fundamental human right.

    e. Nothing worthwhile comes without an amount of responsibility.

    f. In order to promote the common good, the Constitution was written.

    g. Bing Crosby was a renowned and famous singer.

    h. The plane experienced a completely total loss of power.

    i. The President's first initial tour was a disappointment.

    j. The senator contended and maintained that he was innocent and guiltless.

2. Read the very wordy paragraph below and rewrite it, eliminating as many unnecessary words as you can. The first sentence has been revised and put in brackets as a model.

> After school the kids rush to their room, drop their books on the first clean surface they can find and rush to the kitchen for dinner. [After school the kids rush home to dinner.] Dinner is no longer the contemplative social gathering for the family where everyone sits down to summarize the activities of the day while articulating the digestive system on a very satisfying meal to comfort and console through a restful night's sleep. Instead it is a mad onrush to the serving table and then to the magic living room for a daily dose of "The Three Stooges," "Transformers," and "He-Man."

3. Below is another, more sophisticated piece of writing that requires some word surgery:

> At 7:15 on a cold spring morning, at least an hour before the kids came to school, Power's junior varsity baseball coach walked up the narrow stairs to post the names of those boys who had survived cuts and made the team. Only a fringe player himself, a pitcher with brains, desire, and no fastball, the coach had suffered enough setbacks in his own playing career to make him sensitive to the feelings of kids with high hopes and poor skills. The list of survivors, he felt, was the most humane way of letting kids know whether or not they had made the team; they wouldn't suffer the indignity of finding their name on a "cut list." As he was about to tack up his list, he barely noticed someone hugging the early morning shadows in the corridor—Jim Murphy, a freshman from Queens who had left his house at dawn to find his name among the chosen. It wasn't there. Without missing a beat, the coach hurriedly pocketed his list and went downstairs to add the name of Jim Murphy.

SENTENCE FRAGMENTS

One of the most serious problems in writing is the sentence fragment, part of a sentence written as if it were a complete sentence. To be a sentence, a group of words must have three characteristics:

1. Someone or something takes action.
2. The action is specified.
3. The word unit is not set up to be joined to another unit.

Sentence fragments fail to meet one or more of these qualifications.

Understanding the causes of sentence fragments can make you a better writer. Let's look at some of the different types of sentence fragments, why students write them, and how they can be corrected.

1. *Fragmentary clause* (begins with words like "who," "which," "that," "because," "since," "while," "when," "after," "although," "if," and "even if"):

   > Professional people like doctors and lawyers are earning huge salaries. *While high-school dropouts are earning minimum wage.*

   or

   > *While high-school dropouts are earning minimum wage.* Professional people like doctors and lawyers are earning huge salaries.

   The student has written the fragmentary clause "While high-school dropouts are earning minimum wage" as if it were a complete sentence, which it is not. Read it out loud to yourself. What happens "While high-school dropouts are earning minimum wage"? The fragmentary clause depends on the sentence for its meaning:

   > Professional people like doctors and lawyers are earning huge salaries *while high-school dropouts are earning minimum wage.*

   or

   > *While high-school dropouts are earning minimum wage,* professional people like doctors and lawyers are earning huge salaries.

2. Phrase fragment:

   > Disneyland is a source of great entertainment. *For adults as well as children.*
   >
   > REVISED   Disneyland is a source of great entertainment *for adults as well as children.*

3. Example fragment:

   > There are many possible evils of drunken driving. *Such as a head-on collision.*
   >
   > REVISED   There are many possible evils of drunken driving, *such as a head-on collision.*

4. List fragment:

   > Many pleasures beckoned to him. *Like wine, women, and song.*
   >
   > REVISED   Many pleasures beckoned to him *like wine, women, and song.*

5. Absolute (stand-alone) fragment:

   > *His new car flattened by the semi.* John turned to his fiance and cried.
   >
   > REVISED   *His new car flattened by the semi,* John turned to his fiance and cried.

6. An "-ing" fragment:

> The girls went to the mall to finish shopping for those perfect outfits. *Buying the perfect earrings to match their other clothes.*

> REVISED   The girls went to the mall to finish shopping for those perfect outfits, *buying the perfect earrings to match their other clothes.*

Note that in most of the examples above, fragments come *after* the sentence in which they belong. This often happens because students are afraid to write long sentences like the corrected ones above. They write according to some internal "wordometer" that forces them to end the sentence after they have written so many words. Because they panic, they end their sentence too abruptly and write a fragment. It is not the number of words that determines the boundaries of a sentence, but the meaning. One way of testing for fragments is to proofread your writing out loud. Does each sentence make sense? Remember that every sentence must be able to stand on its own; it should make sense without needing a sentence before or after it.

Writing Practice

Read each of the following sentences to yourself out loud. Then (a) underline the fragment, (b) explain what type it is, and (c) rewrite the sentence.

> EXAMPLE   Professionals like doctors and lawyers are earning huge salaries. *While high-school dropouts are earning minimum wage.*

> TYPE   Fragmentary clause.

> REVISED   Professionals like doctors and lawyers are earning huge salaries *while high-school dropouts are earning minimum wage.* [Punctuation note: Remember, if the "while" word group comes after the sentence, it requires a comma only if it adds extra information—not necessary information—to the sentence. If the word group comes first, put a comma after it: *While high-school dropouts are earning minimum wage,* professionals like doctors and lawyers are earning huge salaries.]

> EXAMPLE   Certain professionals earn far more money than others. *Such as doctors, lawyers, and engineers.*

> TYPE   List or example fragment.

> REVISED   Certain professionals earn far more money than others, *such as doctors, lawyers, and engineers.*

> EXAMPLE   He worked at Camp Fish during the long Minnesota summer. *Making enough money to pay for his first year of college.*

> TYPE   "-ing" fragment.

> REVISED   He worked at Camp Fish during the long Minnesota summer, *making enough money to pay for his first year of college.*

1. AIDS presents society with many problems. Such as the need for new and improved health care and protection for the rights of AIDS patients.

2. Well, I got over the fear and played the entire game scoring 12 points and playing my best defense ever. Even though I had to look into the crowd every now and then for that one reassuring face that was always positive and encouraging.

3. Most people are not comfortable driving with the seat belt, or they simply forget to buckle up. While others are more at ease knowing that they are buckled up.

4. On the other hand, research also indicates that it may be safer to wear seat belts. For adults as well as children.

5. As they say, the dog never bites the hand that feeds it. Also seems to be true in other aspects, for instance, insurance for all drivers.

6. In these years I had no choice but to sit back and let the world go on without me. Leaving me behind to dwell on the past and never even thinking about getting back in touch with society.

7. After the initial shock wore off. I came to realize that if I didn't start to take life more seriously, I would end up like my cousin.

8. It was hard for me being a teenager with children, no husband, and living with my parents. Having to do homework every night, doing chores that were expected of me by my parents, and waking up all times of the night for feeding time.

9. My kindergarten teacher told me I could not go to the bathroom until I could ask permission in English instead of the Spanish I spoke at home. So, I learned how to ask in English. Even if it took a lot of changing pants. I sure did learn how to say it pretty quick.

10. A caddy's job consists of a variety of small but essential tasks. Like carrying the clubs, knowing the distances to the green for all eighteen holes, and judging the length of his golfer's shots to advise him which club to use.

11. The twins abandoned as babies by their mother. They certainly started life with many disadvantages.

12. Nutritionists caution us to avoid foods that build up cholesterol. Such as too much beef, cheese, and french fries.

THE RUN-ON SENTENCE

The run-on sentence, in which two or more sentences are punctuated as one, is probably the most common error made by students when writing sentences. There are two basic types of run-ons, the "true" run-on and the comma splice.

The "True" Run-on

The "true" run-on has no punctuation at all:

> The Giants won the Super Bowl then they collapsed the next year.

This sentence has two separate main ideas or main clauses: (1) "The Giants won the Super Bowl" and (2) "then they collapsed the next year." Each of the two parts has both a subject and verb and can stand alone as a separate sentence:

> The Giants won the Super Bowl. Then they collapsed the next year.

One way to combine both related ideas into one sentence is to use a comma and a conjunction, or joining word, like "and," "but," "yet," "or," "nor," or "for":

> The Giants won the Super Bowl, and then they collapsed the next year.

This sentence uses ", and" to show sequence or progression. Another version might be:

> The Giants won the Super Bowl, but then they collapsed the next year.

Here the use of a comma followed by "but" shows contrast between the year the Giants won and the following bad season. Another way to correctly punctuate a run-on sentence is to use a semicolon:

> The Giants won the Super Bowl; then they collapsed the next year.

The use of the semicolon signals sequence or progression.

Which option should you choose? Too many sentences joined by a comma and "and" tend to be stringy:

> The Giants won the Super Bowl, and then they collapsed the next year, and after that season they received a high draft pick, and then they planned to rebuild.

The semicolon functions like a brake or pause in the middle of a sentence to slow down, but not stop, the reader (as a period does):

> The Giants won the Super Bowl; then they collapsed the next year. As a result of their bad season, they received a high draft pick and planned to rebuild.

The best principle to follow when deciding whether to use a comma and conjunction or a semicolon to correct a run-on sentence is variety. Change your sentence patterns by using both techniques.

The Comma Splice

This type of run-on sentence uses a comma by itself to join two thoughts:

> The Giants won the Super Bowl, then they collapsed the next year.

Remember that a comma by itself cannot join two ideas; a comma *and conjunction* can:

> The Giants won the Super Bowl, and then they collapsed the next year.

A semicolon by itself would also correct the comma splice:

> The Giants won the Super Bowl; then they collapsed the next year.

One point to remember about punctuation and run-on sentences is that *a comma and conjunction together are equivalent to a semicolon.*

Writing Practice

1. Use either a comma and conjunction or a semicolon to revise the following run-on sentences.
   a. My teachers were quite understanding they gave me lots of support.
   b. I reached her with my voice, she came running toward me.
   c. That incident caused me to miss graduation, my speech was assigned to someone else.
   d. After the season the rookie returned home to rest and build up for the next season, he wanted to have another big year.
2. There are other options, besides punctuation, that you can use to rewrite run-on sentences. A semicolon followed by "however" and a comma can be used to show contrast:

The Giants won the Super Bowl; however, they collapsed the next year.

Revise the following two run-on sentences using the semicolon and "however."
   a. There was problem after problem, finally I graduated.
   b. Pennsylvania has no laws about seat belts they have more of a solution.

The word "because" can be used to show cause and effect:

Because the Giants had a terrible year, they received next season's highest draft choice.

The word "although" can be used to indicate concession, yielding, or agreement:

Although the Giants won the Super Bowl, they collapsed the next year.

Using either "because" or "although," rewrite the following run-on sentences.
   c. I felt so bad, it seemed there was problem after problem.
   d. There was problem after problem, I finally got my diploma.

Words ending in "-ing" and "-ed" are often used in phrases to depict a time relationship:

After winning the Super Bowl, the Giants collapsed the next year.

or

Defeated by every team in their division, the Giants collapsed the next year.

Revise the following two run-on sentences using a word ending in either "-ing" or "-ed."

   e. The rookie slugger worked for hours each day to hit the curve ball he made the all-star team.

   f. The team was swamped with major injuries, no team had more players on the disabled list.

The words "which" and "who" are usually used for further description:

The Giants, who had won the Super Bowl, collapsed the next year.

or

The horse which won the Derby and Preakness finished second in the Belmont.

Use a "which" or "who" word group to revise these two run-on sentences.

   g. The rookie slugger worked for hours each day to hit the curve ball he made the all-star team.

   h. After a long delay the game was resumed it was for the pennant.

3. Rewrite the following run-on sentence using the indicated method.

My teachers were quite supportive they gave me lots of love and kindness.

   a. , and
   b. ;
   c. -ing
   d. because
   e. who

4. Rewrite the following run-on sentences as short paragraphs using any of the techniques covered in this chapter. Employ variety in your answers.

   a. I learned a lot in that class and ended up passing it, I never liked it, though, and as far as I'm concerned, it was my first and last science class.

   b. This put me in an awkward position usually the nurses were busy with other duties so if someone was going to die I was the first one to know.

5. Using as many revision methods as you can, rewrite the following paragraph.

I personally can't decide about seat belts. I think your choice depends on the type of person you are and the type of accident you fear. Accidents happen quite often, some people choose not to wear seat belts because they're only going a short distance, there is no assurance that an accident won't happen in that short distance. Pennsylvania has no laws about seat belts, they have more of a solution.

6. Revise the sentences in a paper that you wrote earlier in the semester (even if there are no run-ons), using all of the methods covered in this chapter.

READING: "PAMPERED POOCHES CAN LAP UP THE LIFE OF LUXURY IN JAPAN"

The following article by Yumiko Ono uses narration and description to inform. Use your prereading techniques to read the title and subtitle:

Pampered Pooches Can Lap Up the Life of Luxury in Japan

✱ ✱ ✱

Bikinis, Yogurt and Spas Fill Dog Days of Summer; Kitty's $6,000 Necklace

Write down what you think the article is about.

Now read the first paragraph using the three-step prediction strategy:

> KINUGAWA, Japan—After traveling 400 miles from Tokyo to one of Japan's most popular hot spa resorts, Mary decides she doesn't like bathing outdoors, especially with male company. She takes one dip in the steaming water, then springs up, clutching the edge of the tub. She glances indignantly at Harry, who sits relaxed, head back in the water, eyes closed.

1. *Prequest.* Predict the main idea question.
2. *Clarify.* Clarify the meaning of any difficult sentences.
3. *Prenext.* Predict what the next paragraph will say.

Read the second paragraph and the last two paragraphs:

> Mary, an eight-month-old miniature spaniel, and Harry, a two-year-old Chihuahua, are spending a relaxing weekend at the Kinugawa Kokusai Hotel's "pets-only, mixed-bathing" outdoor spa. After the bath, they will get a thorough blow-dry, and then chow down a low-fat dinner of boiled chicken and milk, at the same table as their owners.

> • • •

> A more symbolic ritual proceeds in a planetarium-like dome in the basement of a western Tokyo pet shop. Mourners gaze upward at a $520,000 computer-generated image of a galaxy, while music blares. A pulsing blob of light in a clear pyramid, meant to represent the pet's soul, shoots a spark of light into a star.
> "There," says the funeral director. "The pet has gone back to the land of stars."

Write down a further prediction about the article. Note how the first paragraph fooled us into believing Mary and Harry are humans.

Now read the entire article:

Pampered Pooches Can Lap Up the Life of Luxury in Japan

✳ ✳ ✳

Bikinis, Yogurt and Spas Fill Dog Days of Summer; Kitty's $6,000 Necklace

By Yumiko Ono

Staff Reporter of The Wall Street Journal

KINUGAWA, Japan—After traveling 400 miles from Tokyo to one of Japan's most popular hot spa resorts, Mary decides she doesn't like bathing outdoors, especially with male company. She takes one dip in the steaming water, then springs up, clutching the edge of the tub. She glances indignantly at Harry, who sits relaxed, head back in the water, eyes closed.

Mary, an eight-month-old miniature spaniel, and Harry, a two-year-old Chihuahua, are spending a relaxing weekend at the Kinugawa Kokusai Hotel's "pets-only, mixed-bathing" outdoor spa. After the bath, they will get a thorough blow-dry, and then chow down a low-fat dinner of boiled chicken and milk, at the same table as their owners.

Such are the lengths that Japanese pet lovers go to to pamper their pooches. Californians may have their dog cemeteries and cat psychics, but in the last few years, Japanese pet freaks have become every bit as eccentric, creating a $2 billion-a-year industry. Goods and services now available to Japan's 12 million dogs and cats include diapers, bikinis, dating services, weddings, yoga and funerals.

Better Than Children

"This pet boom is absurd," says Katsumi Hoshino, a lecturer on changing so-cial trends at the University of Tsukuba. "There are more businesses for pets than for people."

The cause of all this is simple. Some Japanese have more money than they know what to do with. Few can afford to buy housing in Japan's overheated real-estate market, so some spend the surplus yen on canned oxygen (used by sports buffs and others) and electric nail shavers. Others, particularly middle-aged women, buy $1,900 Maltese dogs or $3,800 Scottish Fold cats, give them American names, which they think are cute, and then shower the little darlings with luxuries.

"Whenever I see cute pet clothes, I keep wanting to buy them," says Kinue Gunji, a housewife living in the south of Tokyo. "Sure they cost money. But I love my dog more than my child." Mrs. Gunji is staying at the spa with her daughter, her husband, and her Pomeranian, Shelley, who gets a monthly medical check-up, and was recently treated to a new set of rain boots.

Rubbing Noses

Hotel owner Keiko Akutsu began offering pet lodging and meals last year, after she took a trip to Europe and was impressed by the welcome many hotels there extended to animals. Expanding on the European concept, Mrs. Akutsu charges people $110 a night to stay at her hotel, and allows their pets to stay with them for

continued

continued

an extra $4. Her hotel's revenues have nearly doubled.

"The owners are so pleased when we treat the pets like people," says the 55-year-old Mrs. Akutsu, who even has little futon mattresses for the pets. Animal guests, who tend to arrive wearing hats and dresses, are referred to as "little boys" and "little girls." Owners are discreetly handed a plastic pick-up bag and a packet of tissues before they go for a walk.

These boys and girls are free to socialize in the lounge beside the pet souvenir shop, while their owners chat. Squeezed into a tight denim jumpsuit, Chuji, a chubby male Pomeranian, bounces off the table, flapping the red ribbons tied around his ears. Two of his buttons have burst. "We have a jumpsuit just like that one," says Mrs. Gunji, the devoted owner of Shelley. "But ours has a little pocket to put tissues in."

Chuji and Mary rub noses, and their owners coo in delight. Shingo, a two-pound Chihuahua wrapped in a red kilted vest, is jealous. Seeking attention, he strolls over to the bar and urinates on the carpet, making Mrs. Akutsu rush over with a can of deodorant spray. His owner, a middle-aged woman in pink pajamas, gives him a little slap, then cuddles him tightly.

Those looking for more things to put on the dog, will enjoy the Osaka pet fair this month. Along with pet clothes, wigs and good luck charms, there will be $380,000 cats prancing around wearing $6,000 necklaces. Then, there will be the wedding. Two Shetland sheepdogs, one dressed in a tuxedo and the other in a wedding dress, will exchange collars in front of a human "priest," as bow-tied St. Bernards and Pomeranians watch and wag.

Actually, the groom is lucky to have found a bride. In Japan, where many pet owners live in apartments, most male house pets can't sneak out at night, and thus have no chance to meet girls. They end their lives single and sad, says Isoroku Kimura, a Tokyo pet-shop owner. He felt so sorry for them that last year, he set up a pet dating service. Twenty dogs, each of whose owners has dished out snap shots, resumes and $75 for each date, have high hopes for the coming mating season this fall.

Kitty Kimonos

Even pets' everyday food and clothing are becoming more upscale. At Adachiya, a pet fashion boutique in Tokyo's Asakusa district, a baseball uniform, with cap and socks, hangs next to a raincoat and a dress with huge sunflower patterns. (Sunflowers are also the fashion for human girls in Japan this summer.)

"We sometimes wonder if these things are really necessary," confesses Yoshio Iida, an Adachiya executive. But the tiny store sold 170 pet garments one cold winter day. The clothes, priced $30 and up, are made in all sizes, to fit anything from Chihuahuas to Great Danes. A simpler T-shirt, jumpsuit, or cotton kimono is recommended for sharp-nailed cats. There are also a red bikini for the beach, a knapsack for the mountains, a $300 kimono and a $7,600 white mink coat for special photo-taking occasions.

Sogo department store in Yokohama prepares elaborate take-out meals for pets. The most popular, says a store official, is the $75 pet steak dinner of premium rare beef, unsalted ham, sausages and cheese, and white chocolate for dessert. Yasuaki Ohmori, a Tokyo high-school teacher, confesses to having stolen a bite of his dachshund's meal, a meat dish in a special sauce. "It was quite tasty," he says in embarrassment.

Pulling Hares

When too much rich food starts showing as flab, Fido can turn to jogging machines and yogurt, made especially for dogs. At Japan Trimming School, pets can take a 45-minute private yoga lesson for $35: An instructor personally stretches them into 15 poses, intended to improve blood circulation and relax muscles. (Concentration is said to be essential, so distracting observers aren't allowed.) Although most students are canines, someone once brought a rabbit for a stretch.

After the prized pet eventually passes away, a funeral service will cremate the pet right outside the owner's door. Jippo Corp., a truck company, sends a young woman ceremony director in the "Pet Angel Service" truck. Clad in a pink jumpsuit to give the event a rosier image, she instructs tearful owners to place flowers on the pink altar, next to the truck's incinerator. "Thank you for taking care of me up till now," says a recorded woman's voice. The ashes are placed in a candy jar.

A more symbolic ritual proceeds in a planetarium-like dome in the basement of a western Tokyo pet shop. Mourners gaze upward at a $520,000 computer-generated image of a galaxy, while music blares. A pulsing blob of light in a clear pyramid, meant to represent the pet's soul, shoots a spark of light into a star.

"There," says the funeral director. "The pet has gone back to the land of stars."

Reading for Meaning

1. What is the main idea of the article?
2. How does the writer support the main idea?
3. How does the first paragraph about Mary and Harry throw us off?
4. What is the *tone* (the writer's attitude—straightforward, sarcastic, humorous, etc.) of the article?
5. What does the article point to as the root cause for these excesses about pets?
6. How do the last three paragraphs present a fitting end to the article?
7. What are some of the services that make up the $2 billion-a-year pet industry?
8. Why is there a need in Japan for a pet dating service?

Vocabulary in Context

Write down the definition of each of the italicized words below taken from the article. Try to guess the meaning from the context. Use a dictionary only if you have to.

1. "Californians may have their dog cemeteries and cat *psychics* . . ."
2. "A simpler T-shirt, jumpsuit, or cotton *kimono* is recommended for cats."

Writing from Reading

For each of the following assignments, remember to consider your *subject, purpose,* and *audience.*

1. Have you ever seen, or been a part of, something unusual? Try to recall such an incident, brainstorming as many specifics as you can remember. Then try to put the items on your list in chronological order. Write a first and a final draft of a paper.

2. Anecdotes are short, often amusing stories placed within larger narratives. Read this step-by-step description from the article, seeing how each detail contributes to the overall effect:

   > Chuji and Mary rub noses, and their owners coo in delight. Shingo, a two-pound Chihuahua wrapped in a red kilted vest, is jealous. Seeking attention, he strolls over to the bar and urinates on the carpet, making Mrs. Akutsu rush over with a can of deodorant spray. His owner, a middle-aged woman in pink pajamas, gives him a little slap, then cuddles him tightly.

   Try to recall a short, funny incident that you have witnessed and think would make a good anecdote. Tell the anecdote step-by-step like the one above, allowing the reader to see the humor.

3. *Peer reading assignment.* Do one of the two assignments above, sharing your work at each stage of the writing process with the other students in your group.

CHAPTER

5

Paragraph Development from Reporter's Questions

THE REPORTER'S QUESTIONS

Reporters get facts to the reader quickly, usually in the very first paragraph. By answering a series of questions, called reporter's questions, they provide the reader with the main information: *who, what, when, where,* and sometimes *how* and/or *why.* Look at *Chicago Tribune* reporter Gary Washburn's first paragraph in his article on Chicago Transit Authority security (see pp. 107–108).

The Regional Transportation Authority board agreed Tuesday to provide $500,000 next year for added security on the Chicago Transit Authority, but officials acknowledged that the money is largely symbolic and won't rid the CTA of crime.

Who? RTA Board.
When? Tuesday.
What? Provide $500,000 for more CTA security.
Where? Obviously Chicago, but naming the exact site of the meeting is not necessary.
Why? Answered in the body of the article.

The reporter's questions can be used to describe any incident or to tell a story. In a student paper the questions don't always have to be answered in the opening paragraph, but they should be contained in the entire piece.

Writing Practice

Use the reporter's questions in each of the following assignments to make your writing clear to the reader.

1. Describe an accident that involved you.
2. Tell of a time when you were really afraid.
3. Relate an incident when you were truly proud of yourself.
4. Tell of a terrible moment for you in school one day.
5. Describe a great day you had in school.

THE PARAGRAPH AND THE TOPIC SENTENCE

After the sentence, the paragraph is the basic unit of writing. Each paragraph should be based on one controlling idea, usually stated in a topic sentence and often placed at the beginning. The paragraph should be long enough to develop and support the main idea fully. When you turn to a new idea, you begin a new paragraph. Consider the following paragraph from a newspaper article by reporter John Shannon describing the charitable work of John Wetterer, founder of *Mi Casa*, a home and school for orphans in Guatemala:

> No one skims from the money or goods donated to *Mi Casa*. Pat Coles, the corporation's secretary, uses her own stamps to mail the checks from New York. Mary Tyre uses her own boxes to send the clothing. She also sponsors a child. It costs about $17 per month to feed, clothe, and educate a child in the home. This year she will put up two of Wetterer's oldest, who will be studying business at Miami-Dade Community College.

The first sentence—"No one skims from the money or goods donated to *Mi Casa*"—is the topic sentence. The rest of the paragraph supports this idea: Pat Coles uses her own stamps, Mary Tyre uses her own boxes, Tyre sponsors a child, and she houses two of Wetterer's graduates in her own home as they attend college. Each of these four examples develops the topic sentence.

See how this paragraph about AIDS from an article in the magazine *U.S. News & World Report* by Stacy Wells (see pp. 199–200) also begins with the topic sentence:

> Compared with plagues of the past, AIDS is relatively difficult to contract. Unlike the Black Death, it is not spread by insect bites. Unlike smallpox, it is not spread by casual skin contact. Unlike influenza, it is not spread through coughs and sneezes. And unlike typhus, it is not spread through contaminated water.

The topic sentence states that AIDS is difficult to contract, an idea supported by comparisons with four other diseases: the Black Death, smallpox, influenza, and typhus. The pattern of development here is comparison and contrast, and the paragraph is tightened by the use of parallel structure in similar phraseology—"unlike . . . , it is not spread. . . ." Also note the transition "and" at the beginning of the last sentence.

PARAGRAPH DEVELOPMENT

Paragraphs may be developed in different ways: by examples, as in the piece about *Mi Casa*; by facts; and by rhetorical modes—that is, patterns of writing such as cause and effect or comparison/contrast—like the paragraph on AIDS (rhetorical modes will be examined in detail later in the book).

For many paragraphs, however, the writer can check for completeness of development by using the reporter's questions of *who, what, when, where,* and sometimes *how* and/or *why.* Analyze this paragraph from Roger Cohen's article in the *Wall Street Journal,* "Brazilian Youths Get Macho Thrills Riding Atop Trains" (see pp. 118–21) to see how he answers some of these questions:

Riding the tops of trains is a stunt popular among the poor youths of north Rio. Their counterparts in the wealthy south of the city surf the waves; they surf the trains—despite 200 deaths and 500 injuries over the past 18 months. The so-called "surfistas" abound on the early-morning and evening trains into and out of the city center. Adopting nicknames like Rambo, Stallone and Pistoleiro, or Gunman, they are drawn by the macho appeal of defying danger and a camaraderie that bears the fervid intensity of a blood rite.

The topic sentence answers what—*riding the tops of trains, and* who *and* where—*the poor youths of north Rio.*

More what—*facts and statistics.*
When—*present time.*

More who—*nicknames.*

Why—*macho appeal and camaraderie.*

Although it is only part of a longer article, this paragraph still answers the basic questions of *who, what, when, where,* and *why.*

Writing Practice

For each of the following assignments, write a paragraph that begins with a topic sentence and that answers as many of the reporter's questions as possible.

1. Describe an injury you suffered.
2. Relate an embarrassing moment for you.

3. Tell of a humorous incident in school.

4. Discuss some award or honor you received.

5. Analyze how you solved some personal dilemma.

ACHIEVING COHERENCE IN SENTENCES AND PARAGRAPHS

The good writer strives for coherence in writing, always looking for ways to tie his or her sentences and paragraphs together. Parallel structure, discussed in Chapter 4, is one way of accomplishing this. Three other ways of achieving coherence are the use of transitions (see Chapter 9, pp. 128–31), the use of pronouns to replace nouns (naming words) and, finally, the repetition of nouns:

1. Transitions are words like "and," "but," "first," "second," "finally," and so on that link other words, thoughts, sentences, and parts of a paragraph or essay.

2. Pronouns are words that can be substituted for nouns, and usually follow the first mention of a noun. For example, "John built the home, and then *he* moved in." Or, "Mary answered the man's question, but *she* refused to talk with him further."

3. Key words, usually nouns, are repeated for emphasis: ". . . government of the *people*, by the *people*, for the *people*. . . ."

Read the paragraph below from William Least Heat Moon's *Blue Highways*. All the words used for coherence—transitions, pronouns, and repeated nouns, as well as words used for parallel structure—are underlined.

A car whipped past, the driver eating and a passenger clicking a camera. Moving without going anywhere, taking a trip instead of making one. I laughed at the absurdity of the photographs and then realized that I, too, was rolling effortlessly along, turning the windshield into a movie screen in which I, the viewer, did the moving while the subject held still. That was the temptation of the American highway, of the American vacation (from the Latin *vacare*, "to be empty"). A woman in Texas had told me that she often threatened to write a book about her family vacations. Her title: Zoom! The drama of their trips, she said, occurred on the inside of the windshield with one family crisis after another. Her husband drove a thousand miles, much of it with his right arm over the backseat to hold down one of the children. She said, "Our vacations take us."

Of the 152 words in the paragraph, 38, or 25 percent, are used for coherence. A good writer spends much of his or her time chiseling words, sentences, and paragraphs that unify the paper.

Writing Practice

1. Take one of the paragraphs that you wrote early in the semester and (a) try to add meaningful transitions to it; (b) substitute pronouns for some of the nouns; and (c) attempt to repeat a key noun (like "vacation" in the paragraph from *Blue Highways*) once or twice.

2. Repeat the exercise above with one of your longer papers.

Peer Evaluation of Paragraph

1. Take one of your paragraphs—for example, the one you wrote in exercise 1—and read it out loud to a small group of students. Have them then read it to themselves and respond, in writing, to the following checklist.
   a. Explain the type of prewriting used.
   b. What is the main point or topic sentence of the paragraph?
   c. What is the subject of the topic sentence?
   d. List the support the writer gives for his or her topic sentence.
   e. Explain why the content of the paragraph is or is not interesting.
   f. List any transitions used in the paragraph.
   g. Write down any sentences that are not clear or correct.
   h. List any spelling errors the writer has made.
   i. List any sentence fragments the writer has written.
   j. List any run-on sentences the writer has written.

2. As a writer you are responsible for what goes into your paper. While still reserving the right to follow or ignore the views of your peers, you must respond to their advice and comments. You should have reasons for either adopting or rejecting material from your checklist. After reviewing the suggestions and criticisms of the other students, write down responses to the following questions.
   a. What ideas will you adopt from your peer checklist?
   b. What are your reasons for adopting those ideas?
   c. What ideas from the checklist will you not use?
   d. What are your reasons for not using those ideas?
   e. Write down corrections of any spelling errors found by your peers.
   f. Write down revisions of any sentence fragments.
   g. Write down revisions of any run-on sentences.

READING: "HOPI LAND"

The book *Blue Highways* is William Least Heat Moon's autobiographical journal of his year-long trip on the backwoods' roads of America (on maps these roads are designated as Blue Highways). The author, a 38-year-old of mixed ancestry—part Sioux Indian and part white—lived in his van as he drove across rural America on a journey of self-discovery. His journal reveals to us as readers much of what he learned about America and himself.

The following chapter from *Blue Highways*, "Hopi Land," describes William's trip through the Navajo and Hopi Indian reservations of the Southwest. Like any good journal, its point of view is personal, reflecting what William thinks of himself as part Indian in relation to the full-blooded Indians he meets on his journey. As you read pay close attention to what the writer says about himself. What does he reveal about his own self-image?

First look at the first two paragraphs and the last two paragraphs:

TUESDAY morning: the country east of Heber was a desert of sagebrush and globe-shaped junipers and shallow washes with signs warning of flash floods. I turned north at Snowflake, founded by Erastus Snow and Bill Flake, and headed toward the twenty-five thousand square miles of Navajo reservation (nearly equal to West Virginia) which occupies most of the northeastern corner of Arizona. The scrub growth disappeared entirely and only the distant outlines of red rock mesas interrupted the emptiness. But for the highway, the land was featureless.

Holbrook used to be a tough town where boys from the Hash Knife cattle outfit cut loose. Now, astride I-44 (once route 66), Holbrook was a tourist stop for women with Instamatics and men with metal detectors; no longer was the big business cattle, but rather rocks and gems.

• • •

Intimidated by my ignorance of Navajo and by fear of the contempt that full-bloods often show lesser bloods, I again failed to stir a conversation. After the storn blew on east, I followed the old men back outside, where they squatted to watch the day take up the weather of an hour earlier. To one with a great round head like an earthen pot, I said, "Is the storm finished now?" He looked at me, then slowly turned his head, while the others examined before them things in the air invisible to me.

I took a highway down the mesa into a valley of the Painted Desert, where wind had textured big drifts of orange sand into rills. U.S. 89 ran north along the Echo Cliffs. Goats grazed in stubble by the roadsides, and to the west a horseman moved his sheep. Hogans here stood alone; they were not ceremonial lodges but homes. For miles at the highway edges sat little cardboard and scrapwood ramadas, each with a windblasted sign advertising jewelry and cedar beads. In another era, white men came in wagons to trade beads to Indians; now they came in stationwagons and bought beads. History may repeat, but sometimes things get turned around in the process.

Using your prediction techniques, write down what main point you think the author is trying to make.

Now read the entire passage:

Hopi Land

TUESDAY morning: the country east of Heber was a desert of sagebrush and globe-shaped junipers and shallow washes with signs warning of flash floods. I turned north at Snowflake, founded by Erastus Snow and Bill Flake, and headed toward the twenty-five thousand square miles of Navajo reservation (nearly equal to West Virginia) which occupies most of the northeastern corner of Arizona. The scrub growth disappeared entirely and only the distant outlines of red rock mesas interrupted the emptiness. But for the highway, the land was featureless.

Holbrook used to be a tough town where boys from the Hash Knife cattle outfit cut loose. Now, astride I-44 (once route 66), Holbrook was a tourist stop for women with Instamatics and men with metal detectors; no longer was the big business cattle, but rather rocks and gems.

North of the interstate, I entered the reserve. Although the area has been part of the Navajo homeland for five hundred years, settlers of a century before, led by Kit Carson, drove the Navajo out of Arizona in retribution for their raids against whites and other Indians alike. A few years later, survivors of the infamous "Long Walk" returned to take up their land again. Now the Navajo possess the largest reservation in the United States and the one hundred fifty thousand descendants of the seven thousand survivors comprise far and away the largest tribe. Their reservation is the only one in the country to get bigger—five times bigger—after it was first set aside; their holdings increased largely because white men had believed Navajo land worthless. But in fact, the reservation contains coal, oil, gas, uranium, helium, and timber; those resources may explain why Navajos did not win total control over their land until 1972.

Liquor bottles, beercans, an occasional stripped car littered the unfenced roadside. Far off the highway, against the mesa bottoms, stood small concrete-block or frame houses, each with a television antenna, pickup, privy, and ceremonial hogan of stone, adobe, and cedar. Always the hogan doors faced east.

In a classic scene, a boy on a pinto pony herded a flock of sheep and goats—descendants of the Spanish breed—across the highway. A few miles later, a man wearing a straw Stetson and pegleg Levi's guided up a draw a pair of horses tied together at the neck in the Indian manner. With the white man giving up on the economics of cowpunching, it looked as if the old categories of cowboys and Indians had merged; whoever the last true cowboy in America turns out to be, he's likely to be an Indian.

At the center of the reservation lay Hopi territory, a large rectangle with boundaries the tribes cannot agree on because part of the increase of Navajo land has come at the expense of the Hopis. A forbidding sign in Latinate English:

YOU ARE ENTERING THE EXCLUSIVE HOPI RESERVATION AREA. YOUR ENTRANCE CONSTITUTES CONSENT TO THE JURISDICTION OF THE HOPI TRIBE AND ITS COURTS.

continued

continued

Although the Hopi have lived here far longer than any other surviving people and consider their mile-high spread of rock and sand, wind and sun, the center of the universe, they are now, by Anglo decree, surrounded by their old enemies, the Navajo, a people they see as latecomers. In 1880, Hopis held two and one half million acres; today it has decreased to about a half million.

Holding on to their land has been a long struggle for the Hopi. Yet for a tribe whose name means "well behaved," for Indians without war dances, for a group whose first defense against the conquistadors was sprinkled lines of sacred cornmeal, for a people who protested priestly corruption (consorting with Hopi women and whipping men) by quietly pitching a few padres over the cliffs, Hopis have done well. But recently they have fought Navajo expansion in federal courts, and a strange case it is: those who settled first seeking judgment from those who came later through laws of those who arrived last.

Because the Navajo prefer widely dispersed clusters of clans to village life, I'd seen nothing resembling a hamlet for seventy-five miles. But Hopi Polacca almost looked like a Western town in spite of Indian ways here and there: next to a floral-print bedsheet on a clothesline hung a coyote skin, and beside box houses were adobe bread ovens shaped like skep beehives. The Navajo held to his hogan, the Hopi his oven. Those things persisted.

Like bony fingers, three mesas reached down from larger Black Mesa into the middle of Hopi land; not long ago, the only way onto these mesas was by handholds in the steep rock heights. From the tops, the Hopi look out upon a thousand square miles. At the heart of the reservation, topographically and culturally, was Second Mesa. Traditionally, Hopis, as do the eagles they hold sacred,

prefer to live on precipices; so it was not far from the edge of Second Mesa that they built the Hopi Cultural Center. In the gallery were drawings of mythic figures by Hopi children who fused centuries and cultures with grotesque Mudhead Kachinas wearing large terra-cotta masks and jackolantern smiles, dancing atop spaceships with Darth Vader and Artoo Deetoo.

At the Center, I ate *nokquivi*, a good hominy stew with baked chile peppers, but I had no luck in striking up a conversation. I drove on toward the western edge of the mesa. Not far from the tribal garage (TRIBAL VEHICLES ONLY) stood small sandstone houses, their slabs precisely cut and fitted as if by ancient Aztecs, a people related to the Hopi. The solid houses blended with the tawny land so well they appeared part of the living rock. All were empty. The residents had moved to prefabs and doublewides.

I couldn't see how anyone could survive a year in this severe land, yet Hopis, like other desert life, are patient and clever and not at all desperate; they have lasted here for ten centuries by using tiny terraced plots that catch spring rain and produce a desert-hardy species of blue corn, as well as squash, onions, beans, peppers, melons, apricots, peaches. The bristlecone pine of American Indians, Hopis live where almost nothing else will, thriving long in adverse conditions: poor soil, drought, temperature extremes, high winds. Those give life to the bristlecone and the Hopi.

Clinging to the southern lip of Third Mesa was ancient Oraibi, most probably the oldest continuously occupied village in the United States. Somehow the stone and adobe have been able to hang on to the precipitous edge since the twelfth century. More than eight hundred Hopis lived at Oraibi in 1901—now only a few. All across the reservation I'd seen no more than a dozen people, and on the dusty streets of the old town I saw just one bent woman struggling against the wind. But somewhere there must have been more.

To this strangest of American villages the Franciscan father, Tomás Garces, came in 1776 from Tucson with gifts and "true religion." Hopis permitted him to stay at Oraibi, looking then as now if you excluded an occasional televison antenna, but they refused his gifts and god, and, on the fourth day of July, sent him off disheartened. To this time, no other North American tribe has held closer to its own religion and culture. Although the isolated Hopi had no knowledge of the importance of religious freedom to the new nation surrounding them, several generations successfully ignored "the code of religious offenses"—laws designed by the Bureau of Indian Affairs to destroy the old rituals and way of life—until greater bureaucratic tolerance came when Herbert Hoover appointed two Quakers to direct the BIA.

A tribal squadcar checked my speed at Hotevilla, where the highway started a long descent off the mesa. The wind was getting up, and tumbleweed bounded across the road, and sand hummed against the Ghost [the name William had given his van]. West, east, north, south—to each a different weather: sandstorm, sun, rain, and bluish snow on the San Francisco Peaks, that home of the Kachinas who are the spiritual forces of Hopi life.

Tuba City, founded by Mormon missionaries as an agency and named after a Hopi chieftain although now mostly a Navajo town, caught the sandstorm full face. As I filled the gas tank, I tried to stay behind the van, but gritty gusts whipped around the corners and stung me and forced my eyes shut. School was just out, and children, shirts pulled over their heads, ran for the trading post, where old Navajo men who had been sitting outside took cover as the sand changed the air to matter. I ducked in too. The place was like an A&P, TG&Y, and craft center.

In viridescent velveteen blouses and violescent nineteenth-century skirts, Navajo women of ample body, each laden with silver and turquoise bracelets, necklaces, and rings—not the trading post variety but heavy bands gleaming under the patina of long wear—reeled off yards of fabric. The children, like schoolkids anywhere, milled around the candy; they spoke only English. But the old men, now standing at the plate glass windows and looking into the brown wind, popped and puffed out the ancient words. I've read that Navajo, a language related to that of the Indians of Alaska and northwest Canada, has no curse words unless you consider "coyote" cursing. By comparison with other native tongues, it's remarkably free of English and Spanish; a Navajo mechanic, for example, has more than two hundred purely Navajo terms to describe automobile parts. And it might be Navajo that will greet the first extraterrestrial ears to hear from planet Earth: on board each *Voyager* spacecraft traveling toward the edge of the solar system and beyond is a gold-plated, long-playing record; following an aria from Mozart's *Magic Flute* and Chuck Berry's "Johnny B. Goode," is a Navajo night chant, music the conquistadors heard.

Intimidated by my ignorance of Navajo and by fear of the contempt that fullbloods often show lesser bloods, I again failed to stir a conversation. After the storm blew on east, I followed the old men back outside, where they squatted to watch the day take up the weather of an hour earlier. To one with a great round head like an earthen pot, I said, "Is the storm finished now?" He looked at me, then slowly turned his head, while the others examined before them things in the air invisible to me.

continued

continued

I took a highway down the mesa into a valley of the Painted Desert, where wind had textured big drifts of orange sand into rills. U.S. 89 ran north along the Echo Cliffs. Goats grazed in stubble by the roadsides, and to the west a horseman moved his sheep. Hogans here stood alone; they were not ceremonial lodges but homes. For miles at the highway edges sat little cardboard and scrapwood ramadas, each with a windblasted sign advertising jewelry and cedar beads. In another era, white men came in wagons to trade beads to Indians; now they came in stationwagons and bought beads. History may repeat, but sometimes things get turned around in the process.

Reading for Meaning

1. At the end of this excerpt, William Least Heat Moon describes how the old Navajo men at the trading post react to him. How do they treat him and why? Have you ever been fearful of racial hostility, or had it directed against you? Using the reporter's questions of *who, what, when, where, how,* and/or *why,* give a good description of your experiences.

2. What is unique about the Navajo language?

3. What is the dispute between the Navajo and Hopi?

4. Why did the Navajo reservation increase in size? What is ironic about this?

5. How do the Hopi and Navajo differ in how they group themselves for living arrangements?

6. What physical hardships have the Hopi always overcome?

7. How do the Hopi traditionally demonstrate their love for their religion?

8. What is the historical twist revealed at the end of this passage?

9. What does the author reveal to us about white treatment of the Indian?

Vocabulary in Context

Write down the definition of each of the italicized words below taken from the passage. Try to guess the meaning from the context. Use a dictionary only if you have to.

1. ". . . only the distant outlines of red-rock *mesas* interrupted the emptiness."

2. "Kit Carson . . . drove the Navajo out of Arizona in *retribution* for their raids . . ."

3. "the . . . survivors *comprise* far and away the largest tribe."

4. ". . . against the mesa bottoms . . . stood small concrete-block or frame houses, each with a television antenna, pickup, *privy,* and ceremonial *hogan* of stone adobe, and cedar."

5. ". . . a man wearing a straw *Stetson* . . ."
6. ". . . whose first defense against the *conquistadors* . . ."
7. ". . . priestly corruption (*consorting* with Hopi women and whipping men) . . ."
8. ". . . adobe bread ovens shaped like *skep* beehives."
9. "At the heart of the reservation, *topographically* and culturally, . . ."
10. ". . . Hopis, as do the eagles they hold sacred, prefer to live on *precipices*; . . ."
11. ". . . fused centuries and cultures with grotesque Mudhead *Kachinas* wearing large *terra-cotta* masks and jackolantern smiles, dancing atop spaceships with Darth Vader and Artoo Deetoo."
12. ". . . *hominy* stew . . ."
13. "In *viridescent* velveteen blouses . . ."
14. ". . . heavy bands gleaming with the *patina* of long wear . . ."
15. ". . . wind had textured big drifts of orange sand into *rills*."

Writing from Reading

For each of the following assignments, remember to consider your *subject*, *purpose*, and *audience*.

1. In this passage the author twice mentions his inability to strike up a conversation with other Indians, once at the Hopi Cultural Center and later at the store in Tuba City. He says he was "intimidated by [his] ignorance of Navajo and by fear of the contempt that full-bloods often show lesser bloods. . . ." His fears are borne out by the fact that one of the old Navajo men refuses to answer his question. Have you ever been in a situation where, like William Least Heat Moon, you have felt alienated from those around you? Try to recall and to describe the circumstances you were in and how you feel now looking back at the incident. Do your prewriting, one draft, and a revision.

2. "The bristlecone pine of American Indians, Hopis live where almost nothing else will, thriving long in adverse conditions: poor soil, drought, temperature extremes, high winds. Those gave life to the bristlecone and the Hopi." Discuss the struggles of another racial or religious group that, like the Hopi, has survived difficult times. Write your prewriting, one draft, and a revision.

3. Write what you know about the relationship between Indians and whites in the context of both American history and today's world.

4. *Peer reading assignment.* Do any of the assignments above, sharing your work at each stage of the writing process with the other students in your group.

PART TWO

The Process at Work: Learning from Writing Models

▲▲▲

CHAPTER

6

Drafting and Revising: Organizing from Prewriting and Narrowing Focus

ORGANIZING FROM PREWRITING

We will now return to the process of drafting and revising a paper from prewriting to final draft. Recall the prewriting techniques you learned in Chapter 1 to get started (see pp. 2–9). Keeping in mind what you have learned since about narrowing the focus of your writing to a main idea or thesis, examine the following student brainstorming list and final draft to see *how much she uses* from her brainstorming and *how she arranges her paper* based on the contents of that list:

Brainstorming List

a best friend
childhood partners
always willing to give a hand
quick-tempered
very musical
not judgmental
stands up for what he believes in

glad he married someone I am friends with
electronic engineer
lives on north side
very handy around the house
introverted as much as I am
has two children
scared me with his sleepwalking
stood by me with moral support at one of the hardest times in my life
has a lot of feeling
gives impartial advice
good with my kids
three years younger than I
together we gave other siblings a hard time
stubborn

Brainstorming List	**Final Draft of "Twice a Favorite"**
	Our first meeting has been recounted so often by older family members that I feel as though I may even remember it. Because I was
three years younger than I	only three years old when my parents brought Michael home, I could not really recall our first meeting—but the love I have always had for him tells me the story is true. Our private family legend tells of how from the day I peeked at the new baby a special bond was formed between us. This attachment has flourished through 31 years into one of the strongest relationships I have. We are bound not only by ties of blood, but also of spirit—which has given us the additional treasure of
a best friend	friendship.
childhood partners	As children, Michael and I were cohorts in skillfully plotted pranks against our
together we gave other siblings a hard time	other siblings, heedless of the chaos we caused in our

continued

continued

Brainstorming List

**Final Draft of
"Twice a Favorite"**

parents' lives. On one occasion, we fooled our younger sister, Maralee, who was seven and fanatical about being on time for school. We awoke her at midnight, and told her we had overslept, so she had better hurry or she would be late for school. So engrossed in dressing for school, she was oblivious to Michael and me, who by now were doubled over with laughter. The look on her face when my mother informed her it was the middle of the night and to go back to bed still makes me smile today.

As we matured to adulthood, our relationship grew also, deepening in love and trust. Michael has always been the person I could express my thoughts to, knowing they would be held in respect, if not in agreement. He is not judgmental of me, and gives me impartial advice. When I decided it was all right for my oldest son, who is 13, to date, some of our relatives felt I was being too liberal. If I allowed him this privilege now, what would he want to be allowed to do at 16? I asked Michael's opinion, and although he felt my son was too young to date, he agreed it was my decision to make. I let my son date.

not judgmental
gives impartial advice

stood by me with moral support at one of the hardest times of my life

good with my kids

always willing to give a hand

very handy around the house

has two children

electronic engineer

Michael has been support-ive through many hard times in my life. Since my hus-band died, Michael comes to visit me and my children regularly and to see if there is anything I need help with in the house, which always needs some-thing. If something needs to be repaired, Michael is always willing to help me. When my oldest son desper-ately wanted his own bed-room, Michael helped build one for him. He is one of the most important people in my boys' lives; and I have already seen their friend-ships forming with him. He has taken them fishing, to baseball games, and when they are playing football on their school team, Michael comes to cheer them on.

In addition to the impor-tance Michael has in my own family, he is a loving hus-band and father of two, and he lets nothing or no one take precedence over his family. He works hard and long hours as an electronic engineer, so they may have a comfortable life. Employed by Netcom Engineering in Northbrook, a company which handles many government jobs, Michael helps design and build the computerized controls of our missiles and other equipment used in space programs.

Michael's character is not flawless, but even his

continued

continued

Brainstorming List	**Final Draft of "Twice a Favorite"**
	faults intensify who he is. He can be stubborn and quick—tempered. The day Michael and his wife, Chela, moved from their apartment into a new house was one occasion he revealed both emotions. Michael was placing everything not already packed for the trip in a large box, but the box had a weak bottom. We tried to tell him the box would never make it, but he insisted on using it. When he was carrying the box, the bottom collapsed, its contents crashing down three flights of stairs. Michael started yelling and swearing, as though he had not been warned this could happen. He was so loud, the other residents of the building were glad to see him move.
stubborn, quick-tempered	
has a lot of feeling	Michael is passionate in his feelings for others, whether of love, happiness, or anger, making him capable of leaving an impression on others' lives. I have been blessed with many ''favorite'' relatives, but I am blessed twice with Michael, because he is a "favorite" friend.

From her brainstorming list of 21 items, the student used 15 in her paper, choosing not to include:

very musical
stands up for what he believes in
glad he married someone I am friends with

lives on north side
introverted as much as I am
scared me with his sleepwalking

She felt that Michael's being musical, where he lives, and his sleepwalking were not relevant to her description. Her audience of teacher and classmates would not need to know those things. Because the student could not think of a concrete example for "stands up for what he believes in," she doesn't develop it. She also felt it was obvious that she was "glad he married someone I am friends with" and so did not pursue that idea. As an audience of readers, we would like to know more about their being "introverted," but perhaps that is too personal for her to write about.

Although there is no particular order to the student's brainstorming list, her paper is very well-organized:

Paragraph 1— Introduction to best friend (*thesis*: Michael is a relative *and* best friend).

Paragraph 2— Their pranks as siblings.

Paragraph 3— Michael advises her about her children; he is not judgmental.

Paragraph 4— She explains how important Michael is to her and her sons since her husband's death.

Paragraph 5— Michael's own life and job.

Paragragh 6— Michael's flaws.

Paragraph 7— Conclusion, return to thesis of Michael as relative and best friend.

Suggestion: Organize your brainstorming list into some kind of order. This will help you to structure your paper.

The student might have saved herself some time and work by putting her list into the same structure she used in her paper:

Paragraph 1— three years younger than I
a best friend

Paragraph 2— childhood partners
together we gave other siblings a hard time

Paragraph 3— not judgmental
gives impartial advice

Paragraph 4— always willing to give a hand
good with my kids
very handy around the house
stood by me with moral support at one of the hardest times of my life

Paragraph 5— electronic engineer
has two children

Paragraph 6— stubborn
                 quick-tempered
Paragraph 7— has a lot of feeling

As you organize your paper, think of a working title to give it. A title should not be merely a label; it should say something meaningful about your paper. The student's title, "Twice a Favorite," reflects her thesis—the last sentence of the first paragraph and the last sentence of the paper—that she has been "blessed twice with Michael, because he is a 'favorite' friend."

NARROWING FOCUS

Notice that after doing her brainstorming and before beginning her first draft, the student analyzed her *subject,* her "favorite relative"—"a best friend"; her *purpose,* to explain how special her brother is to her; and her *audience,* teacher and classmates. Studying these three components of writing led to her *thesis,* the last line of paragraph 1: "We [she and Michael] are bound not only by ties of blood, but also of spirit—which has given us the additional treasure of friendship." The four questions of *subject, purpose, audience,* and *thesis* can be used before or after the prewriting. Along with the prewriting—whether looping, freewriting, brainstorming, or clustering—answering the four questions can help you to pinpoint the main idea or thesis of your paper.

An important part of narrowing focus is content and sentence revision. Writers revise first for *content*—the ideas contained in their paper—and, at a later stage, for the clarity of their sentences. Analyzing the first draft of her paper about her brother Michael, the student discovered that readers needed to know more about Michael. She added more information to her final draft: Michael is a happily married engineer, he gives her advice about problems at home like her son's dating, and he has an explosive temper. *After* adding this information to the content of her paper, she turned to sentence revision. Let's examine the first paragraph of her first and final drafts to see just how she revised her sentences:

First Draft	Final Draft
A recounting of our first meeting has been told many times through the years by older family members that I feel as though I may even remember it. Though consciously I do not recall this blessed event for I was only three years old, what I	Our first meeting has been recounted so often by older family members that I feel as though I may even remember it. Because I was only three years old when my parents brought Michael home, I could not recall our first meeting—but the love I have

```
have always felt for him in      always had for him tells me
my heart tells me the story      the story is true.  Our pri-
is true.  Our private legend     vate family legend tells of
tells of how from the day I      how from the day I peeked at
peeked at the new baby my        the new baby a special bond
brother Michael my parents       was formed between us.  This
brought home, a special bond     attachment has flourished
was formed between us.  This     through 31 years into one of
bond has flourished through      the strongest relationships
31 years into one of the         I have.  We are bound not
strongest relationships I        only by ties of blood, but
have ever shared.  Many of       also of spirit—which has
the characteristics we share     given us the additional
are ones that bind us by         treasure of friendship.
blood, but the ones we share
in spirit have given us the
treasure of friendship.
```

A comparison of these two drafts reveals that the content remains the same, but that each sentence has been revised. In the final draft, the first sentence is tightened by substituting the verb "recounted" for the redundant (repetitive) "recounting . . . has been told." Also, "recounted" is a more forceful word than the more bland "told."

The second sentence in the original draft is awkward and unclear: "Though consciously I do not recall. . . ." The student revises the sentence by showing that the relationship of its two parts is *cause and effect*: "*Because* I was only three years old when my parents brought Michael home, I could not recall our first meeting. . . ." That is, because she was too little, she could not remember their first meeting.

The third sentence is shortened by omitting the repetitive phrase "my brother Michael" from the final draft. In the fourth sentence the writer drops the redundant "ever shared."

The last sentence in the original draft is clumsy and wordy: "Many of the characteristics we share are ones that bind us by blood, but the ones we share in spirit have given us the treasure of friendship." While keeping the parallel structure of "not only . . . but also," the student substitutes the more compact "We are bound not only by ties of blood, but also of spirit— which has given us the additional treasure of friendship." The last part of the sentence, ". . . which has given . . .," clarifies the relationship; the friendship is almost a bonus.

Again, sentence revision should always be done *after* content revision. First examine your rough draft to see if you have said everything you wanted and to make sure the meaning is clear. Only then should you focus on the draft sentence by sentence, clearing up redundancies (wordiness and repetition) and other problems of meaning. Most of the problems with the student's first draft come from being too wordy, and she solves them by using the principles of "sentence economy" (see Chapter 4, pp. 53–55).

READING: "UNCLE WILLIE"

In this chapter you have read about one student's favorite relative. The following reading is about another relative, Maya Angelou's "Uncle Willie," described in her book *I Know Why the Caged Bird Sings.* Focus on each paragraph of the reading using your prediction strategies—What question would get at the main idea? Are there any sentences that need to be clarified? What will come in the next paragraph? Consider, for example, this short paragraph:

> Only once in all the years of trying not to watch him, I saw him pretend to himself and others that he wasn't lame.

1. *Prequest*—What question would you ask to determine the main idea here? The question might be, Did Uncle Willie ever try to hide his being crippled?
2. *Clarify*—Is there any meaning to be clarified?
3. *Prenext*—Can you predict what will come in the next paragraph? We will learn of the one instance where Maya saw Uncle Willie hide his lameness.

As you read this selection, see how the writer answers the reporter's questions, organizes the story, and uses quotations.

Read the first paragraph and the last two paragraphs:

> Uncle Willie used to sit, like a giant black Z (he had been crippled as a child), and hear us testify to the Lafayette County Training Schools' abilities. His face pulled down on the left side, as if a pulley had been attached to his lower teeth, and his left hand was only a mite bigger than Bailey's, but on the second mistake or on the third hesitation his big overgrown right hand would catch one of us behind the collar, and in the same moment would thrust the culprit toward the dull red heater, which throbbed like a devil's toothache. We were never burned, although once I might have been when I was so terrified I tried to jump onto the stove to remove the possibility of its remaining a threat. Like most children, I thought if I could face the worst danger voluntarily, and *triumph*, I would forever have power over it. But in my case of sacrificial effort I was thwarted. Uncle Willie held tight to my dress and I only got close enough to smell the clean dry scent of hot iron. We learned the times tables without understanding their grand principle, simply because we had the capacity and no alternative.
>
> • • •
>
> He must have tired of being crippled, as prisoners tire of penitentiary bars and the guilty tire of blame. The high-topped shoes and the cane, his uncontrollable muscles and thick tongue, and the looks he suffered of either contempt or pity had simply worn him out, and for one afternoon, one part of an afternoon, he wanted no part of them.
>
> I understood and felt closer to him at that moment than ever before or since.

Write down a prediction about what you think the story is about.

Now read the entire piece:

"Uncle Willie"

Uncle Willie used to sit, like a giant black Z (he had been crippled as a child), and hear us testify to the Lafayette County Training Schools' abilities. His face pulled down on the left side, as if a pulley had been attached to his lower teeth, and his left hand was only a mite bigger than Bailey's, but on the second mistake or on the third hesitation his big overgrown right hand would catch one of us behind the collar, and in the same moment would thrust the culprit toward the dull red heater, which throbbed like a devil's toothache. We were never burned, although once I might have been when I was so terrified I tried to jump onto the stove to remove the possibility of its remaining a threat. Like most children, I thought if I could face the worst danger voluntarily, and *triumph*, I would forever have power over it. But in my case of sacrificial effort I was thwarted. Uncle Willie held tight to my dress and I only got close enough to smell the clean dry scent of hot iron. We learned the times tables without understanding their grand principle, simply because we had the capacity and no alternative.

The tragedy of lameness seems so unfair to children that they are embarrassed in its presence. And they, most recently off nature's mold, sense that they have only narrowly missed being another of her jokes. In relief at the narrow escape, they vent their emotions in impatience and criticism of the unlucky cripple.

Momma related times without end, and without any show of emotion, how Uncle Willie had been dropped when he was three years old by a woman who was minding him. She seemed to hold no rancor against the baby-sitter, nor for her just God who allowed the accident. She felt it

necessary to explain over and over again to those who knew the story by heart that he wasn't "born that way."

In our society, where two-legged, two-armed strong Black men were able at best to eke out only the necessities of life, Uncle Willie, with his starched shirts, shined shoes and shelves full of food, was the whipping boy and butt of jokes of the underemployed and underpaid. Fate not only disabled him but laid a double-tiered barrier in his path. He was also proud and sensitive. Therefore he couldn't pretend that he wasn't crippled, nor could he deceive himself that people were not repelled by his defect.

Only once in all the years of trying not to watch him, I saw him pretend to himself and others that he wasn't lame.

Coming home from school one day, I saw a dark car in our front yard. I rushed in to find a strange man and woman (Uncle Willie said later they were schoolteachers from Little Rock) drinking Dr. Pepper in the cool of the Store. I sensed a wrongness around me, like an alarm clock that had gone off without being set.

I knew it couldn't be the strangers. Not frequently, but often enough, travelers pulled off the main road to buy tobacco or soft drinks in the only Negro store in Stamps. When I looked at Uncle Willie, I knew what was pulling my mind's coattails. He was standing erect behind the counter, not leaning forward or resting on the small shelf that had been built for him. Erect. His eyes seemed to hold me with a mixture of threats and appeal.

I dutifully greeted the strangers and roamed my eyes around for his walking stick. It was nowhere to be seen. He said, "Uh . . . this this . . . this . . . uh, my

continued

continued

niece. She's . . . uh . . . just come from school." Then to the couple—"You know . . . how, uh, children are . . . th-th-these days . . . they play all d-d-day at school and c-c-can't wait to get home and pl-play some more."

The people smiled, very friendly.

He added, "Go on out and pl-play, Sister."

The lady laughed in a soft Arkansas voice and said, "Well, you know, Mr. Johnson, they say, you're only a child once. Have you children of your own?"

Uncle Willie looked at me with an impatience I hadn't seen in his face even when he took thirty minutes to loop the laces over his high-topped shoes. "I . . . I thought I told you to go . . . go outside and play."

Before I left I saw him lean back on the shelves of Garret Snuff, Prince Albert and Spark Plug chewing tabacco.

"No, ma'am . . . no ch-children and no wife." He tried a laugh. "I have an old m-m-mother and my brother's t-two children to l-look after."

I didn't mind his using us to make himself look good. In fact, I would have pretended to be his daughter if he wanted me to. Not only did I not feel any loyalty to my own father, I figured that if I had been Uncle Willie's child I would have re-ceived much better treatment.

The couple left after a few minutes, and from the back of the house I watched the red car scare chickens, raise dust and disappear toward Magnolia.

Uncle Willie was making his way down the long shadowed aisle between the shelves and the counter—hand over hand, like a man climbing out of a dream. I stayed quiet and watched him lurch from one side, bumping to the other, until he reached the coal-oil tank. He put his hand behind that dark recess and took his cane in the strong fist and shifted his weight on the wooden support. He thought he had pulled it off.

I'll never know why it was important to him that the couple (he said later that he'd never seen them before) would take a picture of a whole Mr. Johnson back to Little Rock.

He must have tired of being crippled, as prisoners tire of penitentiary bars and the guilty tire of blame. The high-topped shoes and the cane, his uncontrollable muscles and thick tongue, and the looks he suffered of either contempt or pity had simply worn him out, and for one afternoon, one part of an afternoon, he wanted no part of them.

I understood and felt closer to him at that moment than ever before or since.

Reading for Meaning

1. What is the main idea of the piece?

2. How does Angelou support the main idea?

3. What explanation does Angelou give for the impatience and criticism of young children for the handicapped?

4. How does Maya Angelou compare Uncle Willie to her father?

5. What caused Uncle Willie's lameness?

6. In discussing Willie's deformity, why does Momma always take pains to point out that he wasn't "born that way"?

7. Why did Uncle Willie hide his cane?

8. Why does Angelou think Uncle Willie tried to hide his lameness that day?

Vocabulary in Context

Write down the definition of each of the italicized words taken from the story below. Try to guess the meaning from the context. Use a dictionary only if you have to.

1. "She seemed to hold no *rancor* against the baby-sitter . . ."

2. ". . . Black men were able at best to *eke out* only the necessities of life . . ."

3. "Fate not only disabled him but laid a double-*tiered* barrier in his path."

4. "He put his hand behind that dark *recess* . . ."

Writing from Reading

For each of the following assignments, remember to consider your *subject*, *purpose*, and *audience*.

1. Tell your audience—teacher and classmates—about *your* "favorite or least favorite relative." Show what the person is like through a story or examples, answering the reporter's questions (*who*, *what*, *when*, *where*, *how*, and/or *why*), having a clear order, and by using quotations where appropriate. Begin with a ten-minute brainstorming or freewriting; then write a rough draft. Revise your rough draft twice, the first time for content, the second time for sentence sense and mechanics of punctuation and spelling.

2. In the second paragraph of the selection about Uncle Willie, Angelou gives us a reason for children's cruelty to those with physical defects: "In relief at the narrow escape [from being crippled], they vent their emotions in impatience and criticism of the unlucky cripple." Do you think this is true? Explain your answer, using any examples drawn from your own experience.

3. *Peer reading assignment.* Do one of the assignments above, sharing your work at each stage of the writing process with the other students in your group. Use the following checklist to review each other's papers.
   a. Does the writer answer the reporter's questions?
   b. Are sights, sounds, and feelings described?
   c. Give examples of any effective quotations.
   d. Does the writer tell how he or she feels now looking back at the story?
   e. Is the writer's story clear?

ACTIVE AND PASSIVE VOICE

Active Voice

The subject in most sentences is the doer of an action: "Jaime clobbered the curveball." In this sentence Jaime—the subject—is a doer because he clobbers the ball. The verb here, "clobbers," is active voice; its subject is the doer of the action. Here are some more sentences which have active-voice verbs:

> Fred struck the policeman.
>
> Alfredo sprinted home and proudly told mama the good news.
>
> The sky promised snow at the start of the day.
>
> During the talent show Edwina and Mary belted out a duet.

Most sentences in English are written in the active voice. As in each of the above examples, the subject is clearly identified and the verb may show action or make a statement. It's also important for the writer to use *specific*, rather than general, verbs:

> Alfredo *sprinted*, not *ran* home.
>
> During the argument, Tracey *screamed at*, not *talked to* her mom.
>
> At the end of the school, children *scurried out*, not *left*.
>
> During the talent show Edwina and Mary *belted out* a duet, not *sang*.

Passive Voice

The subject in a sentence can also be a *receiver* of an action or be *acted upon*: "The curveball was clobbered into the upper deck in left field." This sentence is written in passive voice—the subject "curveball" is acted upon ("clobbered"). The emphasis in this sentence is on how hard the ball was hit and how far it went. If the sentence were to emphasize who hit the ball, it would be written in active voice: "Lou Gehrig clobbered the ball into the upper deck in left field." Here are some more examples of sentences written with the verb in the passive voice:

> The policeman was struck by a thrown bottle.
>
> The good news was soon brought home to mama by Alfredo.
>
> During the talent show a duet was belted out by two burly sisters.
>
> Before the night was over, the crowd was thoroughly stirred up.

One use of the passive voice is to depict pity or sorrow; for example, "The school bus was hit by an eastbound train at the crossing" or "The men in the tiny fishing boat were crushed by the tidal wave." The passive voice may also be used when the real doer of the sentence remains anonymous: "The papers were collected hurriedly." Collected by whom? The teacher? Or, "The rock was thrown at the principal's large front window."

By whom was the rock thrown? The sentence doesn't tell the real doer of the action.

The passive voice should be used sparingly. Over-reliance on the passive voice results in writing that lacks specificity and power; consider this example where *all* the verbs are written in passive voice:

> The car *was struck* by an oncoming train. Injured passengers *were driven* by neighborhood residents to the hospital where the seriously hurt *were given* prompt treatment. Soon after the accident, a petition *was circulated* in the town demanding that railroad barriers *be erected* by the state at the dangerous crossing.

Now look at the same paragraph with a mixture of active and passive voice verbs:

> The car *was struck* [passive voice] by an oncoming train. Neighborhood residents *drove* [active voice] the injured passengers to the hospital where an emergency team of doctors and nurses *gave* [active voice] prompt treatment to the most seriously hurt. Soon after the accident, the townspeople *circulated* [active voice] a petition demanding that railroad barriers *be erected* [passive voice] by the state at the dangerous crossing.

Writing Practice

Rewrite the following paragraph using the correct form of the verb—active or passive—in each instance. Remember that the active voice is used with a specific subject that is a doer of some action, and that the passive voice is used when the doer is not emphasized or when the writer wishes to express sadness.

The Baseball Hall of Fame (was built, built) in Cooperstown, New York, as a shrine to this American sport. Residents of the area (claimed, were claimed) that baseball (originated, was originated) there by its founder, Abner Doubleday, a native son. In its earlier years, baseball (called, was called) "rounders," a relative of the British game of cricket. The builders of the Hall of Fame (chose, were chosen) this quiet, beautiful little town, two hours outside of New York City, to memorialize the game's greatest players. When the first selections for the Hall (made, were made), Babe Ruth and Ty Cobb, perhaps the game's greatest players, (dominated, were dominated) the voting. Over the years the Baseball Hall of Fame (has grown, has been grown) in importance for baseball players who now (hunger, are made hungry) for its honors.

Learning from Revision

A STUDENT REVISES

Writers can learn more about the writing process from revising their own work. As they reflect on what they have written, new ideas or new ways of looking at things may occur to them. Revising is *not* editing or proofreading, in which writers look to correct cosmetic errors in spelling, punctuation, grammar, and mechanics; it is the more creative, demanding process of *rewriting*—using what has already been written as a starting point for further writing. Revising is similar to prewriting by furnishing new ideas and insights into the writing.

Read the following student essay about a powerful personal experience the writer had. Compare the final version with the first draft to see what she learned as she revised her work. Particularly note the difference between the feelings she had at the time of her experience and those she has now as she reflects on it.

Hospital Nightmare

First Draft	Final Draft
While I was in high school I took a night course in cardiology technology. This deal with the diagnosing to heart diseases. Af-	While I was in high school, I took a course in cardiology technology. The course dealt with the diagnosis and treatment of car-

ter I got out of high school I got a job as a monitor tech at LUMC. I was in the ICU for open heart surgery. My job was to watch the heart monitors for all the patients' chart changes and notify the nurses. This put me in an awkward position usually the nurses were busy with other duties so if someone was going to die I was the first one to know. Then I had to watch and record their final heart beats.

diac diseases. This enabled me to get a job in a hospital in the intensive care unit for open heart surgery. My job was to monitor the patients' hearts on a screen set overhead. I recorded any changes and kept the nurses informed while they tended to other duties. I was usually the first to know if someone was going to die. I was also responsible for recording their last heart beats if they couldn't be saved.

In this first paragraph the student introduces the reader to her job. All of the problems with punctuation, grammar, and mechanics in the first draft are corrected in the final draft. She has written out "ICU" as "intensive care unit" for the reader unfamiliar with hospital terminology. The main difference between these two versions is the number of careless mistakes; the hastily written version contains many such errors that are corrected in the revised one.

First Draft

My worst experience was with a 3 month old baby. She had a congenital H D which means from birth and had several operations to try and correct the defect. She came directly from surgery into the ICU where I began to monitor her heart. The doctors and parents looked hopeful so I really wasn't worried. It never crossed my mind that this little baby would die. Just as the parents were going to step into the room I saw her go into V F or H F. I had to scream it out. I will never forget the terror on the parents faces as I

Final Draft

My worst experience began when a three-month-old baby was brought into our unit directly after surgery. The child looked pale and lifeless as her tiny body, laden with bandages and tubes, was rolled into the room. Shortly after the baby entered, the parents were brought in. It was hard to guess their ages because the long hours of worrying through surgery had taken a great toll on their faces. They were both dressed in faded blue jeans and T-shirts. Looking at them I wondered how they, even with insurance, could

continued

continued

First Draft	Final Draft
called the DrCART or Code Blue. The monitors were set up to everyone could see so I had to stand next to the parents and we watched their little baby die together. This memory of her last heart beats will stay with me forever. After it was over nurses were crying and I was totally numb all over. I told my sup I had to get out the walls were closing in on me. As I walked out I began to cry not even knowing why.	afford such an expensive hospital. They had just begun to don their masks and gowns when their daughter's heart began to fail. As I frantically alerted everyone, the parents were pushed aside as the doctors rushed into the room. Through the confusion I caught a glimpse of the horror on the parents' faces as their eyes glued to the screen. We watched their baby's life fade away. After it was over, the tearful nurses led the parents into the room where they would hold their baby for the last time. Not having children of my own didn't stop me from identifying with the parents and sharing their pain. My own mortality was also thrust upon me at a time in my life when I rarely thought about it. All of these emotions flooded my mind, heart, and eyes.

In these two paragraphs the student describes the incident that is the central focus of her essay. Notice how the revised description is more complete—the baby is "laden with bandages and tubes"; the parents are "dressed in faded blue jeans and T-shirts." During her revising, she has learned how to fill in incomplete pictures with more details. Looking back on the incident, she portrays the parents with more sympathy; she realizes the ordeal "had taken a great toll on their faces." She has also dropped all the technical terms hospitals use—"H D," "V F," "H F," "DrCART," and "Code Blue"—from the final version.

The student has made a new paragraph from the last three sentences in the first draft—a natural break from the main incident that begins with the transitional or connecting phrase, "After it was over. . . ." She realizes that shorter paragraphs are easier to read, the last one a natural conclusion to the essay.

In this last paragraph, the student reveals to her readers why she cried and, in doing so, what she has learned during her revising process—she had "identified with the parents," witnessing and sharing in their pain. She adds that the "parents would hold their baby for the last time." This is a simple, yet poignant description. The writer has also learned that her "own mortality was thrust upon" her after seeing this baby die.

The process of revising has provided the writer the time and the opportunity to gain insight into a painful but valuable learning experience. For her readers, she has illustrated that some of the most important lessons in life are taught through sorrow and pain. Her emotions are in plain view.

In writing this piece, the student considered her *subject*, the experience at the hospital; her *purpose*, describing and understanding the incident; and her *audience*, teacher and classmates. From her analysis of these three elements, she fashioned her *thesis*, the first sentence of the second paragraph: "My worst experience began when a three-month-old baby was brought into our unit directly after surgery." The first paragraph of her rough draft led her to this main point, which the rest of the essay explains.

The structure of the student essay is simple and natural:

First paragraph—Introduction: a description of her job at the hospital.
Second paragraph—Main incident: a recounting of the death of the baby and the reactions of the parents.
Third paragraph—Conclusion: a reflection upon the incident providing the writer with the insight that she identified with the parents and that the baby's death reminded her of her own mortality.

To write any personal narrative, imitate the natural plan the writer has used here—an introduction to the story, a telling of the crisis or main event and, finally, a conclusion revealing what you have learned from the experience.

Personal Narrative Checklist

Use the following checklist as a guide to help you write the personal narrative.

1. What subject or incident am I going to describe?
2. For what purpose am I telling this story?
3. What is my thesis or main idea?
4. Who is my audience?
5. Why is the incident most important to me?
6. How did I feel then about the incident?
7. How do I feel now looking back on the incident?
8. What will the audience need to know to understand the narrative?
   a. Sights
   b. Sounds

    c. Feelings

    d. Things people said

9. What is the structure of my narrative (for example, introduction, incident, and reflection)?

Writing Assignment

Now that you have read one student's account of an important event in her life, try to write one of your own. It doesn't have to be terrifying and painful like hers. In writing about the incident, try to recall where you were when it happened, your thoughts and feelings at the time and now, and those of the people around you. Also, think about how you want to *order* what happened; the student used chronological order—order according to time, from beginning to end—in her essay. Here are three possibilities for you to write about:

1. Think about something that happened in your life that made you more mature, that changed you in some way. For ten minutes, prewrite about this and then write an account of it.

2. Focus on some important decision that you made in your life. Prewrite for ten minutes about this and then write a paper about it.

3. *Peer reading assignment.* Prewrite for ten minutes about an accident you were in or about a time when you were afraid. Once you have finished your prewriting, share it with the other students in your group by reading it out loud and by getting their reactions to it. Using your prewriting as a start, write a paper about this incident.

    Now that you have completed your prewriting and paper, try to think of your paper as a first draft, a step toward writing a final draft. Such an idea may be new to you. Most students are happy to do their prewriting and paper. They believe their work is over if their paper looks neat and clean. Revising, however, can make your paper much better.

    Consider your paper as a starting point. For example, what else would a reader want to know? Are all the events in your incident clear? Does the reader know how you were changed by what happened to you? In her essay, the student tells us how she was changed by her frightening experience— that before she had never thought of death affecting her personally. If you are working in a group, get some feedback from the other students in your group by asking them the same questions. Try to give good feedback yourself to your peers about their papers.

    Because all students are afraid to be criticized, be gentle and positive with your comments in the beginning. Later, when the students in your group have built up more trust in each other, you can be more direct with your suggestions. If your teacher does not assign you to work on your writing in groups, you should still have a reader or several readers, if possible, review your work. It's best to have readers from your own class because they will be following the same instructions as you.

READING: FROM *I KNOW WHY THE CAGED BIRD SINGS*

Because this excerpt is from a longer work, there are no illustrations or subtitles to help you with prereading. Also, this selection is a narrative, like "Hospital Nightmare," so the writer must fill in the setting, or time and place of the story. Notice that the story is told in natural or chronological order—from beginning to end—and that it uses quotations from the characters involved to fill in the picture for us. As you read, pay attention to how Angelou answers the reporter's questions:

1. *Who* is in the story?
2. *What* happened?
3. *When* did the story occur?
4. *Where* did the incident take place?
5. *How* and/or *why* did it happen?

Answering these questions makes for completeness in the narrative.
Read the first paragraph:

> Our presiding elder had heard the story of Reverend Taylor and Sister Monroe, but I was sure he didn't know her by sight. So my interest in the service's potential and my aversion to Reverend Thomas caused me to turn him off. Turning off or tuning out people was my highly developed art. The custom of letting obedient children be seen but not heard was so agreeable to me that I went one step further: Obedient children should not see or hear if they chose not to do so. I laid a handful of attention on my face and tuned up the sounds in the church.

Using your prediction strategies, answer the following questions on a piece of paper:

1. *Prequest*—What question would get at the main idea of the paragraph?
2. *Clarify*—Are there any difficult vocabulary words that need to be clarified?
3. *Prenext*—What will the next paragraph say?

Now read the next paragraph and the last two paragraphs:

> Sister Monroe's fuse was already lit, and she sizzled somewhere to the right behind me. Elder Thomas jumped into the sermon, determined, I suppose, to give the members what they came for. I saw the ushers from the left side of the church near the big windows begin to move discreetly, like pallbearers, toward Sister Monroe's bench. Bailey jogged my knee. When the incident with Sister Monroe, which we always called simply "the incident," had taken place, we had been too astounded to laugh. But for weeks after, all we needed to send us into violent outbursts of laughter was a whispered "Preach it." Anyway, he pushed my knee, covered his mouth and whispered, "I say, preach it."

• • •

Laughter so easily turns to hysteria for imaginative children. I felt for weeks after that I had been very, very sick, and until I completely recovered my strength I stood on laughter's cliff and any funny thing could hurl me off to my death far below.

Each time Bailey said "Preach it" to me, I hit him as hard as I could and cried.

Write down what you think will happen in the story.

Now read the entire excerpt:

Our presiding elder had heard the story of Reverend Taylor and Sister Monroe, but I was sure he didn't know her by sight. So my interest in the service's potential and my aversion to Reverend Thomas caused me to turn him off. Turning off or tuning out people was my highly developed art. The custom of letting obedient children be seen but not heard was so agreeable to me that I went one step further: Obedient children should not see or hear if they chose not to do so. I laid a handful of attention on my face and tuned up the sounds in the church.

Sister Monroe's fuse was already lit, and she sizzled somewhere to the right behind me. Elder Thomas jumped into the sermon, determined, I suppose, to give the members what they came for. I saw the ushers from the left side of the church near the big windows begin to move discreetly, like pallbearers, toward Sister Monroe's bench. Bailey jogged my knee. When the incident with Sister Monroe, which we always called simply "the incident," had taken place, we had been too astounded to laugh. But for weeks after, all we needed to send us into violent outbursts of laughter was a whispered "Preach it." Anyway, he pushed my knee, covered his mouth and whispered, "I say, preach it."

I looked toward Momma, across that square of stained boards, over the collection table, hoping that a look from her would root me safely to my sanity. But for the first time in memory Momma was staring behind me at Sister Monroe. I supposed that she was counting on bringing that emotional lady up short with a severe look or two. But Sister Monroe's voice had already reached the danger point. "Preach it!"

There were a few smothered giggles from the children's section, and Bailey nudged me again. "I say, preach it"—in a whisper. Sister Monroe echoed him loudly, "I say, preach it!"

Two deacons wedged themselves around Brother Jackson as a preventive measure and two large determined-looking men walked down the aisle toward Sister Monroe.

While the sounds in the church were increasing, Elder Thomas made the regrettable mistake of increasing his volume too. Then suddenly, like a summer rain, Sister Monroe broke through the cloud of people trying to hem her in, and flooded up to the pulpit. She didn't stop this time but continued immediately to the altar, bound for Elder Thomas, crying "I say, preach it."

Bailey said out loud, "Hot dog" and "Damn" and "She's going to beat his butt."

But Reverend Thomas didn't intend to wait for that eventuality, so as Sister Monroe approached the pulpit from the right he started descending from the left. He was not intimidated by his change of venue. He continued preaching and moving. He finally stopped right in front of the collection table, which put him almost in our laps, and Sister Monroe rounded the altar on his heels, followed by the deacons, ushers, some unofficial members and a few of the bigger children.

Just as the elder opened his mouth, pink tongue waving, and said, "Great God of Mount Nebo," Sister Monroe hit him on the back of his head with her purse. Twice. Before he could bring his lips together, his teeth fell, no, actually his teeth jumped, out of his mouth.

The grinning uppers and lowers lay by my right shoe, looking empty and at the same time appearing to contain all the emptiness in the world. I could have stretched out a foot and kicked them under the bench or behind the collection table.

Sister Monroe was struggling with his coat, and the men had all but picked her up to remove her from the building. Bailey pinched me and said without moving his lips, "I'd like to see him eat dinner now."

I looked at Reverend Thomas desperately. If he appeared just a little sad or embarrassed, I could feel sorry for him and wouldn't be able to laugh. My sympathy for him would keep me from laughing. I dreaded laughing in church. If I lost control, two things were certain to happen. I would surely pee, and just as surely get a whipping. And this time I would probably die because everything was funny—Sister Monroe, and Momma trying to keep her quiet with those threatening looks, and Bailey whispering "Preach it" and Elder Thomas with his lips flapping loose like tired elastic.

But Reverend Thomas shrugged off Sister Monroe's weakening clutch, pulled out an extra-large white handkerchief and spread it over his nasty little teeth. Putting them in his pocket, he gummed, "Naked I came into the world, and naked I shall go out."

Bailey's laugh had worked its way up through his body and was escaping through his nose in short hoarse snorts. I didn't try any longer to hold back the laugh, I just opened my mouth and released sound. I heard the first titter jump up in the air over my head, over the pulpit and out the window. Momma said out loud, "Sister!" but the bench was greasy and I slid off onto the floor. There was more laughter in me trying to get out. I didn't know there was that much in the whole world. It pressed at all my body openings, forcing everything in its path. I cried and hollered, passed gas and urine. I didn't see Bailey descend to the floor, but I rolled over once and he was kicking and screaming too. Each time we looked at each other we howled louder than before, and though he tried to say something, the laughter attacked him and he was only able to get out "I say, preach." And then I rolled over onto Uncle Willie's rubber-tipped cane. My eyes followed the cane up to his good brown hand on the curve and up the long, long white sleeve to his face. The one side pulled down as it usually did when he cried (it also pulled down when he laughed). He stuttered, "I'm gonna whip you this time myself."

I have no memory of how we got out of church and into the parsonage next door, but in that overstuffed parlor, Bailey and I received the whipping of our lives. Uncle Willie ordered us between licks to stop crying. I tried to, but Bailey refused to cooperate. Later he explained that when a person is beating you you should scream as loud as possible; maybe the whipper will become embarrassed or else some sympathetic soul might come to your rescue. Our savior came for neither of these reasons, but because Bailey yelled so loud and disturbed what was left of the service, the minister's wife came out and asked Uncle Willie to quiet us down.

continued

continued

> Laughter so easily turns to hysteria for imaginative children. I felt for weeks after that I had been very, very sick, and until I completely recovered my strength I stood on laughter's cliff and any funny thing could hurl me off to my death far below.
>
> Each time Bailey said "Preach it" to me, I hit him as hard as I could and cried.

Now that you have finished the story, go back to your predictions to see how accurate you were. Don't worry if they seem off track; the act of prereading is more important than the accuracy of your predictions. Following the strategy of *prequest, clarify,* and *prenext* will make you a more conscious, alert reader, and will improve your comprehension.

Reading for Meaning

1. What is the main idea of the story?
2. How does Angelou support her main idea?
3. Answer the reporter's questions:
    a. *Who* was the story about?
    b. *What* happened?
    c. *When* did it occur?
    d. *Where* did it happen?
    e. *How* and/or *why* did it happen?
4. What attitude did Maya have at the beginning of the sermon?
5. What were Maya's feelings about Reverend Thomas?
6. Why did Bailey advise Maya to scream out loud during a whipping?
7. Why did Maya hit Bailey every time he said "Preach it"?

Vocabulary in Context

Write down the definition of each of the italicized words below taken from the passage. Try to guess the meaning from the context. Use a dictionary only if you have to.

1. ". . . my *aversion* to Reverend Thomas caused me to turn him off."
2. ". . . the ushers from the left side of the church near the big windows begin to move *discreetly* . . ."
3. "He was not intimidated by his *change of venue*."
4. ". . . we got out of church and into the *parsonage* next door . . ."

Writing from Reading

For each of the following assignments, remember to consider your *subject, purpose,* and *audience.*

1. Near the end of the story, the writer states:

   > Laughter so easily turns to hysteria for imaginative children. I felt for weeks afterward that I had been very, very sick, and until I completely recovered my strength I stood on laughter's cliff and any funny thing could hurl me off to my death far below.

   Put into your own words what you think Angelou means here, and then examine your own life for anything similar that may have happened to you. Did you ever lose control, or were you ever afraid to lose your grip on reality? Describe the situation in which you found yourself, remembering to use the reporter's questions of *who, what, when, where, how,* and/or *why* to give readers a complete picture. Freewrite or brainstorm about that time—what sights, sounds, and feelings can you associate with that time? Were there any consequences for you like the whipping Maya and Bailey took?

   In her story, Angelou uses quotations effectively; for example, "Bailey pinched me and said without moving his lips, 'I'd like to see him eat dinner now.'" Quotations give a sense of reality and immediacy to a story. In your narrative, try to imitate Angelou's use of short quotations that fit the character. Also, like Angelou, tell your story in chronological order, commenting on how you felt *afterward* looking back on the incident.

2. Perhaps you never experienced the loss of control over laughter described in the story. If not, was there ever a time that you really lost your temper or self-control for whatever reason, and were later embarrassed by it? Using the same method outlined above, re-create and describe the incident.

3. *Peer reading assignment.* After finishing your first draft of either of the assignments above, share your paper with another student or group of students. Use the following checklist below to review each other's papers.
   a. Does the writer answer the reporter's questions?
   b. Are sights, sounds, and feelings described?
   c. In what order is the story told?
   d. Give examples of any effective quotations.
   e. Does the writer tell how he or she feels looking back on the story?
   f. Is the writer's story clear?

4. Revise your first draft and write a better paper. Don't be content just with proofreading; build on or condense what you have already written to see what you have learned during the process of revision. Think about your reader and go back to the checklist. What else would a reader wish to know about the incident you are describing? What effect did the incident have on you or others at the time? How do you feel about it now?

   If you are working in a group, each student should serve as an audience for each other. To vary the work, have another student read *your* paper back to you out loud and then have him or her read it silently. Does the reader have any suggestions from the checklist to make your paper better? Do you have any ideas for the other writers in your group?

DICTION

It is important to use the right words, or what is called correct "diction," in writing. In the student essay "Hospital Nightmare," strong action words are used to communicate ideas:

". . . the doctors *rushed* [not *came*] into the room."
"We watched their baby's life *fade away* [not *leave*]."
"My own mortality was also *thrust upon* me [not *occurred* or *shown* to me.]"
"All of these emotions *flooded* [not *filled*] my mind, heart, and eyes."

Writing Practice

Below are some sentences from the student essay that could have used more specific, powerful action words. After considering the original wording, substitute more vivid words of your own.

EXAMPLE   After *it was over* . . .
ANSWER   After *the baby died* . . .

1. My worst experience *began when* . . .
   My worst experience _____ . . .
2. After I *got out* of high school . . .
   After I _____ from high school . . .
3. I *was in* the ICU for open heart surgery.
   I _____ in the ICU for open heart surgery.
4. . . . the long hours of worrying through surgery *had taken a great toll* on their faces.
   . . . The long hours of worrying through surgery _____ their faces.

CHAPTER
8

A Reporter Revises

In this chapter we will analyze the work of a professional reporter for a very large urban newspaper to see what we can learn to improve our own methods of composition.

Gary Washburn has been a reporter since 1960, when he began working for the City News Bureau of Chicago. With B.S. and M.S. degrees in Journalism from Northwestern University, he joined the *Chicago Tribune* in 1972 as neighborhood and suburban reporter. The following year he was named real estate editor. In 1983 he was appointed to his current position of transportation writer, which includes coverage of the building and maintenance of the highway system as well as the urban mass transit system in the Chicago area. Gary writes under a deadline. The *Tribune* goes to press at 11:00 each night, requiring him to have his copy completed by 8:30. Because his work day isn't over until his assignment has been completed, he has great incentive to get his leg work and writing done quickly and efficiently.

Gary was kind enough to share with us the prewriting and drafts of a September 28, 1988 article he wrote for the *Chicago Tribune* about security on Chicago's mass transit system. He first had to cover a morning meeting of the board of the Regional Transportation Authority (RTA), which controls the funding for the Chicago Transit Authority (CTA), the inner-city public transportation system. After the meeting, Gary had to interview key personnel, go back to his office and conduct more interviews on the phone, and then write the story for the next day's paper. The phone interviews were a necessary part of the story because the meeting raised questions that needed some comment and debate. Normally a meeting about establishing funding levels for Chicago's mass transit system fails to create much of a stir. But because of some serious crime on the CTA in the preceding few months, this meeting was different—as his article will reveal to us.

In analyzing Gary's writing and revising process, we'll work backwards, reading through his completed draft first and then looking back at the process he used to write his article. Gary's published article will follow the prereading work. The paragraphs have been numbered so that you can refer to them more easily.

READING: "CTA SECURITY FUNDS WIN RTA APPROVAL"

Remember in your reading first to *prequest*—predict what question would be asked to discover the main idea of each paragraph; second, to *clarify*—see if any clarification of the text is needed; and finally, to *prenext*—predict what the next paragraph will say. Making predictions as you read will help focus your reading.

Begin with the title:

CTA security funds win RTA approval

What can we learn about the article from the title?

Next, read the first two and last two paragraphs of the article:

> The Regional Transportation Authority board agreed Tuesday to provide $500,000 next year for added security on the Chicago Transit Authority, but officials acknowledged that the money is largely symbolic and won't rid the CTA of crime.
>
> One transit official marveled privately that so much attention was being focused on the allocation by the media and the RTA board. ''It's a drop in the bucket,'' he said. ''It's really a token.''
>
> • • •
>
> CTA and Metra officials expressed satisfaction with their allocations, but Pace chairman Florence Boone contended that her agency suffered unfairly. While the CTA and Metra will get between 3 and 4 percent more than in 1988, Pace will suffer a freeze, she complained.
>
> RTA officials countered that Pace received a generous increase in subsidies this year and has won $11.5 million in special grants over the last two years.

Write down what you think the article will say.

Now read the entire article:

CTA security funds win RTA approval

By Gary Washburn
Transportation writer

1 The Regional Transportation Authority board agreed Tuesday to provide $500,000 next year for added security on the Chicago Transit Authority, but officials acknowledged that the money is largely symbolic and won't rid the CTA of crime.

2 One transit official marveled privately that so much attention was being focused on the allocation by the media and the RTA board. "It's a drop in the bucket," he said. "It's really a token."

3 CTA Chairman Clark Burrus, who requested the extra money, said that it "sends a sign to the public that we do recognize that there is this problem and we want to address it."

4 The CTA has not yet decided how to spend the funds, Burrus said, but it would be enough to pay the salaries of five or six extra Chicago police officers and several additional canine teams to patrol the transit system.

5 The CTA operates up to 1,780 buses a day over routes totaling 2,092 miles, and 923 rail cars over a 215-mile rapid transit system that has 142 stations.

6 With the new money, the CTA is expected to spend $5.5 million for security in 1989, including $5 million that will pay for operation of an existing Chicago police unit that patrols the bus system. That is less than 1 percent of the CTA's planned $662 million budget and slightly more than the agency spent last year to clean graffiti from buses, rail cars and stations.

7 Separately, the Chicago Police Department spends about $12 million annually to operate its Mass Transit Unit, which patrols the CTA rail system.

8 Critics contend that the amount of money devoted to CTA security is important, but that the quality and commitment of officers assigned to trains and buses is even more crucial.

9 Some officials, both inside the CTA and out, say that members of the bus unit make a minimal effort to monitor routes; that the ranks of the Mass Transit Unit, which is about 240 officers strong on paper, shrink dramatically with temporary assignments to special events such as Taste of Chicago; and that many Mass Transit Unit members routinely loaf on the job.

10 State Rep. James Stange (R., Oak Brook) said Tuesday that he has received calls recently from seven Chicago police officers, all currently or formerly assigned to the CTA, who have told him the same thing: "Police officers on both buses and trains work for 15 minutes or half an hour when they start their shifts and they are gone until it is time to go home.

11 "They're at coffee shops, whatever, and they are not working," Stange charged. "There is no supervision whatsoever."

12 Cmdr. Carlo Maggio of the Mass Transit Unit and Deputy Chief of Patrol Sherwood Williams were unavailable for comment Tuesday. But police officials have defended the performance of the Mass Transit Unit overall as well as the department's general oversight of the CTA.

continued

continued

13 Stange was a friend of Bruce Plattenberger, an Oak Park lawyer who was shot to death on a CTA train on Sept. 12. The shooting was followed less than a week later by the killing of Anthony Bruno, 17, who was stabbed on a Fullerton Avenue bus.

14 Pressure for increased security mounted last Thursday when a woman was forced off a CTA train by a man and sexually assaulted at the Randolph Street elevated station.

15 "The whole point is being missed," one local transit official said of the $500,000 RTA allocation. "Nobody is asking questions about how many [officers] are out there and what they are doing."

16 RTA Chairman Samuel Skinner has credited the police with doing "a pretty good job" with limited resources, and he said that police Supt. LeRoy Martin has shown a willingness to cooperate in an effort to improve security.

17 Recent attacks on the CTA are "tragedies," but "we should not get too hysterical," Skinner said Tuesday.

18 Skinner termed the new money for CTA security "a step in the right direction." But, he added, "I firmly believe that we are not going to solve the problems of crime through the RTA budget, and we shouldn't be expected to."

19 By a 10-3 vote, the RTA board also approved 1989 funding levels for its three operating subsidiaries—the CTA, Metra and Pace.

20 Under the board's action, the CTA will receive $321 million in operating subsidies, down about $10 million from the amount it had requested, while Metra will get $125 million, down about $2 million from its original request, and Pace will receive about $50 million, roughly $1 million under what it had requested.

21 CTA and Metra officials expressed satisfaction with their allocations, but Pace chairman Florence Boone contended that her agency suffered unfairly. While the CTA and Metra will get between 3 and 4 percent more than in 1988, Pace will suffer a freeze, she complained.

22 RTA officials countered that Pace received a generous increase in subsidies this year and has won $11.5 million in special grants over the last two years.

For paragrahs 1–18 in the article, (a) predict the main idea question, (b) clarify the meaning of any difficult sentences, and (c) predict what the next paragraph will say. The first three paragraphs, and some of the later ones as well, are done for you.

Paragraph 1

a. *Prequest*—What do the officials say about the extra money?
b. *Clarify*—Nothing.
c. *Prenext*—The article will explain why the money is only symbolic.

Paragraph 2

a. *Prequest*—What is the transit official's view on the new money?
b. *Clarify*—"allocation"—"money planned for spending."
c. *Prenext*—The article will tell why the new funds are only a "token."

Paragraph 3

a. *Prequest*—What did Mr. Burrus say about the extra money?
b. *Clarify*—Nothing.
c. *Prenext*—The article will explain the problem Burrus cites.

Paragraph 6

a. *Prequest*—How much of a financial commitment does the CTA make for security?
b. *Clarify*—Nothing.
c. *Prenext*—The article will discuss more about the financial needs of the CTA.

Paragraph 8

a. *Prequest*—What is more important to CTA security than money?
b. *Clarify*—Nothing.
c. *Prenext*—We will learn more about the quality of the officers.

Paragraph 13

a. *Prequest*—What two tragedies had recently occurred on the CTA?
b. *Clarify*—Nothing.
c. *Prenext*—The article will tell about more CTA crime.

Reading for Meaning

1. What is the thesis of the article?
2. How does Gary support his thesis?
3. What factual information do paragraphs 1 and 2 give us, and what important comments on that information do they make?
4. According to paragraph 3, how does Mr. Burrus's opinion of the money differ from the source mentioned in the preceding paragraph?
5. What contrast does Gary draw in paragraphs 4 and 5?
6. In paragraph 6 Gary tells us that the money added for security is less than 1 percent of the full budget, and that it is only a little more than the amount spent on removing graffiti. What point does Gary want us to make with this information?
7. What new concern is raised in the transitional paragraph 8?
8. What are some of the criticisms of CTA security detailed in paragraphs 9 through 11?
9. After quoting Representative Stange's harsh assessment of CTA police in paragraphs 10 and 11, why does Gary mention that the two police officials in charge of CTA security were unavailable for comment?

10. Paragraphs 13 and 14 describe the terrible incidents that sparked the renewed interest in CTA security. Why in paragraph 15 does Gary quote the local RTA official about the added money for security?

11. In paragraphs 16 through 18, Gary quotes RTA Chairman Samuel Skinner. Summarize Skinner's remarks.

12. A good reporter like Gary Washburn is fair and balanced. Give some examples of these qualities from the article.

Writing from Reading

1. *Peer writing assignment—simulation argument.* A simulation argument is structured as a real-life situation. Your teacher, in the role of Gary Washburn, moderates a TV panel debate on CTA security. Each student in a group of five must assume one of these roles:

   CTA police officer
   CTA user
   Representative Stange
   unnamed transit official in paragraph 2
   CTA Chairman Burrus or RTA Chairman Skinner

   a. Using the facts in Gary Washburn's article, write a ten-minute argument of your position in the debate.
   b. Read your statement to the other members of your group for comments and revision.
   c. Polish your argument at home for a debate in the next class.
   d. In the following class, each group reads its *two* best arguments to the rest of the class; as Gary Washburn, your instructor decides which ones are the most effective.

2. Drunk driving is another good topic for a simulation agrument. Divide into groups of four and choose for yourself one of these roles: a mother, a member of MADD (Mothers Against Drunk Driving), whose child has been killed by a drunk driver; a local restaurant and bar owner whose family depends on the sale of liquor for their livelihood; a state highway patrolman who has made numerous arrests of drunk drivers only to see them repeat their offenses; and a middle-aged businessman who has been arrested several times for drunk driving and who, because he denies he has a problem, has never undergone rehabilitation.
   a. Do a ten-minute freewriting of your position in the argument.
   b. Read your freewriting to the other members of the group for comment and revision.
   c. Develop your argument at home into a longer paper.
   d. In the next class, choose the best arguments from the group to be read to the entire class.

3. Problems with urban transportation or drunk driving may not interest you. If that is the case, write an essay about some local problem where

you live, for example, racism or drug use. In the first half of your paper, use the reporter's questions of *who, what, when, where, how,* and/or *why* to fully explain the problem. In the other half of your paper, propose some possible solutions.

GARY WASHBURN'S REVISING PROCESS

Gary writes his articles using a computer word-processing program, which allows him to make revisions fairly easily. Working from a great number of notes taken at the RTA meeting (Gary takes his notes in a form of shorthand called "notehand," which enables him to get a lot of information down in a short time), personal interviews after the meeting, and earlier phone interviews, Gary composed his first draft at 12:12 and his eighth and last draft at 4:49, some four-and-a-half hours later.

To give you an idea of just what he chose to include in his article and why, Gary's published article is reprinted below with notes explaining material added between first and final draft. There are three important points to keep in mind as you reread the article:

▲ Gary's *"lead," or beginning, and the conclusion remain the same* throughout the revising process—new ideas and quotations are added later. Gary presents the main information first, and supports it later with details.

▲ Gary *establishes himself as an authority* on CTA security.

▲ Gary *selects* what to use from a mass of information.

Material Added to First Draft	Final Draft
Paragraphs 1–4: Same as first draft.	The Regional Transportation Authority board agreed Tuesday to provide $500,000 next year for added security on the Chicago Transit Authority, but officials acknowledged that the money is largely symbolic and won't rid the CTA of crime.
	One transit official marveled privately that so much attention was being focused on the allocation by the media and the RTA board. "It's a drop in the bucket," he said. "It's really a token."
	CTA Chairman Clark Burrus, who requested the extra money, said that it "sends a sign to the public that we do recognize that there is this problem and we want to address it."
	The CTA has not yet decided how to spend the funds, Burrus said, but it would be enough to pay the salaries of five or six extra

continued

continued

Material Added to First Draft	Final Draft
	Chicago police officers and several additional canine teams to patrol the transit system.
Paragraph 5: CTA facts.	The CTA operates up to 1,780 buses a day over routes totaling 2,092 miles, and 923 rail cars over a 215-mile rapid transit system that has 142 stations.
Paragraph 6: Contrast money spent on graffiti with money spent on security.	With the new money, the CTA is expected to spend $5.5 million for security in 1989, including $5 million that will pay for operation of an existing Chicago police unit that patrols the bus system. That is less than 1 percent of the CTA's planned $662 million budget and slightly more than the agency spent last year to clean graffiti from buses, rail cars and stations.
Paragraph 7: Same as first draft.	Separately, the Chicago Police Department spends about $12 million annually to operate its Mass Transit Unit, which patrols the CTA rail system.
Paragraph 8: CTA security.	Critics contend that the amount of money devoted to CTA security is important, but that the quality and commitment of officers assigned to trains and buses is even more crucial.
Paragraph 9: CTA—minimal effort to monitor routes.	Some officials, both inside the CTA and out, say that members of the bus unit make a minimal effort to monitor routes; that the ranks of the Mass Transit Unit, which is about 240 officers strong on paper, shrink dramatically with temporary assignments to special events such as Taste of Chicago; and that many Mass Transit Unit members routinely loaf on the job.
CTA police used for special events.	
	State Rep. James Stange (R., Oak Brook) said Tuesday that he has received calls recently from seven Chicago police officers, all currently or formerly assigned to the CTA, who have told him the same thing: "Police officers on both buses and trains work for 15 minutes or half an hour when they start their shifts and they are gone until it is time to go home.
Paragraph 10: Rep. Stange received calls from former CTA police.	
Paragraph 11: No supervision of CTA police.	"They're at coffee shops, whatever, and they are not working," Stange charged. "There is no supervision whatsoever."

Paragraph 12: Police brass unavailable for comment.

Paragraph 13: Two murders.

Paragraph 14: Rape.

Paragraph 15: Point being missed is number and quality of officers.

Paragraphs 16–17: More on RTA Chairman Skinner.

Paragraph 18: Conclusion of first draft—"I think it is a step in the right direction," said RTA Chairman Samuel Skinner. "Mr. Burrus and I are committed to looking at this problem. . . . I firmly believe that we are not going to solve the problems of crime through the RTA budget and we shouldn't be expected to."

Cmdr. Carlo Maggio of the Mass Transit Unit and Deputy Chief of Patrol Sherwood Williams were unavailable for comment Tuesday. But police officials have defended the performance of the Mass Transit Unit overall as well as the department's general oversight of the CTA.

Stange was a friend of Bruce Plattenberger, an Oak Park lawyer who was shot to death on a CTA train on Sept. 12. The shooting was followed less than a week later by the killing of Anthony Bruno, 17, who was stabbed on a Fullerton Avenue bus.

Pressure for increased security mounted last Thursday when a woman was forced off a CTA train by a man and sexually assaulted at the Randolph Street elevated station.

"The whole point is being missed," one local transit official said of the $500,000 RTA allocation. "Nobody is asking questions about how many [officers] are out there and what they are doing."

RTA Chairman Samuel Skinner has credited the police with doing "a pretty good job" with limited resources, and he said that police Supt. LeRoy Martin has shown a willingness to cooperate in an effort to improve security.

Recent attacks on the CTA are "tragedies," but "we should not get too hysterical," Skinner said Tuesday.

Skinner termed the new money for CTA security "a step in the right direction." But, he added, "I firmly believe that we are not going to solve the problems of crime through the RTA budget, and we shouldn't be expected to."

By a 10-3 vote, the RTA board also approved 1989 funding levels for its three operating subsidiaries—the CTA, Metra and Pace.

Under the board's action, the CTA will receive $321 million in operating subsidies, down about $10 million from the amount it had requested, while Metra will get $125 million, down about $2 million from its original request, and Pace will receive about $50 million, roughly $1 million under what it had requested.

continued

continued

Material Added to First Draft	Final Draft
Paragraphs 19–22: Information added to the first draft about other business of the meeting not having to do with CTA security.	CTA and Metra officials expressed satisfaction with their allocations, but Pace chairman Florence Boone contended that her agency suffered unfairly. While the CTA and Metra will get between 3 and 4 percent more than in 1988, Pace will suffer a freeze, she complained. RTA officials countered that Pace received a generous increase in subsidies this year and has won $11.5 million in special grants over the last two years.

What can student writers learn form Gary Washburn's revising process?

Throughout the eight drafts of Gary's article, the lead and the conclusion remain the same—except for the final four paragraphs added to the article having to do with business other than CTA security. They form a five-paragraph (paragraphs 1–4 and 18) frame for the discussion of CTA security that Gary fills in with thirteen paragraphs of information from his sources—"critics," "officials both in the CTA and out," "State Representative Stange," "police officials," and "one local transit official."

In his own comments on this piece, Gary says that he often refines the lead and conclusion as he works through the various drafts, but that he always has a good idea of where he wants to start and end. For beginning writers, the point to remember is that in expository writing, that is, explaining or reporting, the information you have in hand before you start writing should determine where the piece will go.

In personal writing, such as the student essay "Hospital Nightmare" (see Chapter 7, pp. 94–96), the writing itself sparks further writing as one discovery leads to another. The student's earlier drafts served as a kind of "prewriting" for the final draft of her paper. You have already learned how to use brainstorming, freewriting, and other prewriting techniques as ways of getting started in your personal writing.

Although Gary's task in the *Tribune* article—and yours in expository writing—is different from that in more personal writing, Gary builds on his first draft in the same way. He first gathers facts and interpretation of those facts—attending the budget hearing and then interviewing various officials in person and by telephone—all in a few hours. He has the added burden of trying to balance conflicting views on the quality of CTA security and whether or not more money should be allotted to it. But he gets something down on paper *fast*—it is the first draft that Gary builds on in writing his entire article.

In analyzing the material Gary adds to the first draft, we find that it all supports the thesis in the lead paragraph—that the extra security money "won't rid the CTA of crime." In paragraph 4, Gary quotes Chairman

Burrus that the extra money will pay for "five or six extra Chicago police officers and several additional canine units." In the next paragraph Gary provides the facts of the CTA operation—"1,780 buses," "923 rail cars," "215-mile system," and "142 stations." In paragraph 6 he shows that the budget for removing graffiti and for security are about the same. Gary's following paragraphs further explain why the money is not enough. Gary cites allegations that transit police are often given other duties, that they "loaf," and that they have "no supervision." Gary quotes Representative Stange's charges and then presents the balancing opinions of "police officials" and Chairman Skinner.

THE WRITER AS AN AUTHORITY

The good writer proves to the reader that he knows what he is talking about, that he is an "authority" on his subject. One way for the writer to show this is to use facts and quotations from important sources.

Consider just a few of the facts Gary uses: $500,000 was added to the $5 million CTA budget for security; the CTA has 1,780 buses over 2,092 miles, and 923 rail cars over 215 miles with 142 stations; the money allocated for security is less than 1 percent of the CTA's $662 million budget; the Chicago Police Department spends about $12 million on its Mass Transit Unit, in which there are 240 officers. Gary also gives us the date of Bruce Plattenberger's death (September 12th), mentions the murder of Anthony Bruno which followed less than a week later, and notes the sexual assault that occurred "last Thursday."

By using these facts, Gary demonstrates that he has the information he needs to present his argument to his readers. In addition to the factual information, Gary records the words of important figures in the story: Chairman Burrus of the CTA, Chairman Skinner of the RTA, Representative Stange, and other transit officials who didn't want their names used. These quotations again show us that Gary knows the people and the ideas he is writing about.

Gary's article demonstrates that you must present yourself as an authority on any subjects you examine in your work if you are to be convincing. Whether you are writing a personal essay or a term paper, you must prove to the reader that you know the subject and are in command of the facts.

THE WRITER'S PRINCIPLE OF SELECTION

Let's now look at some of the ideas and quotations that Gary chose *not* to use in his article. Here, for example, are two quotations from Representative Stange that Gary chose to omit:

> "One police officer told me he received 2 or 3 awards, and he was warned by his commanding officer that if he won one more award, he would be transferred to another detail because it looked bad for the officers not doing their jobs."

and

> "Another thing they [officers of the Mass Transit Unit] mention is how appalling having 55- or 60-year-old men working on trains. They couldn't run after an 18-year-old robber if their lives depended on it."

Both of these quotations are pertinent to Gary's discussion of CTA security. Why, then, didn't he use them? Gary explained that he used some of this information in a later article that focused more on CTA security police. The lesson for beginning writers is to not use *too much* information; you must *select* from the original material only what you need to make your point.

Choosing what to use and what to leave out involves judgment. Consider some other quotes Gary got after the RTA board meeting. First, RTA Chairman Skinner said that he thought riders of the CTA are more protected "than newspapers lead us to believe." Chairman Burrus of the CTA expressed a similar viewpoint: "The more you talk about it [danger on the CTA], the more people think it is unsafe, the more stop riding [the CTA]. Commenting on why he decided not to use these quotes, Gary said that such statements are "knee jerk" responses to bad publicity from transit officials, and that it is the writer's "judgment call" to use or reject them. In this case, Gary chose to leave them out. As a writer, you must learn that you alone are responsible for the material you choose, and that it is up to you to judge what is and what is not fit to include.

When Gary received the assignment to write this story, his editor told him to write an article of so many inches of news space. To make sure he had enough material, Gary actually wrote more paragraphs than he needed. The following three paragraphs added to draft eight of Gary's article were designated as "optional trim"—material left to the discretion of the editor to choose or exclude and still leave the story intact:

> Pastora Cafferty, a member of the RTA board, asserted that the CTA is safer than areas of the city it passes through, despite the headlines generated by the recent series of attacks.
>
> "The truth is that you are safer riding . . . than walking the streets," Cafferty said. "You are better off on the CTA than parking your car. . . . The trouble is that when we talk about police protection, the public gets the perception that it is unsafe."
>
> RTA board members Kathleen Parker and William Walsh, who had called for belt-tightening and a freeze for all three subsidiaries, voted against the funding levels. Philip Raffe voted no because of the increased funding for CTA security. He contended that police protection is the responsibility of the city.

The first two paragraphs about Pastora Cafferty that the editor excluded from the final article follow Chairmen Skinner and Burrus' comments that the CTA is not as unsafe as the press depicts. The last paragraph about RTA members Parker and Walsh merely presents another dissenting opinion.

From this use of "optional trim," we again see that the writer usually has more material than he or she needs. The writer must judge what is essential from what is not.

READING: "BRAZILIAN YOUTHS GET MACHO THRILLS RIDING ATOP TRAINS"

Like Gary's piece in the *Chicago Tribune*, the following *Wall Street Journal* article by Roger Cohen is also about problems in the big city—in this case poverty and juvenile delinquency in Rio de Janeiro. Cohen, however, focuses on the shocking waste of human life. Using your prereading skills, read the title and subtitle:

Brazilian Youths Get Macho Thrills Riding Atop Trains

Rail 'Surfing' Is a Blood Rite With Often-Fatal Kicks; Losing a Little Brother

Write down a prediction about the content of the article.

Now read the first two paragraphs and the last two paragraphs of the article:

> RIO DE JANEIRO—McDonald's brother died two months ago. The pudgy 15-year-old was electrocuted by the 3,300-volt cable as he stood atop a fast-moving suburban train here. For a train surfer, it was a typical death.
>
> "He shriveled to the size of a ham. The electricity ate through his fat," says McDonald, whose real name is Joabe Pereira da Silva. Though he is distressed by his brother's death, McDonald has been unable to shake his own train-surfing habit. "I got used to it," he says, "and I can't stop."
>
> • • •
>
> As the packed 7:30 p.m. train pulls out from the Central station, the gang seems happy. They pass around a bottle of wine. Russa introduces her friend Beth, who has given up surfing for the moment because she is pregnant. Then, pulling on woolen hats or tying scarves around their heads, Pistoleiro and several others climb out the window and up on top of the train. They scream and wail and stamp on the roof.
>
> The train picks up speed, swaying and jolting. Suddenly, another train whooshes past, and there is a blue flash of electricity. Russa is worried and, after a moment, strains her head out the window of the car to see if anyone has been hurt. "Don't worry," says Rogerio, who is inside the car playing cards for small stakes. "Somebody would have said something if one of them were dead."

Can you add anything to your prediction? Write down your answer.

Now read the entire article. Pay attention to how the writer answers the reporter's questions of *who, what, when, where, how,* and/or *why.* In this piece *why*—the reasons for this bizarre, self-destructive behavior—is very important. Also observe how he uses direct quotations from those involved to support his position and present himself as an authority.

Brazilian Youths Get Macho Thrills Riding Atop Trains

Rail 'Surfing' Is a Blood Rite With Often-Fatal Kicks; Losing a Little Brother

---

By ROGER COHEN

Staff Reporter of THE WALL STREET JOURNAL

RIO DE JANEIRO—McDonald's brother died two months ago. The pudgy 15-year-old was electrocuted by the 3,300-volt cable as he stood atop a fast-moving suburban train here. For a train surfer, it was a typical death.

"He shriveled to the size of a ham. The electricity ate through his fat," says McDonald, whose real name is Joabe Pereira da Silva. Though he is distressed by his brother's death, McDonald has been unable to shake his own train-surfing habit. "I got used to it," he says, "and I can't stop."

The 7:40 a.m. train pulls into Nilop-olis station, in the midst of Rio's abject northern suburbs. McDonald, so nick-named because he once worked for a local outlet of the U.S. hamburger chain, is wearing red laceless basketball shoes, yellow Bermuda shorts labeled Windsurfer and a plaid shirt. He shuns the packed interior of the train. As it pulls out, he clambers onto the window ledge, and from there claws his way onto the roof. He stands dangerously close to the cable,

which is a few feet above the roof, as the train moves toward a top speed of 75 miles per hour. The 16-year-old is surfing.

A Blood Rite

Riding the tops of trains is a stunt popular among the poor youths of north Rio. Their counterparts in the wealthy south of the city surf the waves; they surf the trains—despite 200 deaths and 500 injuries over the past 18 months. The so-called "surfistas" abound on the early-morning and evening trains into and out of the city center. Adopting nicknames like Rambo, Stallone and Pistoleiro, or Gunman, they are drawn by the macho appeal of defying danger and a camaraderie that bears the fervid intensity of a blood rite.

"It's our sport," says Artur, who is revered because he break-dances on the train. "If you fall, you've gone soft and you're finished. That's it."

Before you finish the article, read the next paragraph and (a) predict the main idea question, (b) clarify the meaning of any difficult words or sentences, and (c) predict what the next paragraph will say:

Rambo, whose real name is Jose Lira de Minezes, was once king of the surfers. A clean-cut 23-year-old worker in a curtain factory, he was known for his stylish surfing. But he knew the sport was madness. Last December, he went on television to make an appeal to other surfers. Of his 20 closest friends, he told viewers, 19 were dead. Looking straight into the camera, he added, "This is stupid. It's not worth it. We should stop."

Check these answers against yours:

a. *Prequest*—Why did Rambo go on TV?
b. *Clarify*—Nothing.
c. *Prenext*—The next paragraph will talk about the effect of Rambo's words.

Now read the next paragraph to see how close our prediction was:

Rambo's Death

But a few weeks later, Rambo was surfing again. Three months after his television appearance, he died after falling from a train as it rounded a bend. Lucio Alves, nicknamed Stallone, took over as top surfer. He was killed in June. His cousin, Maria di Fatima Barbosa, or Russa, is one of the few female surfers. "Surfing is a joke that leads to nothing," she says. "But the air up there is so good."

In this case, our prediction was wrong. The paragraph reveals that Rambo didn't follow his own advice and was killed in a fall from a train. Remember that

even if your prediction is not always correct, the process of predicting is valuable in itself because it forces you to concentrate on the reading.

Here is the rest of the article:

The new leader is Pistoleiro, a handsome 21-year-old who will only give his first name, Nelson. He and the gang gather at the Central Station around 6:30 every evening. They are a motley crew. There is Formigao, or Giant Ant, with his arm in a sling from a fall three months ago; Orelinha Eletrica, or Electric Ear, who has hit the cable three times and survived; and Indio whose younger brother lost his legs two months ago when he fell. What did Indio feel about that? "Nothing," he says.

Some surfers, among them McDonald, are street hawkers. Others work as office boys, carpenters or glass-cutters, earning roughly the equivalent of $50 to $100 a month. They insist vehemently that press images of them as drug addicts or thieves are false. They are regular guys, they say—except for the fact that they are hooked on a deadly sport.

The surfers worship film heroes, such as Charles Bronson and Arnold Schwarzenegger. They proudly display their wounds: burns, bald patches, and scars. They don't want to die, they say, but death doesn't scare them. Death is the only thing that will stop them, they say. They seem remarkably untouched by the loss of friends or even family. Asked about the death of his friend Rambo, Pistoleiro says, "Whoever falls, was."

Only talk of their parents seems to move the youths. They realize it's tough to be a surfer's parent. Carlos Maciel, an office boy, says his mother has implored him to stop. McDonald is protective about his mother, who is still in shock from his brother's death. But her grief isn't enough to stop him.

continued

continued

'A Form of Suicide'

Francisco Machado, a retired railway worker, lost his son a couple of years ago. The boy's legs were sliced off in a fall from a train. Mr Machado barely holds back his tears as he talks about the tragedy. "I feel it in my skin," he says. He seems tortured by trying to understand why his son did it. "It's a form of suicide," he says. "Brazilian youth is suffering so much, they see no reason to live."

Train surfing has caught on as the nation's economic crisis has deepened over the last 18 months. Inflation of nearly 800% over the past year is tough on everyone, but it bites particularly hard in the Baixada Fluminense, a poverty-stricken sprawl just a few miles north of the plush opulence of south Rio. On the average, five people a day are murdered in this slum, which 2.6 million people—including many surfers—call home. Here, death squads roam, drugs abound, police connive and corpses are regularly dragged from the rivers.

"Train surfing stems from the acute social problems here. As inflation multiplies, so does crime," says Evandro Steele, a state prosecutor who has handled several cases involving train surfers. Debt-ridden, Brazil does not have the money to police its trains, he argues. Nor, it seems, can it offer the education or jobs to instill a greater attachment to life.

Selling Candy to Survive

McDonald's life illustrates the misery. When he arrives in town in the early morning, he takes it easy for a while. Then he goes to a wholesale candy store and buys a box of 30 chocolate bars for 1,800 cruzados, or about $4. During the day, he sells the bars on trains. His daily profit of about $2.70 will go to help pay his family's rent of roughly $23 a month. McDonald dreams of a better life. He says

he would like to be a chauffeur for a "Madame." In the meantime, he surfs.

The state-owned Brazilian Urban Trains Company, or CBTU, has tried to stop the surfers, but it is beset by other problems. When trains are late, angry passengers sometimes stone them or set them on fire. Copper is stolen from wires, stalling signals and causing accidents.

Fighting Surfing With Photos

CBTU's fare, about seven cents, covers less than a third of its operational costs. Chronically underfinanced, the company lacks the resources to hire guards to prevent surfing. Nonetheless, it is required to compensate surfers and their families for deaths and injuries. Over the past 18 months, CBTU paid out $500,000 in compensation.

"We've tried everything to put an end to the madness of train surfing, but we can't," says spokesman Helio Barros. Earlier this year, CBTU organized an exhibition featuring photographs of dead or crippled surfers. Some photos showed limbs mutilated by falls; others showed electrocuted surfers, attached in hideous contortions to the electric cable. The exhibition drew crowds but didn't discourage the surfers.

A $2 Fine

The company has tried prosecuting surfers. It took nine of them to court this year and charged them with disrupting train service. But the case was thrown out after the prosecutor, Mr. Steele, conceded there was no proof that train-surfing had ever caused a rail disaster. So surfing still carries only a $2 fine.

As the packed 7:30 p.m. train pulls out from the Central station, the gang seems happy. They pass around a bottle of wine. Russa introduces her friend Beth, who has given up surfing for the moment because she is pregnant. Then, pulling on woolen hats or tying scarves around their heads, Pistoleiro and several others climb out the window and up on top of the train. They scream and wail and stamp on the roof.

The train picks up speed, swaying and jolting. Suddenly, another train whooshes past, and there is a blue flash of electricity. Russa is worried and, after a moment, strains her head out the window of the car to see if anyone has been hurt. "Don't worry," says Rogerio, who is inside the car playing cards for small stakes. "Somebody would have said something if one of them were dead."

Reading for Meaning

1. What is the main idea of the article?
2. How does the writer support his thesis?
3. What is "rail surfing"?
4. Explain how the "surfistas" are killed.
5. How do the "surfistas" explain the reasons for their behavior?
6. Why do the "surfistas" boast of their wounds and injuries, and have as their heroes Charles Bronson and Arnold Schwarzenegger?
7. How does Francisco Machado, who lost his son to rail surfing, explain the reasons for it?
8. How has the train company tried to stop the rail surfing?
9. Can you think of any parallels of such destructive behavior as rail surfing to activities among American youth?
10. Why does the writer give so many examples of rail-surfing tragedies?

Vocabulary in Context

Write down the definition of each of the italicized words below taken from the article. Try to guess the meaning from the context. Use a dictionary only if you have to.

1. "Adopting nicknames like Rambo, Stallone and Pistoleiro, or Gunman, they are drawn by the macho appeal of defying danger and a [a.] *camaraderie* that bears the [b.] *fervid* intensity of a blood rite."

2. ". . . in the midst of Rio's *abject* northern suburbs . . ."
3. "Their *counterparts* in the wealthy south of the city surf the waves . . ."
4. "They are a *motley* crew."
5. "They insist *vehemently* . . ."
6. ". . . his mother has *implored* him to stop."
7. ". . . police *connive* . . ."

8. "Inflation of nearly 800% over the past year is tough on everyone, but it bites particularly hard in the Baixada Fluminense, a poverty-stricken [a.] *sprawl* just a few miles north of the [b.] *plush opulence* of south Rio."

Writing from Reading

For each of these assignments, prewrite, write a first draft, and then write a final draft. Remember to consider your *subject, purpose,* and *audience.*

1. Read the following paragraph again.

Selling Candy to Survive

McDonald's life illustrates the misery. When he arrives in town in the early morning, he takes it easy for a while. Then he goes to a wholesale candy store and buys a box of 30 chocolate bars for 1,800 cruzados, or about $4. During the day, he sells the bars on trains. His daily profit of about $2.70 will go to help pay his family's rent of roughly $23 a month. McDonald dreams of a better life. He says he would like to be a chauffeur for a "Madame." In the meantime, he surfs.

This paragraph, developed by example from the topic sentence "McDonald's life illustrates the misery," makes real the facts of poverty in Rio. Imitate the structure of this paragraph by developing a similar example of a poor youngster in a large American city. Use this as your topic sentence: "Jack's day in New York was one long struggle for survival."

2. Why does it seem that the rail surfers feel sorrow only for their parents, and not for each other?

3. Do you or your friends and acquaintances ever endanger yourselves, though not so dramatically as the rail surfers?

4. Explain why you think the photos of mutilated surfers don't discourage the others. Can you think of other wrong-headed attempts to deter destructive behavior, for example, photos of car crashes, dirty drug needles, or even AIDS victims? Or do you think some of these warnings work?

5. The picture of poverty and needless suffering in Rio de Janeiro may seem remote to us in America, but we have our own serious problems with the poor and homeless, too, especially in large cities. Describe an area you have seen near where you live or in your travels that is filled with people who have no hope—like the youth of Rio described in Cohen's article. What do you see? What do you hear and smell? What are its worst features? What are the people like? What are the causes and possible solutions for these problems?

PART THREE

Types of Writing

▲▲▲

CHAPTER

9

The Five-Paragraph Essay

Many of the essays you will be required to write in school will follow the basic structure of *introduction with thesis, body with supporting reasons,* and *conclusion.* Before examining in detail the structure of the five-paragraph essay, let's walk through a student example to review the writing process once again. The student follows the same pattern you have learned throughout this book: brainstorming (or some other form of prewriting), revised brainstorming, outline, and essay. For this assignment the student was required to "role play," that is, pretend to be a parent disturbed by Surgeon General C. Everett Koop's controversial brochure, *Understanding AIDS* (see pp. 191–97), mailed to every home in America.

Original Brainstorming List

concerned for the sex education of my daughters
sex education is the parents' responsibility
is this the government of Big Brother?
My church beliefs—abstinence until marriage
brochure implies sexual freedom, sex with one partner not abstinence
stirs unhealthy interest in sex—oral and anal sex
suggests condom use, not abstinence
turns a personal moral issue into a health concern
more to sex than facts
characterizes sins as "safe behavior"
by urging condom use, advocates promiscuity

As a basis for his outline, the student revised his original list according to the importance of the items:

Revised Brainstorming List

parents are responsible for the sex education of their children
brochure so explicit, promotes unhealthy curiosity about anal and oral sex
brochure downplays morality
our religious belief is abstinence until marriage, then a single partner 'til
    "death do us part"
brochure characterizes sins as "safe behavior"
no moral standards in brochure, just health concerns
urging use of condoms suggests they are not a moral concern

From the many ideas suggested in his revised brainstorming list, he derived an outline: the thesis "The AIDS brochure advocates immoral sexual behavior," with supporting reasons listed in order of importance. Each of the three reasons serves as a topic sentence in one of the middle paragraphs of his essay:

1. By being explicit about how one can get AIDS, the brochure suggests new immoral ways to have sex.
2. The brochure encourages immoral sexual habits by explaining how to avoid getting AIDS, thereby encouraging sexual activity.
3. Rather than encouraging abstinence, the brochure promotes sex with one partner, which is immoral outside of marriage.

Because his third reason is the most important, he uses it to begin the last of the middle paragraphs in the body of his essay. You should always offer your strongest reason last to leave a lasting impression on the reader's mind.

Now read the finished essay. Look for the pattern of thesis at the end of the first paragraph, reasons supporting the thesis as topic sentences in the three middle paragraphs, and a concluding paragraph. You may or may not agree with the thoughts the writer expresses here, but bear in mind that the student had to assume a role for this assignment.

AIDS Brochure

As a parent of two teenage daughters, I am outraged by the AIDS brochure I received in the mail. If I wanted my daughters to learn about AIDS, I would have told them myself. The U.S. government should not have mailed out the AIDS brochure; my daughters saw it in the mail before me. I was shocked to learn after they read the brochure that it was so explicit. My daughters never should have seen that brochure. The AIDS brochure advocates immoral sexual behavior.

By being explicit about how one can get AIDS, the brochure suggests new immoral ways to have sex. As soon as my daughters read the brochure, they started asking me about oral and anal sex. I am angry that I cannot convince them that anal and oral sex are immoral. They argue that it must be okay if it is in the brochure. They should not have heard about having sex with different partners. I have always told them that sex should only happen within a marriage, something the brochure does not consider important.

The brochure encourages immoral sexual habits by explaining how to avoid getting AIDS, thereby encouraging sexual activity. With the AIDS scare, my daughters are less likely to have sex. Once they learn that they can escape the AIDS virus, they can freely engage in sex without any fear. I think that using condoms is immoral. Once my daughters get married, I do not want them using condoms or any form of birth control.

Rather than encouraging abstinence, the brochure promotes sex with one partner, which is immoral outside of marriage. I do not want my daughters to have sex at all, but the brochure tells them that sex is okay with one faithful, uninfected partner. Sure, the brochure mentions abstinence; I think it should make abstinence more important than sex with one faithful partner.

The AIDS brochure encourages immoral sexual behavior. The brochure is just too explicit. I wish my daughters never saw it in the mail. Next time I hope the U.S. government will talk to some parents before sending out a similar brochure.

THE FIVE-PARAGRAPH ESSAY

After you have developed your thesis and supporting arguments through brainstorming or other prewriting, try to structure the outline of your essay in this five-paragraph pattern:

Paragraph 1—Introduction, thesis.
Paragraph 2—First supporting reason.
Paragraph 3—Second supporting reason.
Paragraph 4—Third supporting reason.
Paragraph 5—Conclusion, restatement of thesis.

Let's look again at the student's outline:

Thesis (last sentence of paragraph 1)—"The AIDS brochure advocates immoral sexual behavior."
First reason (first sentence of paragraph 2)—"By being explicit about how one can get AIDS, the brochure suggests new immoral ways to have sex."
Second reason (first sentence of paragraph 3)—"The brochure encourages immoral sexual habits by explaining how to avoid getting AIDS, thereby encouraging sexual activity."
Third reason (first sentence of paragraph 4)—"Rather than encouraging abstinence, the brochure promotes sex with one partner, which is immoral outside of marriage."

Thesis restated (first sentence of paragraph 5)—"The AIDS brochure encourages immoral sexual behavior."

Writing Practice

For each of the following thesis statements, think of three supporting reasons. Always put your strongest reason last.

1. "People on welfare should be required to work for their checks."
2. "People on welfare should not be required to work for their checks."
3. "Traffic in our major cities has become almost impossible."
4. "The cost of college has recently become almost prohibitive."
5. "Inner-city education must be improved."

The First Paragraph

The first paragraph is an introduction to your essay. It begins with a generalization or broad observation on the topic, and it ends with your thesis statement. If you become stuck trying to begin the first paragraph, take a noun from your thesis—for example, "AIDS brochure" from the student essay—and write a sentence about it. Look again at the student's first sentence: "As a parent of two teenage daughters, I am outraged by the AIDS brochure I received in the mail." This statement about the brochure leads to the thesis in the last sentence: "The AIDS brochure advocates immoral sexual behavior." Some other first sentences might be "The AIDS brochure mailed to every home in America is an invasion of privacy" or "The AIDS brochure may have been well-intended, but it takes over the role of the parent in sex education."

The Middle Paragraphs

The middle paragraphs make up the body of the essay, and they all follow the same pattern—a topic sentence followed by other sentences that support it with facts, examples, or explanations. The second paragraph of the student essay, for example, begins with the topic sentence, "By being explicit about how one can get AIDS, the brochure suggests new immoral ways to have sex." The writer supports this claim with examples of sexual behavior implicitly condoned by the brochure—"anal and oral sex" and "having sex with different partners."

The third paragraph of the student's essay begins with the second argument of his thesis—"The brochure encourages immoral sexual habits by explaining how to avoid getting AIDS, thereby encouraging sexual activity." He supports this argument with the example that "using condoms is immoral. Once my daughters get married, I do not want them using condoms or any form of birth control."

In the fourth paragraph, the student offers the most convincing case for his thesis. "Rather than encouraging abstinence," he writes, "the brochure promotes sex with one partner, which is immoral outside of marriage." He explains his reason: "I do not want my daughters to have sex at all, but the brochure tells them that sex is okay with one faithful, uninfected partner."

The fifth and final paragraph of the student essay begins with a restatement of the thesis—"The AIDs brochure encourages immoral sexual behavior"—and concludes with a summary of the three reasons, in the same order, that he gave in the middle paragraphs to support his thesis.

The five-paragraph structure can be adapted to many other general essay topics. Although it is not the only way to write an essay, the five-paragraph form provides the writer a system with which to write on many subjects. With some adjustments, of course, this basic structure can be expanded to include as many middle paragraphs as needed to develop more reasons supporting the thesis. The introduction and conclusion can still have the same format.

Writing Practice

For each of the following assignments, try to imitate the five-paragraph structure of the student essay on the AIDS brochure. First do your brainstorming or other prewriting, using the revised prewriting to fashion an outline with a thesis and three supporting reasons to be used as topic sentences for the middle paragraphs.

1. Consider the neighborhood in which you live. Are there any changes you can suggest to improve it?
2. Some people believe that television is wasting the minds of many of America's youth. What is your view?
3. Health officials have recommended that birth control clinics and sex education offices be made part of public high schools throughout America's cities. What is your opinion?
4. There has recently been a lot of criticism of America's grammar and high schools. Can you suggest any ways to improve American education?

Transitional Words

Another way to organize your writing besides reordering the sequence of your brainstorming list or other prewriting is to use transitions. The word "transition" is derived from two Latin roots, *trans* (across), as in "transatlantic" and "transfer," and *ire* (to go). Transitions help you cross from or connect one idea to another. Why study transitions? Transitions are to writing what mortar is to bricks—something to hold the structure together. In stories or jokes we use them naturally: *first*, this happened; *then*, that happened; and *finally*, the last thing happened. But it is also important for you to make conscious use of transitions to connect ideas together for the reader. You have probably noticed that the five-paragraph pattern of the essay lends itself particularly well to the use of transitions at the beginning of each of the middle paragraphs.

Transitions may be divided according to the kinds of signals they give to the reader, for example, sequence or contrast. Some transitional words or phrases may give more than one type of signal. Here are some of the major types of transitional word and phrase groups:

Addition

These words add ideas together:

and	Tamara was beautiful *and* seductive; *furthermore*, her parents were filthy rich.
furthermore	
in addition	

Cause and effect

These words and phrases show cause-and-effect relationships or results:

as a result	After the war many lives were shattered. *As a result*, normal domestic living was impossible for years.
therefore	
thus	
consequently	
because	

Sequence

These transitions indicate sequence, or chronological order (order according to time):

first	*First*, the killer crawled along the hall. He *then* slowly pushed open the door, reached quietly inside his coat for his .38 police special, and *finally* took aim and fired into the broad back of Big Tuna.
second	
third	
then	
next	
another	
finally	

Spatial locations

These words indicate direction or some spatial relationship:

here	Strewn *over* the rubble, *here* and *there* were shards of glass, just waiting for the unwary traveler *down* from the hills.
on	
in	
there	
beneath	
below	
above	
under	
over	
beside	

Contrast

These transitions point to contrast or difference:

but	He is handsome, *but* dumb.
yet	Jon was mad at Jill, *yet* still loved her.
however	The Germans won the early battles in World War
nevertheless	II; *however*, they lost in the end.

A note on punctuation is important here. "But" and "yet" are conjunctions and are preceded by a comma. "However" and "nevertheless" are conjunctive adverbs preceded by a semicolon (and followed by a comma) when they are used to join two ideas—as in the example above.

Example

These phrases signal examples:

for example	The Boston Celtics are one of the greatest teams
for instance	in all of professional sports; they have, *for exam-*
in other words	*ple*, won more world championships than any
	other pro team.

Some writers use transitions almost without thinking about it. Most beginning writers, however, have to learn how to use them. Having this list in front of you as you work through your drafts will help you see where transitions can provide links in your paper. It is a good idea to glance over the list of transitions as you complete each draft. If nothing else, having the book open to the section on transitions will make you more aware of the need to use them.

Writing Practice

Write down the correct transitional word or phrase for each of the blank spaces in the passage below:

and	and
one	however
two	that is
three	and
for example	

The Navajo Way is the Southwestern Indian tribe's religion and refers to a Navajo's harmony with the flow of nature (1.) _____ with the natural pattern of life. Practice of the Navajo Way has become more difficult, (2.) _____, for today's Navajo because the outside world of the *Belecani*, (3.) _____, the White Man, keeps imposing its values even on the Reservation. Radio and television have for a long time carried the White Man's "way" to even the most remote parts of the four-state Reservation.

For many young Navajo today, the cable TV preacher has replaced the tribal shaman or medicine man who once taught him how to "walk in beauty." Like the Mormons or Catholic priests whom the Navajo has long allowed to live among him, the TV preacher has little or no knowledge of Navajo beliefs (4.) _____ customs. (5.) _____, the Navajo has no concept of a life after death. He believes that when a man dies, that which was natural in him, and therefore good, exists no longer.

Despite the incursion of the White Man into his life, the Navajo has been able to survive for three basic reasons: (6.) _____, the strength of his family life; (7.) _____, his love of raw nature on the Reservation; (8.) _____, (9.) _____, his refusal to leave his home and migrate from the Reservation.

Transitional Sentences

Sentences, as well as words and phrases, can serve as transitions in writing. Transitional sentences connect ideas from previous paragraphs to later paragraphs. For an example, let's look again at the beginning of Gary Washburn's *Chicago Tribune* article, "CTA security funds win RTA approval" (see pp. 107–108):

> The Regional Transportation Authority board agreed Tuesday to provide *$500,000* next year for added security on the Chicago Transit Authority, but officials acknowledged that the *money* is largely symbolic and won't rid the CTA of crime.
>
> One transit official marveled privately that so much attention was being focused on the allocation by the media and the RTA board. ''It's a drop in the bucket,'' he said. ''It's really a token.''
>
> CTA Chairman Clark Burrus, who requested the extra *money*, said that it ''sends a sign to the public that we do recognize that there is this problem and we want to address it.''
>
> The CTA has not yet decided how to spend the *funds*, Burrus said, but it would be enough to pay the salaries of five or six extra Chicago police officers and several additional canine teams to patrol the transit system.
>
> The CTA operates up to 1,780 buses a day over routes totaling 2,092 miles, and 923 rail cars over a 215-mile rapid transit system that has 142 stations.
>
> *With the new money*, the CTA is expected to spend $5.5 million for security in 1989, including $5 million that will pay for operation of an existing Chicago police unit that patrols the bus system. That is less than 1 percent of the CTA's planned $662 million budget and slightly more than the agency spent last year to clean graffiti from buses, rail cars and stations.

Gary begins the last paragraph here with this sentence: "With the new money, the CTA is expected to spend $5.5 million for security in 1989, including $5 million that will pay for operation of an existing Chicago police unit that patrols the bus system." The phrase "with the new money" refers to an additional $500,000 Gary has described in paragraphs 1, 3, and 4 ("money" and "funds"). The rest of the sentence points to how the overall security budget is to be spent, a subject of the following paragraphs.

Writing Practice

Below are some transitional sentences. Analyze each one and try to summarize what the previous paragraph said and what is likely to come next.

EXAMPLE   After this *rowdy behavior* by the students in the cafeteria, the principal was forced to make strict *new rules*.

ANSWER   The previous paragraphs explained the "rowdy behavior"—for example, screaming in the cafeteria, harrassing the serving ladies, throwing food, and leaving garbage on the floor. The "new rules"—for example, detention or suspension for rowdy behavior—will be explained next.

1. Because of the *heroic efforts* of the firemen, everybody in the burning hotel was *rescued.*

2. To stop further *pollution* of the Hudson River, federal officials began fining the offending *industries.*

3. Any of these *forms of exercise* will help the sincere man or woman lose weight and feel *better.*

4. All these foods are *fattening* and must be avoided if the dieter is to achieve *success.*

5. These cars are the most *expensive* in America, calling for *more money* than an average home used to cost.

The Paragraph Hook

In addition to transitional words and sentences, another device for keeping writing unified and focused is the paragraph hook—repetition of a noun at the end of one paragraph and the beginning of the following paragraph. In the following passage, notice how key nouns are used to link paragraphs:

The Alaskan oil spill created an ecological disaster of mammoth proportions. In addition to the thousands of barrels of oil irretrievably lost in the environment, hundreds of miles of shoreline were fouled. Many species of animals were severely damaged, especially *salmon,* the mainstay of the Alaskan commercial fishing industry.

In the fishing season following the oil spill, the *salmon* catch was only 61% of the normal catch. Other animals in the area were affected, too, including seals, otters, wading birds, and even intertidal creatures like snails, mussels, and mollusks. All this damage was caused by *Exxon,* a giant in the oil industry.

What was *Exxon's* response to the catastrophe it had triggered? For over a year, Exxon mobilized a clean-up force of hundreds of workers. One good came from all the mess—the use of the fertilizer Inipol which hastened the growth of oil-eating microbes. This technique of fighting the spill was so successful that it is sure to help in future similar incidents.

Repeating the nouns "salmon" and "Exxon" keep the paragraphs focused on related ideas.

Writing Practice

1. Use of the paragraph hook does not come naturally. You have to work at it. In the paragraphs below, take a key noun from the last sentence of one paragraph and repeat it in the first sentence of the next paragraph.

    Navajo Indians have no belief in an afterlife. In their view, a *chindi*, or evil spirit, inhabits the body of the deceased and must be released through a hole in the ceiling of the *hogan*, or Navajo home. Unlike their Hopi and Zuni neighbors who believe that the spirit transcends death, the Navajo maintain that all good in man dies with him.

    The _____ differ from the Hopi and Zuni also in their great love for the rodeo. They excel at barrel-racing, calf-roping, and other cowboy events. Perhaps the Navajo interest in horses is explained by their background as migratory or "Plains" Indians, in contrast to the more sedentary Hopi and Zuni who have always been "Pueblo" Indians. For all of the Indians living on the Four Corners Reservation—25,000 square miles of Arizona, New Mexico, Colorado, and Utah—a recent development has been the discovery of valuable natural resources, especially oil and uranium, on their land.

    In a sad replay of history, the white man is again trying to cheat the Indians, this time by stealing his _____. But this time the Indian is more wary, and now he has competent lawyers to guard his rights.

2. Now see if you can use the paragraph hook in your own writing. Take several essays you have already written and see if you can insert paragraph hooks in your middle paragraphs. Remember to repeat them in the last sentence of one paragraph and the first sentence of the next paragraph.

CHAPTER
10

Description and Narration

Essay writing has many purposes—to describe, narrate, explain, amuse and argue, to name a few. Often these purposes overlap or are combined in the same essay. For example, if you were to write a paper arguing against steroid use by young athletes, you would probably first describe what steroids are, explain why and how they are used, and narrate an incident illustrating the physical and psychological consequences to teenagers of long-term steroid use. In this chapter we will examine two major types of writing—description and narration.

DESCRIPTION

A writer describes by appealing to the senses of the reader—what can be seen, heard, smelled, tasted, or felt. Consider again this description of Navajo land from William Least Heat Moon's *Blue Highways*:

> Liquor bottles, beercans, an occasional stripped car littered the unfenced roadside. Far off the highway, against the mesa bottoms, stood small concrete-block or frame houses, each with a television antenna, pickup, privy, and ceremonial hogan of stone, adobe, and cedar. Always the hogan doors faced east.

In a classic scene, a boy on a pinto pony herded a flock of sheep and goats—descendants of the Spanish breed—across the highway. A few miles later, a man wearing a straw Stetson and pegleg Levi's guided up a draw a pair of horses tied together at the neck in the Indian manner. With the white man giving up on the economics of cowpunching, it looked as if the old categories of cowboys and Indians had merged; whoever the last true cowboy in America turns out to be, he's likely to be an Indian.

Write down those words that appeal to your sense of taste, sound, or feeling.

When describing, a writer must also use a clear pattern that the reader can follow. What pattern does William Least Heat Moon use in his description—from near to far, far to near, left to right, or right to left? Look at the key words and phrases he uses to organize his picture spatially:

"unfenced roadside"
"Far off the highway, against the mesa bottoms"
"the hogan doors faced east"
"a boy on a pinto pony herded . . . across the highway"
"A few miles later"

The description is arranged from near ("unfenced roadside") to far ("A few miles later").

Writing from Reading

1. Brainstorm or freewrite about a favorite or least favorite place. It could be a place in the country or the city, a large lake or a small room. Next, list those things you would see, hear, taste, touch, and smell there. Find a pattern for your description—for example, left to right, right to left, or some other spatial organization—and write one long paragraph telling the reader about the place you have chosen.

2. *Peer reading assignment.* Do the assignment above, sharing your paper at each stage of the writing process with the other students in your group.

READING: "A FEW MORE POUNDS, AND THIS PORKER IS IN HOG HEAVEN"

The following *Wall Street Journal* article by Clare Ansberry is an unusual example of descriptive writing. First read the title and two subtitles:

A Few More Pounds, And This Porker Is in Hog Heaven

* * *

Called Chief, He Is in Training For Heaviest-Pig Record; Bellying Up to a Six-Pack

A Few More Pounds Will Place This Plump Pig in Hog Heaven

Write down what you think the article is about.

Now read the first two and last two paragraphs:

> NORTH LEWISBURG, Ohio—"Wanna see him?" asks Bob Corbett, a wad of tobacco the size of a half dollar tucked in his cheek. Without waiting for a reply, the retired prison worker grabs a cane and a wood shield and disappears into the back of a red trailer, where something is snoring loudly.
>
> Seconds later, the corralled snorer appears: Chief, a grunting 1,230-pound hog, with ears the size of mud flaps and a runway for a tongue. A Hula-Hoop would be snug on this porker's eight-foot girth.
>
> • • •
>
> Mr. Corbett initially refused to go because he didn't know "who the heck this Letterman fellow was." He grudgingly accepted. "It wasn't so bad, but I'd never do it again," he says. Driving his big truck and trailer through Manhattan "was enough to make you chew your gum backwards." Then there was the matter of getting Chief up to the studio on the sixth floor of Rockefeller Center, where, in expectation, the furniture had been stacked out of the way and covered with plastic.
>
> Since then, Chief has become quite the ham. He refused to leave the stage after snaring the Indiana State Fair title. And when various award-winning fruits and animals were assembled for a local TV shot, Chief tried to eliminate the 59-pound watermelon by eating it. But he wasn't quick enough. The watermelon's owner outsnatched him.

Write down any further predictions you have about the content of the article.

As you now read the entire piece, try to determine the *tone* of the writing, the author's attitude toward her subject—whether serious, sarcastic, humorous, or playful. The tone of the writing reveals much about its meaning.

A Few More Pounds, And This Porker Is in Hog Heaven

* * *

Called Chief, He Is in Training For Heaviest-Pig Record; Bellying Up to a Six-Pack

BY CLARE ANSBERRY

Staff Reporter of THE WALL STREET JOURNAL

NORTH LEWISBURG, Ohio—"Wanna see him?" asks Bob Corbett, a wad of tobacco the size of a half dollar tucked in his cheek. Without waiting for a reply, the retired prison worker grabs a cane and a wood shield and disappears into the back of a red trailer, where something is snoring loudly.

Seconds later, the corralled snorer appears: Chief, a grunting 1,230-pound hog, with ears the size of mud flaps and a runway for a tongue. A Hula-Hoop would be snug on this porker's eight-foot girth.

"Whaddya think?" asks Mr. Corbett, a man of no small expanse himself, as he nods at the 4-foot-tall, 9-foot-long hog. Standing next to Chief, he rocks on his feet with a proud, that's-my-boy expression.

A Pig in Bloom

No wonder. Chief is the reigning World's Largest Male Hog, or so say the judges at the Indiana State Fair, where he recently won the title. The six-year-old edged out Oscar, a half-ton runner-up from Delphi, Ind., to win $350 in prize money, a plaque and a local television appearance.

But Mr. Corbett believes his boar is destined to bring home far bigger bacon. Next year, Chief will fatten up to go after the known record for the world's heaviest hog: 1,338 pounds.

Last June, Chief came close when he tipped the scales at the local feed elevator at 1,322 pounds. "He was ready to blossom," says Mr. Corbett. But when this summer's heat wave hit, Chief quit pigging out and quickly lost 100 pounds. His owner put three fans in his stall and a water mister overhead, but nothing helped. When Mr. Corbett poured molasses on Chief's feed to make it more appealing, the bored hog merely licked off the syrup. He wouldn't even tuck in to his favorite cherry Jell-O. "The hot weather just about melted him away," Mr. Corbett says with a sigh.

Chief—a Berkshire pig, black with patches of white—descends from a great tradition of hefty hogs. They were the norm through the 1940s, when enormous amounts of lard were needed for the war effort. Some got so large that their sagging stomachs dragged along the ground, and farmers took to tying aprons round them to prevent belly burn. The Perry family of Bethel, Mo., raised a hog of similar girth during the war years. Ol' Lard, they called him. "He ate and slept until he looked like he was going to break," recalls Kathleen Perry.

But like many hog farmers, the Perrys now raise a different breed to cater to a more health-conscious nation. The hogs are taller and slimmer, with less fat and more muscle. The only reason to grow a big hog today, says Mrs. Perry, is for sport. "Some people golf. Some people fish," she explains.

Mr. Corbett is one who raises plump porkers for show. His first few candidates grew like weeds, only to top out at 950 pounds. But Mr. Corbett knew Chief was a

Please Turn To Page A6, Column 3

continued

continued

A Few More Pounds Will Place This Plump Pig in Hog Heaven

Continued From First Page

contender when he was born. He had big bones and more wrinkles than a washboard, a sign he had a lot of skin to grow into.

By his first birthday, Chief was a hefty 590 pounds. At four, he won the title of Ohio State Fair Buckeye Big Boar, catapulting him to fame. About that time, the hog breeder stumbled across a bodybuilding magazine with an article about the digestive system, which he found similar to that of a pig. A hog, he reasoned, should be able to build body mass just like a weight lifter. All it would take is the right diet—high in carbohydrates and protein.

So Chief went into training, bellying up each day to family-sized helpings of ground oats, barley, bran and dehydrated turnips. About the only unhealthful things Chief eats are red and orange gumdrops (he turns up his snout at the green and yellow ones). In all, the hog consumes about 20 pounds of dry feed a day.

And to wash it down? Beer, of course—the real stuff, not light. "Ever see a skinny beer drinker?" asks veterinarian Grant Thompson, an occasional adviser in Chief's training camp. Chief averages a six-pack a day. The hog's weekly meal allowance tops about $30, which is why Mr. Corbett is thinking of finding a sponsor for Chief's run at the heavyweight title.

Like a body builder, Chief also gets a regular regimen of vitamins: iron supplements every other day, vitamin B shots every week and vitamin E shots once a month. (No steroids for this contender.) Mr. Corbett also takes Chief in for X-rays to make sure fat hasn't built up around his heart and lungs. And to help ward off bad health, the prodigious swine walks a half mile every day. The saunter takes more than an hour.

Pork Chops? Never!

Mr. Corbett considers Chief a pet and even wears a badge of his affection pinned to his baseball cap. The button reads: "Have You Hugged Your Hog Today." When Chief dies, says Mr. Corbett, he won't go onto the barbecue but will be buried with dignity in the front yard.

The breeder, though, has also made something of a cash cow out of his pig. Already, Chief rakes in $700 for each county-fair appearance. And Mr. Corbett's sister-in-law is busy selling ceramic Chief piggy banks for $10 a shot, $2 of which comes back to Mr. Corbett. He has even taken out a $5,000 insurance policy on his hog, as a hedge against the pig's premature passing.

Chief may be a pet, but his corpulence shouldn't be underestimated, especially when the hog decides to throw his weight around. Take the time he showed off in front of spectators at a fair by coming up behind Mr. Corbett, sticking his snout between his owner's legs and upending him, face first into the dirt. And once in a while, Chief helps Mrs. Corbett over the fence before she's ready to go. More annoying is when the hog rototills a section of the front lawn with his megaphone-like snout.

He is forgiven these lapses. After all, Chief is the closest thing to a celebrity this town of 1,200 has, and he is treated as such. "Home of the Chief" signs greet visitors on all four roads leading into North Lewisburg. The local bank has a black piggy bank on the counter with the name Chief taped to the side. The hog is a regular at the Labor Day festival, where he helps raise cash for the local fire department. And there is an emerging fan club. Admirers from several states have visited, including a South Carolina woman who stayed a week, taking notes for a book she plans on remarkable animals.

Publicity Hog

"It's quite a thing for us around here," says Patty Woodruff, assistant cashier at the bank. "It's nice to have someone around here who has been on a national TV show."

Indeed, almost everyone in town has a tape of Chief's appearance last year on David Letterman's late-night show. It was a night to remember: Chief shared the stage with two other notables from the Ohio State Fair, a 2,700-pound bull and a life-sized butter sculpture of race-car driver Bobby Rahal.

Mr. Corbett initially refused to go because he didn't know "who the heck this Letterman fellow was." He grudgingly accepted. "It wasn't so bad, but I'd never do it again," he says. Driving his big truck and trailer through Manhattan "was enough to make you chew your gum backwards." Then there was the matter of getting Chief up to the studio on the sixth floor of Rockefeller Center, where, in expectation, the furniture had been stacked out of the way and covered with plastic.

Since then, Chief has become quite the ham. He refused to leave the stage after snaring the Indiana State Fair title. And when various award-winning fruits and animals were assembled for a local TV shot, Chief tried to eliminate the 59-pound watermelon by eating it. But he wasn't quick enough. The watermelon's owner outsnatched him.

Reading for Meaning

1. What is the thesis of the article?

2. How does the writer support her thesis?

3. There are many puns, or humorous uses of wordplay, in Ansberry's article—for example, "*Bellying* Up to a Six-Pack," "Chief has become quite the *ham*," and "the breeder, though, has also made something of a *cash cow* out of his pig." Write down some other puns used in the piece.

4. What signs did Chief give at his birth about his future stardom?

5. What happened to Chief in the summer of the drought?

6. What health precautions does the breeder take for Chief?

7. What does the heading "Pork Chops? Never!" indicate about Chief's future?

8. In the article we are given various descriptions of Chief's physical characteristics:

> Chief, a grunting 1,230-pound hog, with ears the size of mud flaps and a runway for a tongue. A Hula-Hoop would be snug on this porker's eight-foot girth.
>
> the 4-foot-tall, 9-foot-long hog
>
> Chief—a Berkshire pig, black with patches of white

How does the author describe his *personality* or *behavior*?

9. How is Chief regarded in his home town?

10. Why are Berkshire pigs—Chief's breed—raised less often by hog farmers than they used to be?

Vocabulary in Context

Write down the definition of each of the italicized words below taken from the article. Try to guess the meaning from the context. Use a dictionary only if you have to.

1. ". . . when enormous amounts of *lard* were needed for the war effort."

2. ". . . *dehydrated* turnips."

3. "And to help ward off bad health, the *prodigious* swine walks a half mile every day."

Writing from Reading

Consider your *tone* in each of the following assignments, and how it will affect your *subject, purpose,* and *audience.* Because your tone will be lighter, like that in the article on Chief, your *purpose* in writing may be quite different.

1. Clare Ansberry describes Chief with a great deal of humor. Pretend you are a neighbor of Chief's who doesn't like him, maybe because of his smell or because of the visitors he attracts, and describe him in a paragraph or so in a letter to a friend.

2. Have any animals ever struck you as funny, perhaps a dog with a sweater on, or a zoo animal? Describe the animal in a long paragraph.

3. Make believe you are Chief—with the ability to read and write—and you have just read about yourself in the *Wall Street Journal.* Write a letter to the editor commenting on the article.

4. Role play as a smitten sow who has fallen in love with Chief from reading about him and seeing him on David Letterman's show. Write a letter to Chief about your desire to have a family with him.

5. As a member of the local humane society, you feel indignant that the Corbetts are feeding Chief a diet that might result in his early death—all to make money from him as a "show" pig. Write a letter to the Corbetts expressing your concern for Chief's health.

MORE ON TONE

Contrast the humor with which Chief is depicted with this description of a boxer's gym in Panama from another article in the *Wall Street Journal* by Jose De Cordoba:

> The Maranon is a dingy dream factory, as squalid as the slums its young boxers are fighting to leave. The roof leaks. The floor is riddled with holes and, in places, is rotted by rain. Rusty, exposed nails trip and gouge the careless. A stench of sweat, old leather, mildew and urine hangs heavy in the tropical heat.
>
> The ring in the middle of the gym has ropes that are frayed and drooping. A few weeks ago, during an amateur fight, both boxers hit the ropes and fell out of the ring. One sprained his hand, but still managed to win the bout.

Reading for Meaning

1. What words does the writer use in the first paragraph that reveal his *tone*, his attitude toward his subject, to be serious?

2. How does the example the writer gives in the second paragraph support the overall description of the gym?

3. What pattern of organization does the writer use in the first paragraph?

4. To what senses does the writer appeal in his description of the gym?

Writing from Reading

In each of these assignments, try to convey a tone: how do you feel toward the subject? Also, organize your description in a spatial pattern—top to bottom, bottom to top, right to left, and so on—and appeal to the senses of the reader. Describe one or more of the following:

1. A building like a school, gym, or stadium.

2. Someone's home or office.

3. A car, boat, plane, or train.

NARRATION

Narration is the telling of a story, the relating of events. The pattern of organization in this type of writing is usually chronological—order by time. In reading the following account of a day in Maya Angelou's General Store, look for two things: first, the *order* in which the story is told; and second, the *tone* of the author, her attitude toward what she is describing.

The lamplight in the Store gave a soft make-believe feeling to our world which made me want to whisper and walk about on tiptoe. The odors of onions and oranges and kerosene had been mixing all night and wouldn't be disturbed until the wooded slat was removed from the door and the early morning air forced its way in with the bodies of people who had walked miles to reach the pickup place.

"Sister, I'll have two cans of sardines."

"I'm gonna work so fast today I'm gonna make you look like you standing still."

"Lemme have a hunk uh cheese and some sody crackers."

"Just gimme a coupla them fat peanut paddies." That would be from a picker who was taking his lunch. The greasy brown paper sack was stuck behind the bib of his overalls. He'd use the candy as a snack before the noon sun called the workers to rest.

In those tender mornings the Store was full of laughing, joking, boasting and bragging. One man was going to pick two hundred pounds of cotton, and another three hundred. Even the children were promising to bring home fo' bits and six bits.

The champion picker of the day before was the hero of the dawn. If he prophesied that the cotton in today's field was going to be sparse and stick to the bolls like glue, every listener would grunt a hearty agreement.

The sound of the empty cotton sacks dragging over the floor and the murmurs of waking people were sliced by the cash register as we rang up the five-cent sales.

If the morning sounds and smells were touched with the supernatural, the late afternoon had all the features of the normal Arkansas life. In the dying sunlight the people dragged, rather than their empty cotton sacks.

Brought back to the Store, the pickers would step out of the backs of trucks and fold down, dirt-disappointed, to the ground. No matter how much they had picked, it wasn't enough. Their wages wouldn't even get them out of debt to my grandmother, not to mention the staggering bill that waited on them at the white commissary downtown.

The sounds of the new morning had been replaced with grumbles about cheating houses, weighted scales, snakes, skimpy cotton and dusty rows. In later years I was to confront the stereotyped picture of gay song-singing cotton pickers with such inordinate rage that I was told even by fellow Blacks that my paranoia was embarrassing. But I had seen the fingers cut by the mean little cotton bolls, and I had witnessed the backs and shoulders and arms and legs resisting any further demands.

Some of the workers would leave their sacks at the Store to be picked up the following morning, but a few had to take them home for repairs. I winced to picture them sewing the coarse material under a coal-oil lamp with fingers stiffening from the day's work. In too few hours they would have to walk back to Sister Henderson's Store, get vittles and load, again, onto the trucks. Then they would face another day of trying to earn enough for the whole year with the heavy knowledge that they were going to end the season as they started it. Without the money or credit necessary to sustain a family for three months. In cotton-picking time the late afternoons revealed the harshness of Black Southern life, which in the early morning had been softened by nature's blessing of grogginess, forgetfulness and the soft lamplight.

Reading for Meaning

1. What is the thesis of this descriptive passage?
2. How does Maya Angelou support her thesis?
3. What is the tone of the piece?
4. How does Maya organize this scene—chronologically or as a flashback (in which the narration of an earlier event interrupts the normal chronological sequence)? Consider some of the phrases she uses:

The lamplight in the Store . . .

In those tender mornings . . .

The sound of the empty cotton sacks dragging over the floor and the murmurs of waking people . . .

All of these phrases describe the morning. She then goes on to contrast the morning with the afternoon:

If the morning sounds and smells were touched with the supernatural, the late afternoon had all the features of the normal Arkansas life. In the dying sunlight the people dragged, rather than their empty cotton sacks.

The sounds of the new morning had been replaced with grumbles about cheating houses.

In cotton-picking time the late afternoon revealed the harshness of Black Southern life, which in the early morning had been softened by nature's blessing of grogginess, forgetfulness and the soft lamplight.

Vocabulary in Context

Write down the definition of each of the italicized words below taken from the passage. Try to guess the meaning from the context. Use a dictionary only if you have to.

1. "... the staggering bill that awaited them at the white *commissary* downtown."
2. "In later years I was to confront the [a.] *stereotyped* picture of gay song-singing cotton pickers with such [b.] *inordinate* rage that I was told even by fellow Blacks that my [c.] *paranoia* was embarrassing."

Writing from Reading

For each of the following assignments, remember to consider your *subject, purpose,* and *audience.*

1. Have you ever had a day that started out full of promise and then deteriorated? Brainstorm about this topic for ten minutes. Revise your list and put it in chronological order; use Maya Angelou's "before" and "after" pattern, or use the "flashback," where you start with the *last* event and work backwards. Then write a narrative of what happened.

2. Maya Angelou tells us she was filled with "inordinate rage" whenever she was confronted with the "stereotyped picture" of "gay song-singing cotton pickers." Some people feel the same way about the portrayal of chimney sweeps in Walt Disney's *Mary Poppins* as happy-go-lucky little boys, when the reality was that thousands of orphan boys performed this terrible work for slave wages and often got cancer from inhaling soot and coal dust. Have you ever seen anything, perhaps in the media, where the public is given a falsely cheerful picture of some grim reality? Freewrite about this topic and then write a first and final draft about it.

3. *Peer reading assignment.* Do either of the assignments above, sharing your work at each stage of the writing process with the other students in your group.

READING: "SATURDAY MORNING AT MAC'S"

The following student essay uses narration *and* description to inform. Using the prediction techniques you have learned to improve your comprehension, read the title and write down what you think the passage is about:

                    Saturday Morning at Mac's

Now read the first paragraph and the last two paragraphs:

Saturday morning having breakfast at McDonald's again, on Kedzie Avenue right off 26th Street, I order the usual breakfast of eggs and muffin, hashbrowns and coffee. I take my accustomed seat near the window. Lost in thought, I begin to eat. It's cold outside, and the new snow is beginning to stick, blanketing the old pale snow with a thin sheet of virgin white.

                            • • •

As I watch the old lady scramble around outside on the street, I think, ''It's a dog-eat-dog world.''
I wash down the last of my cardboard muffin with this ferocious dirt coffee and head for my goddamn car.

Write down a new prediction.

Saturday Morning at Mac's

Saturday morning having breakfast at McDonald's again, on Kedzie Avenue right off 26th Street, I order the usual breakfast of eggs and muffin, hashbrowns and coffee. I take my accustomed seat near the window. Lost in thought, I begin to eat. It's cold outside, and the new snow is beginning to stick, blanketing the old pale snow with a thin sheet of virgin white.

Outside, the people are rushing by. Across the street by the intersection, I see an old lady with a beaten-up gabardine coat and a scarf wrapped around her head clutching the purse at her side. At the other side of the street, an old man holding a ragged shopping bag scampers to catch the same bus. The woman cuts in front of traffic and jumps in front of the old man. Out of the bus trundles a fat lady with a mob of little kids. The old lady muscles her way onto the bus, but in her panic drops the purse behind her. It hits the bottom step and falls into the slush in the gutter. The old man snatches it up, drops it in his bag, and saunters away as if he were going for a stroll in the park. He turns into the alley and disappears.

By this time the old lady realizes she has lost her purse. The bus crosses the intersection and spits her out. She runs back against traffic to the bus stop, grabbing people and pointing frantically to the ground. Perhaps she lost her social security check or her food stamps or her life savings—perhaps nothing.

What would prompt an otherwise honest-looking old man into stealing a purse? With high unemployment and cuts in social programs, maybe he has suddenly found himself poor after a lifetime of hard work, and stealing doesn't seem so awful.

As I watch the old lady scramble around outside on the street, I think, ''It's a dog-eat-dog world.''

I wash down the last of my cardboard muffin with this ferocious dirt coffee and head for my goddamn car.

Reading for Meaning

1. Where in the article does the writer reveal his attitude about what he saw?

2. What question bothers the writer?

3. Should the writer have gone to the old woman's aid? What would you have done?

Writing from Reading

1. Have you ever witnessed a crime—for example, shoplifting—or seen an instance of someone treating another person with real cruelty? Free-write about the incident, write a first draft, and then write a final draft.

2. Have you ever had the opportunity to help someone in trouble but didn't? Prewrite about the occasion, remembering to answer the reporter's questions—who, what, when, where, how, and/or why. Write a first draft and then a final draft.

3. *Peer writing assignment.* Do any of the assignments above, sharing your work at each stage of the writing process with the other students in your group.

WORD DEMONS (CONTINUED)

We now return to some of the words that often cause students difficulty. Simply ignore those you have no trouble with and move on. The uses, meanings, and parts of speech of the words examined below are not intended to be exhaustive, but reflect the most common occasions when these words cause confusion.

4. Accept, except

The verb "accept" means to "take" or "receive," as in "I *accept* the honor." "Except" can be a preposition or verb with the meaning "to leave out, exclude": "All the players *except* Walter Payton went to the Pro Bowl to play in the game."

Exercises

Complete the following sentences with either "accept" or "except."

a. Please _____ my apology; I was wrong.

b. Every student _____ John could go to the game.

c. Pete seemed to _____ everything Alex said calmly.

d. He has all the right qualities _____ patience.

5. Affect, effect

"Affect" means to "influence, change," as in "Very often the weather would *affect* his feelings—for good or bad." As a noun, "effect" means "result": "a bad *effect*." As a verb, "effect" means to "bring about": "The Senator tried to *effect* a compromise between the President and Congress."

Exercises

Complete the following sentences with either "affect" or "effect."

a. The _____ of the mayor's death was to cast a pall over the city.
b. A prolonged spell of bad weather would so _____ him that he would be in a foul mood for the whole time.
c. President Lincoln at first tried to _____ a compromise between the North and the South.
d. The total _____ of the Vietnam War was one of disillusionment and loss of morale.

6. A lot

"A lot" is the only correct spelling for the phrase meaning "many," as in the sentences "There are *a lot* of problems with that car," or "*A lot* of children seem out of place in that experimental program." Very often students incorrectly write these two words as one word.

7. A, an

The article "a," meaning "one" or "any," is used before words beginning with a consonant or a consonant sound including those spelled with a pronounced "h": "*a* dog," "*a* union." "An" has the same meaning as "a," but is used before words that begin with vowel sounds including the silent "h": "*an* owl," "*an* idiot," "*an* hour."

Exercises

Complete the following sentences with either "a" or "an."

a. We heard that _____ elephant escaped from the zoo.
b. The boys had _____ game of basketball.
c. Not _____ chance of winning remained when the Russians scored the first four goals.
d. The stands were empty _____ hour after the game was over.

8. An, and

"An" is the article referred to above. Never use "an" as a connecting or joining word. "And" is a conjunction that adds things together, as in "Jack *and* Jill."

Exercises

Complete the following sentences with either "an" or "and."

a. Go to the store and buy some bread _____ butter.
b. It's hard to find _____ honest man.
c. I enjoy hearing the music of Peter, Paul, _____ Mary.
d. They went to _____ island near Jamaica.

9. Are, our

"Are" is part of the verb "to be," for example, "The French *are* no longer America's strong ally." "Our" is the possessive pronoun meaning "belonging to us," as in "*our* house."

Exercises

Complete the following sentences with either "are" or "our."

a. The affair is now out of _____ hands.
b. Some females think that most males _____ sexist.
c. Many people in East and West Germany _____ awaiting the day that their two countries are unified as one country.
d. The lawyer is supposed to serve _____ best interests.

10. Change, chance

These words are most often confused when used as nouns. "Change" means "a difference," as in "Every so many years Jack wants a *change* of jobs." "Chance" refers to "an opportunity" or "a possibility," as in "Lamarr is just looking for one last *chance* to prove himself."

Exercises

Complete the following sentences with either "chance" or "change."

a. After thirteen years working in the same school, John wanted a _____ in his job.
b. Joe faced a choice—to jeopardize his health or to make a _____ in his eating habits.

c. Peter took a _____ and became manager of the Peoria Chiefs.

d. Madonna gave Sean one last _____ to be faithful to her.

11. Choose, chose

"Choose" is the present tense of the verb meaning "to select," as in "You can *choose* whatever class you wish." "Chose" is the past tense of "choose": "Last week you *chose* whatever class you wished."

Exercises

Complete the following sentences with the correct tense of "choose."

a. At some point in life, we must _____ our goals and work toward them.

b. Caesar _____ to cross the Rubicon and begin civil war.

c. Thomas More _____ to remain faithful to his ideals and not betray his conscience.

d. Parents have to give their children the freedom to _____ the direction in which their lives are headed.

12. Conscience, conscious

"Conscience" is a noun meaning "the deciding or judging of right and wrong," as in "Stalin had no *conscience*; he murdered the flower of the Russian military leadership in the years before the Germans invaded." It might be helpful to remember this word as meaning "with" (*con-*) "knowledge" (*-science*). "Conscious" is an adjective meaning "to be awake or aware," as in "Hoover was always *conscious* of Roosevelt's distrust." The antonym, or word meaning the opposite, of "conscious" is "unconscious"—"unaware, knocked out, not conscious."

Exercises

Complete the following sentences with either "conscience" or "conscious."

a. Joe Louis was fully _____ even though he had been knocked down in the third round.

b. Bill was too _____ of his faults to ever feel relaxed.

c. The oldest child in a family often has a very tender _____.

d. Macbeth was convinced by his wife to go against his _____.

13. Etc.

"Etc." is an abbreviation of the two Latin words *et cetera*, meaning "and others." Because part of its meaning is "and," "etc." is always written by itself—never preceded by "and"—as in the sentence "John bought blankets, boots, powdered food, etc., for the camping trip." The abbreviation "etc." is always preceded by a comma and is followed by a period whether or not it ends the sentence. The abbreviation "etc." should only be used sparingly—for example, to indicate more items on a list: "Jack went to Dominick's and bought sugar, bread, eggs, milk, etc." Many students overuse "etc." instead of concluding the sentence. Don't substitute "etc." for writing out the rest of the sentence.

14. Idea, ideal

"Idea" means "a thought," as in "I had no *idea* that you were so sick." "Ideal" means "a standard of perfection or excellence," as in "No one has higher *ideals* about education than Betsy; she is almost a perfectionist."

Exercises

Complete the following sentences with either "idea" or "ideal."

a. Thomas More wrote *Utopia* as his expression of the perfect state, one that would serve as an _____ to which all future societies would aspire.

b. In the Renaissance some people erroneously held the _____ that *Utopia*, a work of imagination, referred to a real time and place.

c. The ruler of *Utopia*, the philosopher-king, presented an _____ for the future ruler to emulate.

d. Thomas More had no _____ that his *Utopia*, which advocates communal ownership of property, would later be looked on to justify Communism.

CHAPTER
11

Exposition

One of the most useful types of writing is exposition, which means "to explain" or "to set out." Most term papers, reports, letters, and business correspondence are examples of exposition. Expository writing takes many forms—process, comparison/contrast, exemplification (using examples), cause and effect, division, classification, and definition. In this chapter we will examine each of these forms in detail.

PROCESS WRITING

Process writing is used to explain a step-by-step activity, whether it be following a recipe, tuning a car, or learning how to compose an essay. For the process to work, it's important to include all the steps necessary, and in the right order. For example, a recipe must specify *how much* of each ingredient is needed and *how long* each part is to cook. If you were giving someone directions from your home to school and he or she was unfamiliar with the route, what would you need to tell that person? To give clear and precise directions you would need to specify, in order, all of the signs, stoplights, landmarks, roads, and turns that he or she would encounter between your house and the school.

READING: "TO NEW ENGLANDERS, STONE WALLS LINK LIFE TO SIMPLER PAST"

The following article in the *Wall Street Journal* by Lawrence Ingrassia illustrates process writing. First read the title and two subtitles:

To New Englanders, Stone Walls Link Life to Simpler Past

So People Are Building
Them The Old-Fashioned
Way: Piece by Piece
by Piece

To New Englanders, Stone Walls Are a Link to Simpler Way of Life

Write down what you think the article is about.
Now read the first two paragraphs and the last two paragraphs:

HARTLAND, Vt.—Harvey Bumps, all 235 pounds of him, hops on top of the stone wall. He takes a few steps, then bounces up and down on it for good measure.

The stones wiggle not an inch beneath his burly frame. "It'll hold for 100 years," he declares. "Easily."

• • •

Also, many walls today are built with rough, quarried stone, instead of field boulders. Mr. Bumps dynamites his stone out of a mountainside, and Mr. Snow uses ledge stone that has naturally fallen off mountains. Field stone, generally rounder, is hard to come by because much is already in old stone walls, and few farmers are plowing new fields. Hayden Hillsgrove, a mason in North Sandwich, N.H., says he spends two days a week looking for field stone to buy. "Farmers used to look at me like I was crazy when I wanted to pay for the stones. Now every farmer thinks they're pieces of gold," he says.

With so few of them around, experienced wall builders usually are booked a year in advance. As a result, some folks are constructing their own walls. Robert Butler, of North Dartmouth, Mass., recently built a 210-foot wall on his property, working nights and weekends with friends. With the popularity of stone walls again on the rise, the group has decided to build them for others. "We ended up with four other jobs from people driving by and seeing us do it," he says.

Write down a further prediction about what the rest of the article will say.

As you read the entire article, look for an explanation of the *process* used to build stone walls.

To New Englanders, Stone Walls Link Life to Simpler Past

———

So People Are Building Them The Old-Fashioned Way: Piece by Piece by Piece

———

By Lawrence Ingrassia
Staff Reporter of The Wall Street Journal

HARTLAND, Vt.—Harvey Bumps, all 235 pounds of him, hops on top of the stone wall. He takes a few steps, then bounces up and down on it for good measure.

The stones wiggle not an inch beneath his burly frame. "It'll hold for 100 years," he declares. "Easily."

Mr. Bumps steps down and, with a colleague, resumes building the wall the old-fashioned way—no mortar, no cement, nothing to hold the stones together except the stones themselves. Working from a jigsaw puzzle of pieces, they stack one stone on another, overlap joints, wedge in small stones to secure large ones. "When you're all through and look back after you're done, it feels good," says Mr. Bumps.

A New Popularity

Like the town green and the white-steepled church, the dry stone wall is quintessential New England, a vestige of more simple times gone by. Thousands of miles of walls—many thick with moss and lichen—ramble through backwoods New England, as much a part of the pastoral landscape as the trees now starting to show splashes of red and yellow as summer gives way to fall. Some old walls are crumbling, others still stand as solid as rock. All are memorialized by a figure in a Robert Frost poem who said: "Good fences make good neighbors."

Before you continue, read the next paragraph and (1) predict the main idea question, (2) clarify the meaning of any difficult

continued

continued

words or sentences, and (3) predict what the next paragraph will say.

The farmers who built them over the past few centuries are long gone, and only a handful of masons like Mr. Bumps still put them up the way old-timers did. But after a long decline, the dry stone wall is making a comeback. Old Yankee families are hiring masons to rebuild aging walls, and newly arrived Yuppies are putting up fresh ones. Some hardy do-it-yourselfers are building their own; an envoy from the Dry Stone Walling Association of Scotland has held several workshops to show New Englanders how the job is done.

Check these answers against your own:

1. *Prequest*—What is now happening to the old dry stone wall?

2. *Clarify*—"Yuppies" are "young, upwardly mobile, urban professionals."

3. *Prenext*—The next paragraph will give more details about why the stone wall is making a comeback.

Please Turn To Page A7, Column 1

To New Englanders, Stone Walls Are a Link to Simpler Way of Life

Continued From First Page

New England's early settlers built walls with stone out of necessity. The soil was so rocky that they had to do something with the boulders plowed up in their fields; dry stone walls were built in other, scattered parts of the U.S., but in far smaller numbers. Today, New Englanders are fond of the walls because they link the present to the past. "A stone wall looks like it took a lot of time to build. You can see all of the energy tied up in a wall in the woods," says Jane Dorney, who recently wrote a master's thesis on stone walls in Vermont's Green Mountains. "It's a romanticization of the 19th century."

History Etched in Stone

For some New Englanders, stone walls are monuments to be preserved. Dublin, N.H., earlier this year adopted an ordinance protecting stone walls that border town roads. "They're part of the history of the town," says Betsy Harris, who lives on Stone Wall Farm ("that's always been the name") and is head of Dublin's conservation commission. "When it became clear that individuals were doing away with walls that had been there a couple of centuries, we said we better do something." Moreover, many old walls are legal property boundaries.

Dry stone walls today are built much the same as they were long ago. Wall builders usually dig a shallow trench to start, then lay heavy base stones at the bottom. To strengthen the structure, the bottom of the wall is built wider than the top. Stones are laid close together, generally slanting inward, with each stone touching as many others as possible. Smaller stones—called shims or chink stones—help tighten fits. Big, flat "cap" stones are saved for the top of the wall.

The interlocking construction and the heft of the larger stones—which generally weigh from 50 to several hundred pounds—hold it together. Not all dry stone walls last long, of course. A poorly constructed one may tumble down when the frost heaves the ground. But, when built properly, the dry stone wall is a minor engineering marvel.

"Once you start doing it, it kind of grows on you," says Mr. Bumps, a 43-year-old with a bushy beard and a beer belly. "You get to feeling like you're doing something your grandfather did. Both of my grandfathers were farmers. When they took stones out of the ground, they put them on a wall." Mr Bumps took up masonry about 15 years ago, after he was laid off from a job building log homes.

Working on a 35-foot length of wall here, he moves quickly from the wall to a pile of stones nearby and back, occasionally knocking off a corner of a stone with a hammer to make it fit. The wall, which stands near a quiet country home and faces a tree-covered mountain in the distance, is about three feet high and two feet wide. The stones are big and small, some flat, others curved, some jagged, a few smooth, some triangular, others rectangular. The trick, Mr. Bumps explains, is to catalogue in your mind the shapes of both the stones and the holes in the wall. "When I walked over there, this stone said, 'Here I am,'" he says, plopping one

down in a perfect fit on the wall. "Sometimes you can't put them in fast enough."

What masons love about stone walls is that they all are different. There are no standard parts, no assembly-line shortcuts. Each wall is the product of the builder's skill and the stone at hand. "This is the only one like it," Mr. Bumps notes, gesturing to his half-built project. "If we pulled it down and put it up again, it wouldn't be exactly the same."

Daniel Snow, a lanky 37-year-old wall builder from Brattleboro, Vt., likens constructing a wall to putting together a puzzle—only it is harder. "A puzzle is a two dimensional thing with one solution. This is a three-dimensional thing with infinite solutions," says Mr. Snow, who studied industrial design and worked at general construction before specializing in stone walls. "You want to get it so each stone can take the weight of the rock on top without changing position. Otherwise, the problems would be compounded."

Building a wall this way, of course, takes time. An experienced wall builder, working at a steady clip, can lay only 10 to 20 feet of wall a day. Mr. Snow, building a retaining wall on an estate in Walpole, N.H., a recent fall morning, has a long length of wall under way at all times so there are always a variety of holes to fill. "Once you've picked up a stone, don't put it down till it's in the wall," he explains. "If you pick every one up twice, that's twice as much work."

Because they take so much time, dry stone walls are expensive. Prices vary widely—some masons charge by the hour, others by the job—but $100 a foot isn't uncommon. "I have three times as many jobs as I can do," Mr. Snow says. He usually highballs estimates because of the difficulty of figuring how long a job will take. 'If their eyes roll and they choke, I don't do the job." He says he charges less if the project comes in under his estimate.

continued

continued

There are a few modern conveniences, of course, that make things easier nowadays. Builders haul stones to a site in dump trucks, and some even use tractors to lift the heavy cap stones into place. Mr. Snow, like many masons, puts crushed stone in the below-ground base of his walls for a firmer foundation. He used to do it the old-fashioned way, laying large stones below ground. ''But digging a ditch and laying stone four feet down—it wasn't fun. If they had had crushed stone [long ago], that's what you'd find at the bottom of old walls,'' he figures.

Analyze the next paragraph, part of the conclusion, with the three-step reading strategy:

Also, many walls today are built with rough, quarried stone, instead of field boulders. Mr. Bumps dynamites his stone out of a mountainside, and Mr. Snow uses ledge stone that has naturally fallen off mountains. Field stone, generally rounder, is hard to come by because much is already in old stone walls, and few farmers are plowing new fields. Hayden Hillsgrove, a mason in North Sandwich, N.H., says he spends two days a week looking for field stone to buy. ''Farmers used to look at me like I was crazy when I wanted to pay for the stones.

Now every farmer thinks they're pieces of gold,'' he says.

Again, check your answers against these:

1. *Prequest*—what types of stone do today's builders use?

2. *Clarify*—a ''mason'' is a ''skilled workman who builds with stone or similar material.''

3. *Prenext*—The last paragraph will summarize the changes in building dry stone walls.

With so few of them around, experienced wall builders usually are booked a year in advance. As a result, some folks are constructing their own walls. Robert Butler, of North Dartmouth, Mass., recently built a 210-foot wall on his property, working nights and weekends with friends. With the popularity of stone walls again on the rise, the group has decided to build them for others. ''We ended up with four other jobs from people driving by and seeing us do it,'' he says.

Remember that the accuracy of your predictions is not as important as the prereading process itself. This process gives you a step-by-step way to *attack* what you are reading, to make it less intimidating and complex.

Reading for Meaning

1. What is the main idea of the article?

2. How does the author support the main idea?

3. The process of making stone walls is detailed in the eighth paragraph, reprinted below with all of the transitional words italicized. Note how each step is explained clearly in a separate part of a sentence or in a sentence by itself:

Dry stone walls today are built much the same as they were long ago. Wall builders usually dig a shallow trench *to start*, *then* lay heavy base stones *at the bottom*. To strengthen the structure, the *bottom* of the wall is built wider than the *top*. Stones are laid close together, generally *slanting inward*, with each stone touching as many others as possible. Smaller stones—called shims or chink stones—help tighten fits. Big, flat "cap" stones are saved *for the top of the wall*.

What pattern does the description of the process follow?

4. What modern conveniences have been added to make building stone walls a little easier?
5. Why in the past did New England farmers build stone walls?
6. Why is there renewed interest today in building stone walls?
7. How is each stone wall unique?
8. How is a stone wall a puzzle?
9. Why are dry stone walls expensive?
10. How have farmers changed their attitudes toward field stones?

Vocabulary in Context

Write down the definition of each of the italicized words below taken from the article. Try to guess the meaning from the context. Use a dictionary only if you have to.

1. ". . . *quintessential* New England . . ."
2. ". . . a *vestige*" of more simple times gone by."
3. ". . . *pastoral* landscape . . ."
4. ". . . *romanticization* of the 19th Century.

Writing from Reading

For each of the following assignments, remember to consider your *subject, purpose*, and *audience*.

1. Is there any special hobby, craft, or skill you have whose process you can explain? Freewrite about the topic, write a first draft and then write a final draft. Remember to include all the steps, put them in the right order, and keep them separate to avoid confusion.
2. Write an essay explaining the process you use to write your papers—what you do first, next, and so on.
3. *Peer reading assignment.* Do either of the two assignments above, sharing your work at each stage of the writing process with the other students in your group.

EXPLAINING THROUGH COMPARISON/CONTRAST

One of the most effective forms of expository writing is comparison/contrast, in which the writer analyzes similarities or differences among things, ideas, or even people. For example, suppose you were to compare your high-school and college experiences. There are at least two patterns you could use—*side-by-side* or *one-at-a-time*.

Side-by-Side

Comparison	High School	College
size	small	very large
campus life	regimented	free
relations with teachers	close	more impersonal
costs	free tuition	very expensive

One-at-a-Time

High School

Size: Small
Campus life: regimented
Relations with teachers: close
Costs: free tuition

College

Size: very large
Campus life: free
Relations with teachers: more impersonal
Costs: very expensive

Note that in both patterns, the points that are compared are in the same order.

Writing Practice

Using the side-by-side and one-at-a-time patterns, compare two sports, for example football and baseball.

READING: "SPREAD OF SLEAZE AND LOW AIR FARES REMAKE TWO CITIES"

The following *Wall Street Journal* article by Matt Moffett is a good illustration of expository writing through comparison/contrast. First, use your prediction techniques to better understand the article. Read the title and two subtitles:

Spread of Sleaze And Low Air Fares Remake Two Cities

* * *

Tijuana Loses Its Ill Repute While Acapulco Gains Penny-Pinching Tourists

Spread of Sleaze, Low Air Fares Remake Tijuana and Acapulco

Write down what you think the article is about.

Now read the first two paragraphs and the last two paragraphs:

For decades, lurid Tijuana and alluring Acapulco have shaped the Yankee view of Mexico.

Tijuana, the major border crossing point, was Sin City. "A festering sore," growled a West Coast newspaper of the 1930s. Tijuana's charms included a block-long bar, a gambling joint where Al Capone lost half a million dollars and a floor show headlined by a half-dressed contortionist billed as the Pretzel Woman.

• • •

Dan and Doris Ault, a welder and his wife from Quebec, are doing Acapulco on $40 (Canadian) a day. Their budget air fare, a full picnic cooler and an itinerary heavy on "natural wonders"—that is, free sights—made the trip affordable. "For our money," says Mrs. Ault, "Acapulco is even better than Calgary and not much more expensive." But Mr. Ault bruised his knee when he fell on some craggy seaside rocks. He was sneaking around the admission booth to get a free look at Acapulco's famed cliff divers.

Other people love Acapulco—and don't miss Frank Sinatra. One of them is Irma Mendoza. She came from a mountain village, where the corn crop was too meager to feed her five children. Now her family walks the streets and beaches peddling hand-made yarn dolls. The Mendozas live in a hut made from pieces of an old fishing boat, but even that is so much better than village life that Mrs. Mendoza is inviting her sister's family to join them. "This is a place to come for a better life," she says, as her troupe of tiny vendors surrounds tourists stepping off a bus.

Make another prediction about the content of the article.

As you read the entire article, be aware of which type of comparison/contrast method the writer is using and how it forces the reader to draw conclusions.

Spread of Sleaze And Low Air Fares Remake Two Cities

✶ ✶ ✶

Tijuana Loses Its Ill Repute While Acapulco Gains Penny-Pinching Tourists

BY MATT MOFFETT

Staff Reporter of THE WALL STREET JOURNAL

For decades, lurid Tijuana and alluring Acapulco have shaped the Yankee view of Mexico.

Tijuana, the major border crossing point, was Sin City. "A festering sore," growled a West Coast newspaper of the 1930s. Tijuana's charms included a block-long bar, a gambling joint where Al Capone lost half a million dollars and a floor show headlined by a half-dressed contortionist billed as the Pretzel Woman.

Acapulco, 2,000 miles south of the border, was the "Pearl of the Pacific," a resort for celebrated sophisticates. Errol Flynn gave diving exhibitions off the mast of a yacht at Acapulco, Joe DiMaggio shagged flies on the beach, and Liz Taylor married promoter Mike Todd in the city's glamorous Villa Vera hotel.

Modern mores, cheap air travel and Mexico's economic turns have changed both places.

Malls and Assembly Plants

Tijuana has cleaned up its act. Gone are the U.S. sailors who once took indecent liberty in Tijuana's dives. Now more decorous Americans flock to the city's discos, restaurants—and shopping malls. An economy that once seemed devoted to sex and shoddy souvenirs now flexes its manufacturing muscle. Sanyo, Colgate-Palmolive and some 270 other corporations have opened assembly plants here.

Acapulco, by contrast, has become an underplanned, overbuilt urban muddle. For four decades it was Mexico's top resort for foreign tourists, but newer and glitzier Cancun, off the Yucatan coast, overtook it in the mid-1980s. Acapulco has attracted so many jobless refugees from the Mexican countryside that some aerial photographs show more peddlers on the beach than sun-worshippers.

Tijuana had been a fleshpot since the American experiment with Prohibition in the 1920s. Some 95 bars sprang up on seven blocks in the town, best known until then as an old stagecoach stop. Of 1,091 residents, 200 worked as prostitutes. "Vice was the pillar of our economy," recalls Wulfrano Ruiz, an erstwhile bar owner, and it stayed that way for years.

In the 1970s, a leading Mexico City newspaper went so far as to claim that half the women of Tijuana were whores. Even then, however, a sexual revolution in the U.S. was beginning to spell the end of Tijuana's long debauch. Yankees found it considerably easier to enjoy Tijuana-style frolicking without having to cross town, let alone clear customs. "We lost our monopoly on immorality," says Emilio Ortiz, the manager of a Tijuana cabaret put out of business by U.S. competition.

Read the next paragraph using the three-step reading process. On a piece of paper (1) predict the main idea question, (2) clarify the meaning of any difficult words or sentences, and (3) predict what the next paragraph will say.

Catering to Families

Enter Oscar Escobedo, a young entrepreneur who learned about tourism from working in a Tijuana souvenir shop and studying in an American university.

He bought a notorious bar called the Beast and the Beauty, which featured a comic in a gorilla suit, a dancer dressed far less elaborately, and an audience of U.S. servicemen "too loaded to tell them apart," a bartender recalls.

Compare your answers to those below:

1. *Prequest*—How did Mr. Escobedo get his start in Tijuana?
2. *Clarify*—Nothing.
3. *Prenext*—The next paragraph will tell more about Mr. Escobedo's career in Tijuana.

Please Turn To Page A2, Column 3

Spread of Sleaze, Low Air Fares Remake Tijuana and Acapulco

Continued From First Page

Mr. Escobedo redecorated the place and put a neon sign above the door: "Family Restaurant." The throngs of well-behaved tourists outside the place, called Margarita's Village, made a deep impression on other entrepreneurs. In short order, three dozen other dives closed. Family restaurants took their place. Polo and Calvin Klein clothing shops moved onto a corner where a divorce lawyer had offered curb service. A French pastry shop replaced a package store.

The class of tourists has changed accordingly. Anyone lucky enough to get past the doorman at Club OH, one of the world's top discos, stands a better chance of encountering Tina Turner or Robin Williams than a drunken sailor.

At the same time, foreign and Mexican investors began building apparel and other factories to exploit new U.S. tariff breaks on products assembled along the border. In the past year, such *maquiladora* plants have been locating here at the rate of 11 a month. Four of the Big Eight U.S. accounting firms have established branch offices here in the past year. Some real estate is now advertised in Japanese.

The rest of Mexico—including Acapulco—remains in the worst economic crisis since the Great Depression, with real wages down 50%. Yet Tijuana's commercial and manufacturing boom has pro-

continued

continued

pelled two-thirds of the population into the middle class and created so many jobs that factory foremen cruise the city soliciting workers with bullhorns.

Tijuana's leading hotel, the Fiesta Americana, has started an advertising campaign in the U.S. It's the first time Tijuana has ever been marketed abroad. "To tell you the truth," says hotel manager Roberto Lyle, sheepishly, "we would never have been allowed to advertise most of the attractions here before."

Acapulco's fortunes, meanwhile, have regressed. Since the collapse of the peso in 1982, the city's tourist industry has come to depend on different kinds of visitors: middle-class foreigners and Mexicans who can't afford to vacation elsewhere.

Yet this was Frank Sinatra's kind of town. Carlos Ruiz, a middle-aged motorboat tour guide, can only reminisce about the very good years of his youth. "I remember that when Mr. Sinatra came on my boat, he sang even better than he did on his records," says Mr. Ruiz, pointing to the spot on the beach where he first met the crooner. Now that spot is occupied by a peddler trying to entice some indifferent bathers with sculptures hewn out of coconuts.

Sights and Smells

Old Blue Eyes hasn't put in an appearance on this beach in more than 15 years. Nor has Mr. Ruiz lately seen Sammy Davis Jr., whose gold jewelry and big tips always made quite an impression. "Now the tourists come here in buses, if they come at all," he says. "They pose for pictures next to the boat, but won't pay for a ticket. How could Acapulco have come to this?"

"Where visitors are concerned, we have exchanged quality for quantity," says Hector Zurita Brito, a leading marine ecologist. "But we've kept the infrastructure of a small resort town."

Infrastructural luxuries such as modern sewage treatment weren't missed when Acapulco was smaller. But not now. While the city is building its first sewage-treatment plant, specialists say it needs two more. Now, even before visitors see the large welcome sign at the elegant Hyatt Regency, they are greeted by the stench of an open sewer that flows from the city's biggest slum a few blocks from the hotel. On another beach, a canal leading directly from the town carwash flows into a fetid pool yards from Restaurante Zombie and the bay.

After a decade-long hiatus, Acapulco last year tried to revive a film festival that once had attracted some of the biggest names in Hollywood. It flopped. "Acapulco lost its sizzle," says Bob Osborne, a columnist for the Hollywood Reporter. Canceled this year, the film festival will probably be revived in Cancun.

From (Way) North of the Border

Warren Avis, builder of the rental-car empire and long the owner of one of Acapulco's grandest mansions, remains in town. But, he says, "The downtown's gone honky-tonk and there's no social center for the people they really need to attract here. Places like Acapulco come into fashion and, if they're not taken care of, they can go out just as quickly."

Read the next paragraph using the three-step reading strategy:

Canadians now arrive in droves. A slew of enterprises bear names such as the Rendezvous Canadian Restaurant and the Bazaar Quebec. Local people find the Canadians remarkable for their frugality. One Canadian visitor started a fire in the Hyatt with the hot plate he was using to cook dinner. "That was an exceptional case because they usually pack ham sandwiches," sniffs Nina Quiros, social correspondent for the English-language Mexico City News.

Now check your answers:

1. *Prequest*—What is the dominant characteristic of the Canadian tourist in Acapulco?
2. *Clarify*—Nothing.
3. *Prenext*—The next paragraph will tell more about Canadian tourists.

Dan and Doris Ault, a welder and his wife from Quebec, are doing Acapulco on $40 (Canadian) a day. Their budget air fare, a full picnic cooler and an itinerary heavy on "natural wonders"—that is, free sights—made the trip affordable.

"For our money," says Mrs. Ault, "Acapulco is even better than Calgary and not much more expensive." But Mr. Ault bruised his knee when he fell on some craggy seaside rocks. He was sneaking around the admission booth to get a free look at Acapulco's famed cliff divers.

Other people love Acapulco—and don't miss Frank Sinatra. One of them is Irma Mendoza. She came from a mountain village, where the corn crop was too meager to feed her five children. Now her family walks the streets and beaches peddling handmade yarn dolls. The Mendozas live in a hut made from pieces of an old fishing boat, but even that is so much better than village life that Mrs. Mendoza is inviting her sister's family to join them. "This is a place to come for a better life," she says, as her troupe of tiny vendors surrounds tourists stepping off a bus.

Reading for Meaning

1. What is the thesis of the article?
2. How does the author support his thesis?
3. Why have companies invested in Tijuana?
4. Explain why the people of Acapulco aren't happy with the tourists now coming there.
5. Was such a reversal of roles between Tijuana and Acapulco expected? Is anyone responsible for the change?
6. How did Oscar Escobedo help reform Tijuana's bad image?
7. Why is Tijuana now in much better economic shape than the rest of the country?
8. What environmental problems does Acapulco have?
9. What sentence is used as a transition from the major study of Tijuana to the brief discussion of Acapulco?

Vocabulary in Context

Write down a definition of each of the italicized words below taken from the article. Try to guess the meaning from the context. Use a dictionary only if you have to.

1. "Spread of *Sleaze* . . ."
2. ". . . *lurid* Tijuana . . ."

3. "... *alluring* Acapulco ...!"
4. "... *festering* sore ...!"
5. "... Tijuana *cabaret* ...!"
6. "... Tijuana's long *debauch* ...!"
7. "... a young *entrepreneur* ...!"
8. "... *maquiladora* plants ...!"
9. "... *infrastructure* of a small resort town."
10. "After a decade-long *hiatus* ...!"

Writing from Reading

For each of the following assignments, remember to consider your *subject*, *purpose*, and *audience*.

1. Write an essay contrasting Tijuana with Acapulco, using information from the article. Using either of the comparison/contrast patterns, prewrite, write a first draft, and then write a final draft.

2. Compare two places that you know well, one economically on the upswing, the other on the decline. Use all the writing steps—prewriting, first draft, and final draft.

3. Pick a place that was once a favorite of yours—perhaps a city, restaurant, or resort that has fallen on hard times. Contrast the past condition of the place with its current state. Use all the steps of the writing process.

4. *Peer reading assignment.* Do any of the assignments above, sharing your work at each stage of the writing process with the other students in your group.

EXPLAINING THROUGH EXAMPLES

Examples make writing more concrete, more real to the reader. The statement "New York has many fine restaurants," for example, leaves you wanting some examples—The 21 Club, The Four Seasons, Mama Leone's. Examples make general writing more specific. Here is a student paper that explains much about Chicago by using specific examples:

```
            Where is the Real Chicago?

    Most people don't see the real Chicago—the one they
never make commercials about. They don't see the garbage
and filth in the alleys of the poor neighborhoods. They
don't see the drunks—men and women—out in the cold at 10
below zero at 1:30 a.m. with no coats on. They don't see
```

the little girls with no boots and no decent coat to
wear.

No, most people don't see our hungry and homeless or
the broken-down tenements with no heat, hot water,
lights, or gas. The commercials don't show these things;
the businesses don't salute this Chicago. Instead, the
media focus on Water Tower Place, the Magnificent Mile,
and Lake Shore Drive.

The makers of commercials don't get out to 16th and
Kedzie, 47th and the El, or 43rd Street with its magnificent mile of drunks, druggies, and prostitutes—some
mere teenagers. They don't show up at the General Assistance office on Sacramento and Franklin at 8 a.m.

No, the movers and shakers focus on the Chicago of
money and power, the Chicago of Hiltons and Hyatts,
Palmer Houses and Marriotts—the tourists' city, where
everyone wears mink coats, drives Rolls Royces, eats
hearty steaks and broiled lobsters, and pays for it all
with a gold credit card.

Note that the student cites specific ills and points of luxury in Chicago. By giving examples of places and addresses, types of people, and problems, she makes her paper more clear and forceful.

READING: "KIDS ARE OFTEN LOSERS IN JOINT CUSTODY"

The following *Wall Street Journal* article by Clare Ansberry uses examples
to make its point. Read the title:

Kids Are Often Losers in Joint Custody

What question could you ask to get at the main idea of the article? For
example, *how* and *why* are these kids losers? Now look at the subtitle:

Constant Moves Between Parents Produce Strains

The subtitle tells you more about the kids' problems. On a piece of paper, write down what you think the article is about.

Now read the first two paragraphs and the last two paragraphs:

> Meet the new kids on the block: two-household children.
>
> Four-year-old Ryan Padwo of Baltimore lives with Dad on Mondays and Tuesdays, with Mom on Wednesdays and Thursdays, and alternates the rest of the week with each of them. Asked by his mother if he wants to spend more time with his father, Ryan replies: "No, Mom, I want this to be fair for each of you."
>
> • • •
>
> There are annoyances, of course. Vacations are hard to schedule, and it's bothersome having to check with each other before doing anything—even scheduling a teacher's meeting. They've also had to battle well-meaning teachers, parents and even their marriage counselor who questioned their joint-custody decision.
>
> "We had to fight against the odds," says Ellen. "But it's worth it. Jessica may have lost her family, but we didn't want her losing her parents."

Write down a new prediction.

As you read the piece, look for the examples the author uses to support her thesis.

Kids Are Often Losers in Joint Custody

Constant Moves Between Parents Produce Strains

By Clare Ansberry

Staff Reporter of The Wall Street Journal

Meet the new kids on the block: two-household children.

Four-year-old Ryan Padwo of Baltimore lives with Dad on Mondays and Tuesdays, with Mom on Wednesdays and Thursdays, and alternates the rest of the week with each of them. Asked by his mother if he wants to spend more time with his father, Ryan replies: "No, Mom, I want this to be fair for each of you."

Seven-year-old Jessica Toplin shuttles back and forth between her separated parents four times a week. "I wish I could just split myself in half," the Philadelphia youngster once told them. And then there's Amy, a 16-year-old who alternates weeks with her divorced parents, who live 30 miles apart. The Baltimore-area teenager, tagged "bag lady" by classmates because she often totes her clothes with her to school, says she's disappointed she can't see her friends more often. "My life is more complex, but it's worth it to see my dad," she says.

Children of divorced parents used to live with Mom and see Dad every other weekend. But with more mothers working and many fathers seeking a greater role in parenting, custody arrangements have become more flexible, producing some children who live out of suitcases, have their own frequent-flier cards and keep personal calendars taped to two refrigerator doors. For them, Saturday baseball leagues or piano lessons are often out of the question since weekend schedules are just too crazy. It's the price they pay to be equal children to parents who have gone separate ways.

Read the next paragraph, analyzing it with the three reading steps:

Custody Agreements

Psychologists and child-custody specialists agree that joint or more-flexible sole custody agreements should be beneficial in assuring children that they haven't lost either parent. "How could a kid be harmed because both parents want to spend a lot of time with him?" asks Lynn Gold-Bilkin, a lawyer in Philadelphia.

Check your answers:
1. *Prequest*—What do psychologists and joint-custody specialists agree are the effects of joint custody on children?
2. *Clarify*—Nothing.
3. *Prenext*—The next part of the article will suggest that joint custody has serious flaws.

But such arrangements often work better on paper than in practice. Even when the divorce is amicable, the simple logistics—deciding who takes the child to and from school, to the dentist, and on shopping trips—are difficult enough. It's doubly hard when anger and bitterness linger between the couple.

"The question is: Can you get along better after the divorce than before?" asks Albert J. Solnit, former director of the Yale University Child Studies Center. He believes that since a child remains close to both parents in a shared-custody arrangement, it's especially important for them to put aside their hurt and not undermine each other's parental role.

"Joint-custody arrangements sound so wonderful. Everything is in the 'best interest of the child,'" notes Clare Robinson, a child psychologist at the Cleveland Clinic. But, she adds, too often the child becomes "a secondary consideration" for parents unwilling to care for kids full time or to bear the full financial burden.

For the child, the most direct impact of dividing time between parents is having to physically shuttle back and forth. "It makes me dizzy," says Michelle Black, an eight-year-old from Kingsville, Md. Although her mother has sole custody, she spends the school year with her mother, summers with her father, and alternate weekends at both houses. "Sometimes I don't know where I'm going," she says. "Sometimes I'm confused about whose house I'm supposed to be at."

Such moves are also exhausting. Last year, Bryce Hatch, director of pupil services at public schools in Upper St. Clair, Pa., near Pittsburgh, noticed that a few children were falling asleep Monday mornings. Each had flown in late Sunday night or early Monday morning from weekend visits with a parent. "I think the parents' problems are so great they don't realize what they're doing to the kids," he says.

Judith Wallerstein, a Palo Alto, Calif., divorce researcher and clinical psychologist, worries about the effect on young children who may equate the shuttling as being sent away for bad behavior. Donald Freidheim, a Cleveland child psychologist, recalls a six-year-old boy, who commuted every other week between Cleveland and Philadelphia. The boy appeared introverted and preoccupied with drawing pictures of black clouds. Those clouds started to disappear after the parents

continued

continued

agreed he could stay longer with each parent.

Older children find the constant shifts disquieting as well. "I don't really feel like I have a home," says 16-year-old Laura. When her parents first separated, she lived with each for two weeks at a time. Then it was a month with each, and now she's living with her father until the Christmas holidays and then switches to her mother's.

"You have to be different for each parent. Mom is more lenient than Dad. So you behave differently. I don't have any sense of stability," says Laura, who admits to being "really depressed" at times.

For most two-household children, each home has a different personality and rules. One may use wheat bread, the other white. Bedtime is 8 p.m. at one house, and 9 at another. One young girl notes that soap operas are taboo at Dad's but OK at Mom's. While such differences may seem minor, they're often disquieting, specialists say.

Ms. Robinson, the psychologist, says that to cope, children tailor their behavior to their environment. Ryan Padwo's room at his mother's home is filled with stuffed animals while super heroes fill his room at his father's. "It's like he has two separate identities," says his mother, adding: "I'm the read-the-book parent. His father is the play parent."

Understandably, children often feel caught in the middle since each parent has a say in their upbringing. "When I'm at Dad's, I ask him if I can do something. When I go back to Mom's and tell her, she wonders, 'Why didn't you ask me?'" says one 16-year-old girl. She asks: "Am I supposed to call back over there every time I need to do something?"

Risa Garon, a social worker, says constant shuttling makes it easier for parents and children to gloss over rather than solve problems. "It acts like an escape valve. When things get rough, you can pick up and go to the other house," she says. "Or when you start to work things out, it's time to pack and leave. The continuity isn't there."

Ms. Garon, who runs a support group for children of divorced parents in Columbia, Md., says that children too often get tangled up in their parents' bitterness. She cites a recent picnic where, even though a boy and his father were having a great time when his mother arrived at 6 p.m., she "demanded the child leave because it was 'transfer time.'" And she says some parents have left a child with a baby sitter or at a friend's home while they traveled on business because "it's not the other parent's week."

An Even Split

Ellen and Rick Toplin opted for joint custody because they believed Jessica needed both parents. "I couldn't be Jessica's mother and equally Ellen couldn't be Jessica's father," says Rick. There were also selfish motivations. Both have demanding careers and, says Ellen, "neither of us wanted to let go of her."

They've split everything evenly, even alternating years to claim Jessica as a tax deduction. They bail each other out in emergencies: If Jessica gets sick at school and the parent who has Jessica can't pick her up, the other parent steps in. "We get along better now than when we were married," says Ellen.

There are annoyances, of course. Vacations are hard to schedule, and it's bothersome having to check with each other before doing anything—even scheduling a teacher's meeting. They've also had to battle well-meaning teachers, parents and even their marriage counselor who questioned their joint-custody decision.

"We had to fight against the odds," says Ellen. "But it's worth it. Jessica may have lost her family, but we didn't want her losing her parents."

Note how the writer uses examples in these paragraphs:

Paragraph 9

Main idea: It's hard for kids to divide time between parents.
Michelle's example: Quote from her describing just how hard it is.

Explanation of her example.

Another quote from Michelle.

For the child, the most direct impact of dividing time between parents is having to physically shuttle back and forth. "It makes me dizzy," says Michelle Black, an eight-year-old from Kingsville, Md. Although her mother has sole custody, she spends the school year with her mother, summers with her father, and alternate weekends at both houses.

"Sometimes I don't know where I'm going," she says.

"Sometimes I'm confused about whose house I'm supposed to be at."

Paragraphs 12–13

Main Idea: Older kids find moving hard, too.
Laura's example: Her statement about how difficult it is.

Explanation of her example.

Another quote from Laura.

Older children find the constant shifts disquieting as well. "I don't really feel like I have a home," says 16-year-old Laura. When her parents first separated, she lived with each for two weeks at a time. Then it was a month with each, and now she's living with her father until the Christmas holidays and then switches to her mother's.

"You have to be different for each parent. Mom is more lenient than Dad. So you behave differently. I don't have any sense of stability," says Laura, who admits to being "really depressed" at times.

Reading for Meaning

1. What is the main idea of the article?
2. How does the writer support her main idea?
3. What are some of the causes of this new phenomenon of children being shared by both parents?
4. What are some of the negative effects of joint-custody arrangements?
5. According to psychologist Clare Robinson, how does Ryan Padwo "tailor his behavior to his environment"?
6. Sixteen-year-old Laura states, "You have to be different for each parent." But isn't that also the case in traditional two-parent families where there is no joint custody? Give some examples.
7. When the Toplins decided for joint custody, whom did they have to battle?

Vocabulary in Context

Write down the definition of each of the italicized words below taken from the article. Try to guess the meaning from the context. Use a dictionary only if you have to.

1. "But such arrangements often work better on paper than in practice. Even when the divorce is [a.] *amicable*, the simple [b.] *logistics*—deciding who takes the child to and from school, to the dentist, and on shopping trips—are difficult enough. It's doubly hard when anger and bitterness linger between the couple."

2. ". . . constant shuttling makes it easier for parents and children *to gloss over* rather then solve problems."

Writing from Reading

In analyzing *subject, purpose,* and *audience* for each of the assignments below, consider how the purpose and audience will be different from those of most of your previous writing.

1. Select one or two paragraphs from the article and explain how the writer uses examples effectively.

2. Pretend that you are one of Laura's parents reading her remarks for the first time. Write her a letter about how you feel.

3. Pretend you are a marriage counselor advising a divorced couple about joint custody. What would you tell them?

4. Play the role of Bryce Hatch, the director of pupil services at public schools in Upper St. Clair, Pennsylvania (see paragraph 10), giving a talk to parents in his district about joint custody. What will you say?

5. Writer Clare Ansberry uses a variety of people from different parts of the country to explain the problems of joint custody on children of divorced parents. Would this article be more or less effective if the writer had used *one extended example,* say Ryan Padwo's family, rather than many examples, and focused on details of their situation? Explain.

6. *Peer reading assignment.* Do any of the assignments above, sharing your work at each stage of the writing process with the other students in your group.

SOME TRADITIONAL METHODS OF ESSAY DEVELOPMENT

In addition to process, comparison/contrast, and exemplification, there are four other methods of development in expository writing—cause and effect, division, classification, and definition. As we will see, these methods are also well-suited to the five-paragraph essay structure of introduction, body, and conclusion.

Cause and Effect

In this type of exposition, the writer examines the relationship between some cause and its consequent effects. For example, if a writer wanted to study why so many kids today seem overprogrammed and lacking in creativity (the effect) he or she would examine some of the causes: increased dependence on day care and more reliance on television and adult-supervised sports or hobby instruction because kids' parent(s) must work. In such an essay the pattern would be:

1. *Introduction.* Describe the effect and state the thesis.
2. *Body.* Explain and analyze the causes, writing one paragraph on each cause.
3. *Conclusion.* Restate the thesis and summarize the causes.

If, in the example above, the writer desired to focus on the possible effects of the increased use of day care and organized play to supervise children, the structure of the paper could be:

1. *Introduction.* Explain the cause or causes and state a thesis.
2. *Body.* Detail the results from the causes mentioned in the first paragraph, writing one paragraph on each result.
3. *Conclusion.* Repeat the thesis and show how the effects stem from the cause or causes.

Below is a sample cause-and-effect student essay about the lack of creativity observed in many children today.

Listless Kids: No Time to Play

Many children today appear unable to make decisions for themselves, to be creative in running their own lives. Lacking in personal initiative, these kids wait to be told what to do rather than to rely on themselves to make up things to do, to be able to ''play.'' In the minds of some sociologists and psychologists, this new problem results from the increased reliance on day care and on adult—supervised classes for hobbies and games.

Because frequently both partners in a marriage work today, they need day care for their children. These kids might spend as much as eight to ten hours a day under the direction of adults other than their parents. These

continued

continued

children find their time structured by the demands of
the day-care supervisors; they are not free to plan for
themselves.

The rising divorce rate has left many single mothers
as chief caretakers and, in some cases, chief providers
for the needs of their children. Forced to work, these
single mothers also use day-care facilities to provide
the nurturing that mothers at home once did.

Besides the increased use of day care for their children, many parents also turn to structured after-school,
weekend, and summer classes and lessons in dance,
tennis, swimming, computers, and many others. Between
day care and lessons, these children are left almost no
time to play, to have the freedom to construct their own
activities.

With so much of their time consumed by day care and
extra classes, many children today are robbed of the
precious time and opportunity to structure their own
lives, to play on their own. How sad that, because of
their economic and personal needs, some parents rob
their children of childhood.

Writing Assignment

1. Explain the effects on your life of attending college.
2. If there are some academic skills in which you are deficient, perhaps in reading or math, explain what caused them.
3. Explain the causes of the disease AIDS.
4. What are the effects on young athletes of using steroids?

Division

In this pattern of development, the writer divides the whole or a large unit of something into its parts. For example, the government of the United States is divided into three branches: executive, legislative, and judicial; an essay on this division would be organized in this way:

1. *Introduction.* Explain the whole and state the thesis.
2. *Body.* Describe each of the main parts into which the whole is divided, writing one paragraph on each part.
3. *Conclusion.* Restate the thesis and give a possible explanation of how all the parts fit together.

Below is a sample student essay written in the pattern of division.

Teachers and Class Control

There are many different kinds of high-school teachers. Although teachers have their own unique personalities, they can be easily categorized by how they control or fail to control their classes.

First, the nervous, insecure teacher slinks into the room clutching a mound of materials. This teacher speaks softly, hesitantly, and dares not make eye contact with the students because he or she fears them. Not feeling even equal with the students, the insecure teacher begs them to be good.

Another version of the insecure teacher is the ''buddy'' teacher who wishes to befriend the students, not teach them. The buddy teacher bounces into the room and tries to get down to the students ''at their level.'' Everybody's friend until things go wrong, this teacher feels hurt and betrayed when his ''friends'' act out and need discipline—after all, what are friends for?

Then there is the drill-sergeant teacher, who wishes to carry over into the classroom the strong discipline of the military. ''Yes, sir!'' and ''No, sir!'' ring out through this classroom. This teacher addresses everyone with formality—even a fourteen-year-old freshman is ''Mister'' or ''Miss.'' If the students go wild, the drill sergeant has two choices: either yell and scream and go crazy, or make believe the trouble never happened and ignore it totally.

All teachers, no matter how individual they may seem, can be readily classified according to their ability to manage a classroom. Most of them fall into one of three camps: the insecure teacher, the buddy, and the drill sergeant.

Writing Assignment

1. Describe the types of friends you have.
2. There are many kinds and styles of parenting. What type of parent would you prefer yourself to be?
3. You may be preparing yourself for a future in the job market. What qualities do you wish to have in your ideal job?
4. Describe the attributes of the perfect spouse for you.

Classification

In classification the writer categorizes many people or things (as opposed to one person or thing) according to their similarities. The structure of this kind of essay would be:

1. *Introduction.* Explain the different categories and state the thesis.
2. *Body.* Describe the members or parts of each particular category, writing a paragraph on each category.
3. *Conclusion.* Restate the thesis and summarize the categories.

Below is a sample student classification essay.

```
                    Major League Pitchers

    Major league pitchers have come in all shapes and
sizes from towering J. R. Richard to tubby Luis Tiant
and the slim, trim Billy Pierce. No matter what his size
and strength, every major league pitcher can be cate-
gorized according to how hard he threw, what variety of
pitches he had, and what kind of control he had.
    The ''cute'' pitcher generally had no blinding fast-
ball, but had a variety of pitches and pinpoint control.
Harvey Haddix and Whitey Ford from the fifties, and
later Juan Marichal and Catfish Hunter, and today's Mike
Boddicker and Rick Rueschel belong to this group. Not
relying solely on ''smoke,'' they all had great breaking
stuff and even ''trick'' pitches like the screwball and
forkball. These pitchers did all the little things well—
fielding their position, holding runners on base, and
even hitting, and especially bunting.
    The ''flame thrower'' brings ''heat.'' Usually big
and strong, this type of pitcher overpowers the batter.
From Walter Johnson through Bob Feller, Sandy Koufax,
Nolan Ryan, and Roger Clemens, this pitcher dominates a
game by strikeouts. Most of these pitchers, the greatest
of the game, learned along the way a companion pitch,
usually a sharp-breaking curveball. But their fame came
first from their fastball. Also, most of these players
experienced much wildness in their early years, but
later acquired control.
    A third type of pitcher combined craft and heat. Tom
Seaver and Dwight Gooden come quickly to mind. They not
only had great fastballs and good curveballs, but also a
great third pitch, usually a slider, and/or a change up.
Only the great pitchers have three or even four ''out''
```

pitches. With these two pitchers, too, control was never
a problem. They had complete command of all their
pitches.

   Even though physical strength and skills may vary
greatly among pitchers, every pitcher fits into one of
three recognizable groups: the cute pitcher, the flame
thrower, or a combination of the two.

Writing Assignment

1. Classify the different kinds of friends you have.
2. What categories could you use to describe most TV shows today?
3. Explain the types of colleges there are.
4. Explain the different categories of today's cars.

Definition

The definition paper tells the meaning of a term, explaining what differen-
tiates it from others that are similar. The *extended* definition may use
some other mode, or type, of development like process or comparison/
contrast to define the term further. The typical structure of this paper
would be:

1. *Introduction.* Name the term and state the thesis.
2. *Body.* Define the term, writing a paragraph on each definition or shade
   of meaning.
3. *Conclusion.* Restate the thesis and summarize the definitions.

Below is a sample student definition paper.

Self-Motivation

   Someone once said about pornography, ''I can't define
it, but I know it when I see it.'' The same may be true
of self-motivation. We know very well what those are
like who have it and those who don't. Those who have
self-motivation are self-starters, in need of no outside
influence to get them going. Those who lack this quality
always need goading or prodding. But although we know
its effects well, the term ''self-motivation'' remains
elusive, difficult to define.

   The word ''self'' is important to this definition because self-motivation can't be gotten or imposed from
outside the self. If it could, why would parents have to
nag their children, teachers their pupils, spouses their

continued

continued

marriage partners? Self—motivation springs from the person.

The opposite of self—complacency, self—motivation is not content with doing just enough. The self—motivated person may be hard to please and dissatisfied with any—thing less than continued improvement and achievement. The self—motivated person drives himself or herself to go beyond what is merely satisfactory.

Thousands of young people and adults are bored, unin—terested in ''stretching themselves,'' that is, improv—ing or acquiring new skills. These people are often drop—outs from school and even from life itself. How does an Abraham Lincoln, a Henry Ford, a Maya Angelou, a Lee Iacocca, not born into wealth and prestige, somehow rise above his or her peers? The answer is by self—motivation, whatever that means.

Writing Assignment

1. All people at some time or other experience loneliness. Write a paper defining "loneliness."
2. Grandparents are people that the young often take for granted—until they are gone. Write a definition essay about "grandparents."
3. Write a paper defining "friendship."
4. Pick a personal quality you admire in some friend or loved one and write a definition essay about it.

WORD DEMONS (CONTINUED)

15. Knew, new

"Knew" is the past tense of "know," that is, "to have knowledge," as in "General Patton *knew* he had to strike fast." "New" means "fresh, not old," as in "The German *blitzkrieg* was a *new* war tactic."

Exercises

Complete the following sentences with either "knew" or "new."

a. The English _____ they had to find some way to undermine the mo-rale of the German people.
b. Every year the auto show is the place for people to come who are in the market for a _____ car.

c. Most older pitchers have to come up with a _____ pitch once they lose their fastball and can no longer overpower hitters.

d. The Russians _____ that if they could trap the Nazis in the cold Russian winter, they could turn the tide of the war.

16. Know, no

"Know" refers to "knowledge"; for example, "I *know* the answer." "No" means "negative" or "not any," as in "*No* Parking."

Exercises

Complete the following sentences with either "know" or "no."

a. There was _____ way Dan would obey the baby sitter.

b. I _____ there is only one correct answer.

c. He offered _____ proof, only possibilities.

d. Only a specialist could _____ as much as he does about physics.

17. Lead, led

This is a confusing pair of words, partly because of pronunciation. These words are pronounced the same way when "lead" refers to the metal. Only by considering the context of each word can you choose the right one. "Lead" can mean "to *lead* into battle"; it can also mean the metal, as in "*lead* pencil." The word "led" is the past tense of the verb "lead": "Grant *led* the army of the North."

Exercises

Complete the following sentences with either "lead" or "led."

a. Reverend, will you _____ us in prayer?

b. Some dangerous forms of paint contain _____.

c. Lincoln _____ the cause for the abolition of slavery.

d. Peter will not _____ you astray.

18. Loose, lose, lost, loss

As an adjective, "loose" means "not tight fitting," as in "a *loose* leather jacket." "Lose" is a verb meaning "to miss from one's possession," as in "Kevin would *lose* his gloves three or four times a winter." "Lost" is the past tense of "lose": "The Yankees *lost* the pennant on the last day of the season." Another form of "lost" is the adjective meaning "lacking assurance or self-confidence," as in "a *lost* soul." "Loss" is a noun meaning "the act of losing," as in "Mary suffered the *loss* of her mother and father within the same year."

Exercises

Complete the following sentences with "loose," "lose," "lost," or "loss."

a. Cathy did not want to _____ her way on the sidestreets serving as a detour for the expressway.

b. The traitor Judas is the prototype of the _____ soul, one for whom there is no hope.

c. One of the images in *Macbeth* is that of the false king whose robe is too _____ for him to wear properly.

d. No general wants a victory that will prove costly in the long run, "to win the battle, but _____ the war."

e. For some people, the _____ of their reputations is as important to them as the _____ of life itself.

f. The religious hymn "Amazing Grace" brings comfort to those thinking of themselves as spiritual exiles, _____ to God.

19. Mine, mind

These two words sound alike, but that is their only connection. "Mine" is a possessive pronoun that shows ownership: "The blue Chrysler with the big tail fins is *mine*." As a noun or verb, "mine" refers to the extraction of metals, as from a "gold *mine*." As a noun, "mind" means the "brain" or "intelligence," like a "bright *mind*." The verb "mind" can also mean "permit, allow": "Would you *mind* doing the work today?"

Exercises

Complete the following sentences with either "mine" or "mind."

a. Jack Ruby screamed, "Oswald, you're _____!"

b. Oswald had a tortured _____.

c. Would you _____ seeing Dean Sherman after class?

d. Cancer of the lung comes often to those who work in a coal _____.

20. Passed, past

These two words are especially confusing. "Passed" is the past tense of the verb "pass," meaning "to go by, make it," as in "Julie passed by Throop Street very often" or "Paul passed all the requirements for Notre Dame."

"Past" can be a noun, adjective, preposition, or adverb with the meanings "beyond" or "time gone by," as in "Tim dwells on the *past*" or "*past* events," or "Jack walked *past* the house."

Exercises

Complete the following sentences with either "passed" or "past."

a. Critics of Nixon were glad to see him caught up in events from his murky _____.

b. The White House flunkies had long since _____ the point of worrying about the finer points of ethics.

c. The bullet flew _____ his bobbing head in an instant.

d. Nixon often _____ the buck to his lieutenants.

21. Plus

The word "plus" is generally a term used in mathematics: "Two *plus* two equals four." It is never to be used as a substitute for "and": "Sam gets mad too often, *and* he goes out of his way to look for trouble."

22. Precede, proceed

The word "precede" means "to go before": "The faculty *precede* the students in the graduation procession." "Proceed" means "to go on": "You students are to *proceed* with your homework."

Exercises

Complete the following sentences with either "precede" or "proceed."

a. Jack and Kevin _____ him in age.

b. I will _____ with the investigation.

c. _____ to the next assignment.

d. Coughing and sneezing often _____ the onset of the flu.

23. Principal, principle

"Principal" has three common meanings: (1) "head of a school," as in "Principal Jones" (think of the "pal" in principal"); (2) "chief, main," as in "the principal reason"; and (3) "main sum of money," as in "The principal of the loan was $60,000." "Principle" means "rule, ideal" as in "the principle of freedom of speech." Think of the "*le*" in "ru*le*" and "princip*le*."

Exercises

Complete the following sentences with either "principal" or "principle."

a. The angry mother went directly to _____ Collins.
b. Plato always dealt with the philosophical _____.
c. Bring that child down to the _____.
d. To Thomas More, _____ meant more than life itself.

24. Quiet, quite

"Quiet" is an adjective, noun, or verb meaning "not loud, still." "He is a *quiet* man." "I want some *quiet!*" "Carson tried to *quiet* the crowd." The word "quite" means "very," as in "Joe Grimaldi was *quite* ill."

Exercises

Complete the following sentences with either "quiet" or "quite."

a. The July day was _____ warm.
b. The Redskins proved to be _____ an adversary for the Bears.
c. Only by sitting behind the speaker and glowering at the students was the teacher able to _____ them.
d. John Wayne never seemed like a _____ man.

25. Than, then

"Than" is an adverb or conjunction showing comparison: "Ali was faster *than* Frazier." "Then" is an adverb telling "time when": "*Then* Al Capone was sent to Alcatraz."

Exercises

Complete the following sentences with either "than" or "then."

a. The Chrysler is more expensive _____ a Cadillac.
b. Jesse Owens ran faster _____ the Germans.
c. _____ Napoleon was forced to return to Elba.
d. When the police came, he _____ had to surrender his gun.

26. Thing, think

"Thing" is a noun referring to "a matter of concern" or a "possession," as in "The girl didn't mean a *thing* to him." "Think" is a verb meaning "to form or have in the mind": "I *think* I have the solution to the problem."

Exercises

Complete the following sentences with "thing" or "think."

a. Did you ever _____ that this could happen to me?
b. Sally quickly saw that not a _____ could be done unless she first cleaned the kitchen.
c. The teachers _____ that their school is in a bad location.
d. When Jim moved, he didn't leave a _____ behind.

27. Threw, through (also spelled "thru")

"Threw" is the past tense of the verb "throw," as in "Joe Montana *threw* four touchdown passes." "Through" or "thru" is often used as a preposition or adverb meaning "from one side to the other," as in "Little Red Riding Hood walked *through* the woods to grandmother's house."

Exercises

Complete the following sentences with either "threw" or "through".

a. Tom passed into maturity _____ his military service and subsequent acquisition of a job.
b. Patton _____ all caution to the wind.
c. _____ the whole, long ordeal, Earl acted with nothing but civility to all parties.
d. Feller _____ a fastball that Gomez claimed to the umpire he couldn't see.

28. Want, won't

"Want" is a verb meaning "desire," as in "Denis *wants* money." As a noun, "want" means "something lacking or desired," as in "During the war most of Europe suffered from *want*." "Won't" means "will not": "The Japanese *won't* reciprocate in our trade agreements by buying American products."

Execises

Complete the following sentences with either "want" or "won't."

a. He believes that most students _____ do the extra work required to get an A in his class.
b. Some members of Congress _____ the United States to have tougher trade policies with the Japanese.
c. I _____ you guys to clean the basement.
d. The Bears _____ win the NFC Central this year.

29. Weather, whether, would rather

These words are commonly misused. The difference between the first two can be explained pretty easily. "Weather" is most often a noun referring to "climate," as in "winter *weather*," while "whether" is a conjunction meaning "or," as in "*whether* or not he will come." Students sometimes misuse "whether" for "had or would rather," as in "I would *rather* he come sooner than later." "Rather" is an adverb.

Exercises

Complete the following sentences with either "weather," "whether," or "would rather."

a. Thomas More saw his situation in this way—_____ to choose to follow his king or his conscience.

b. Winter in the Midwest presents some of the coldest _____ in the whole United States.

c. I _____ my son be a good person than merely a successful one.

d. _____ or not he is on time depends on him.

30. When, went

"When" refers to time, as in "When he comes home, he will do his homework." "Went" is the past tense of the verb "to go"—"Phyllis *went* to the store."

Exercises

Complete the following sentences with either "when" or "went."

a. John F. Kennedy _____ to Dallas and met his death there.

b. Jack Ruby was waiting _____ the Dallas police brought Oswald down to the parking garage.

c. _____ Ruby shot Oswald, the whole world could see the shock on the dying Oswald's face.

d. The news of Kennedy's assassination _____ around the world.

31. Where, were

The adverb "where" refers to a place and can be used in a question or a statement: "*where* the crime had been committed" or "*Where* is the milk?" The word "were" is a form of the verb "to be," as in the sentence "The boys were here."

Exercises

Complete the following sentences with either "were" or "where."

a. _____ have all the flowers gone?

b. The Mafia gangs _____ running illegal liquor supplies during Prohibition in Chicago.

c. Chicago Stadium and the old Madison Square Garden _____ centers of college basketball at one time.

d. Jimmy Cagney demands to know _____ the gun was hidden.

PART FOUR

Writing Essays to Explain and Persuade

▲▲▲

CHAPTER

12

Using Facts to Persuade

Although there are many different types of writing—description, narration, exposition, and so on—each tailored to its own specific subject, purpose, and audience, the underlying function of all writing is to *persuade* the reader, to convince him or her of the validity of a particular position, point of view, or just a way of looking at the world.

Official state and federal documents are often written expressly to persuade. A responsible government is obliged to inform its citizens about the important facts of public health, even if that knowledge is highly technical or may offend the religious beliefs or personal convictions of certain segments of the population. No topic has stirred as much controversy and public concern in recent years as AIDS, so much so that the surgeon general of the United States (our highest-ranking health official) took the unprecedented action of preparing and distributing the pamphlet *Understanding AIDS* to every home in the nation.

In this chapter we will first study AIDS in the context of writing that uses factual information to persuade. Later we will focus on another issue of increasing public concern, the use of steroids.

READING: "GOOD DEED GETS HER NOTHING BUT GRIEF"

As an introduction to the painful topic of AIDS, read the following article by *Chicago Tribune* columnist Mike Royko.

First, however, read the title, the first two paragraphs and the last two paragraphs:

Good deed gets her nothing but grief

A couple of weeks ago, I wrote about a kind-hearted woman who gave a stranger mouth-to-mouth resuscitation after he collapsed on a sidewalk and appeared to be dying.

When the city's paramedics arrived, they looked at the man's arms and discovered that he was a mainlining junkie. And, as it turned out, he was not only a junkie, but a gay junkie. And not only a gay junkie, but one with bleeding gums.

• • •

They might have a point, so I want to make it clear that I was not trying to frighten people into ignoring someone in need of help.

On the other hand, it might not be a bad idea to take a couple of seconds and check to see if he has needle marks on his arms and is wearing lipstick.

Write down a prediction about the meaning of the article.

As you read the entire piece, notice that Royko doesn't harangue the reader about the situation he describes; he simply lets the events and people speak for themselves.

Good deed gets her nothing but grief

MIKE ROYKO

A couple of weeks ago, I wrote about a kind-hearted woman who gave a stranger mouth-to-mouth resuscitation after he collapsed on a sidewalk and appeared to be dying.

When the city's paramedics arrived, they looked at the man's arms and discovered that he was a mainlining junkie. And, as it turned out, he was not only a junkie, but a gay junkie. And not only a gay junkie, but one with bleeding gums.

Naturally, the woman was alarmed at the possibility that she might have been exposed to AIDS. So she tried to persuade

the hospital, where the man was treated for a seizure, to give her information, including his name.

The hospital refused, saying the law prevented it from giving out any information on the man.

So she turned to the city's Health Department for help. She told her story in detail to a department employee who listened, then asked: "Did you have sex with him?"

And that was where we left the story of Nancy, the Good Samaritan. Since then, there have been other developments.

"My social life has taken a nose dive," says Nancy, who is divorced.

"There's been someone in my life. I showed him the article, and obviously he's rather hesitant. We haven't broken

continued

continued

up, but I haven't seen him very much in the last couple of weeks.

"My dentist read the article and now he wears a mask when he works on my teeth. Friends who used to shake my hand no longer do.

"I don't know if I can describe it, but my friends seem different now. It's just a feeling I have, a gut reaction. They're concerned about my welfare, but they're also concerned about their own. But with all the misinformation going around about AIDS, I'm not surprised.

"The impression I get from people is, they look at me with amazement, and the look on their faces says: 'Why did you do such a stupid thing?' It's as if I could have somehow known that he was an addict. Or a promiscuous queen. Some of the neighbors have told me about that." (Nancy lives on the North Side, in the heart of the gay community, as it is called.)

The hospital where the man was treated still hasn't done much for Nancy, although it has tried.

"They've tried to get him to come in for a test. They've been in contact with his mother, and she thinks it would be a good idea. But he's refused.

"What really infuriated me is that the hospital told me that he'd like to talk to me and they asked me if they could give him my phone number.

"When they asked me that, I was furious. I told them: 'You won't tell me who he is, but you want to give him *my name and phone number*? Do you think I want some junkie calling me at 2 o'clock in the morning telling me he's sorry?'

"They've offered to give me free blood tests and monitor me every three months. But I'm not going to go there for the tests because they might have some vested, legal interests in the results. I'm going to get the tests, but somewhere else."

A spokesman for the hospital con-cedes that it is in kind of a bind.

"We've been trying to get him to come in to be tested, but we haven't been successful. We've also tried to get him to agree to let her have his phone number, but we haven't been able to ask him. He's hard to get in touch with, so we've had to deal with his mother, and he doesn't live with his mother."

Working on her own, however, Nancy has discovered the man's name. When the paramedics treated him, they took down that information and it is a matter of public record.

But that hasn't helped Nancy track him down because, as the hospital spokesman said, the man seems to be constantly on the move. A busy lifestyle, I assume.

So Nancy is going to go ahead and take the series of tests. There's no great urgency. As a state health official said: "It's not like she can go in and take a shot and change anything." In other words, if she's got it, she's got it and that's that.

The state official also said: "I've talked to our medical experts and they said that her chance of getting AIDS is extremely slim."

Incidentally, after I wrote the first column about Nancy's experience, I heard from an organization that promotes educating the public on how to give cardio-pulmonary resuscitation.

The organization said that I may have been irresponsible in writing the article, because I might discourage others from giving mouth-to-mouth aid to strangers.

They might have a point, so I want to make it clear that I was not trying to frighten people into ignoring someone in need of help.

On the other hand, it might not be a bad idea to take a couple of seconds and check to see if he has needle marks on his arms and is wearing lipstick.

Reading for Meaning

1. What is the thesis of Royko's article?
2. How does Royko support his thesis?
3. What started Nancy's problems?
4. What three dangerous things did the paramedics discover about the stricken man Nancy helped?
5. What have been the long-term effects of Nancy's actions?
6. Even though the hospital wouldn't give Nancy the name of the man she tried to help, what did they offer her?
7. How did Nancy finally discover the name of the man she helped?
8. Why can't Nancy track down the man to try to convince him to be tested for AIDS?
9. What is Nancy going to do about the possibility that she may have contracted AIDS from the man she helped?
10. What tongue-in-cheek advice does Royko have for those who, like Nancy, might be tempted to give mouth-to-mouth resuscitation to a stranger?

Writing from Reading

Recall that a simulation argument is one in which you seriously assume the role of a person in a debate. If you "become" the person, taking his or her point of view as your own, you will be motivated to find good evidence for the position you represent. Get in groups of four or five students, each of you playing the role of one of the five described below. Then, for ten minutes freewrite about the reasons for your actions as described in the article. Keep in mind that you want to *persuade* the others in your group of your point of view.

Nancy. She wants the man she helped to be tested for AIDS.

Junkie who may have AIDS. He is sorry for Nancy but wants to protect his privacy. He is afraid to be tested for AIDS because he might discover he has it.

Junkie's mother. She is terrified that her son might have AIDS, but she feels sorry for Nancy.

Hospital administrator who wouldn't give Nancy the man's name. He doesn't want his hospital to be sued for invading the privacy of the possible AIDS victim.

Nancy's lover. He has abandoned Nancy for fear she may have contracted AIDS.

After each member of your group has finished his or her prewriting, he or she should read it out loud to the others in your group. Suggest changes in each other's work.

Using your prewriting as a basis, write a first draft and a final draft of your argument at home. During the next class, each member of your group should read his or her final draft to the others, who will vote for the most convincing argument. The teacher may then choose to have the best paper from each group read aloud to the rest of the class.

READING: *UNDERSTANDING AIDS*

The government pamphlet that follows was mailed to every home in America in 1988; it was written to give clear facts and explanations about AIDS and to persuade a frightened general public about the realities and fallacies associated with the disease.

Before reading the entire pamphlet, use your prereading techniques to better understand the material by skimming through it, noting the headings and organization. Also read the following headings, taken from the back cover of the pamphlet:

WHAT DO YOU REALLY KNOW ABOUT AIDS?

ARE YOU AT RISK?

AIDS AND SEX

WHY NO ONE HAS GOTTEN AIDS FROM MOSQUITOES

On a piece of paper write down what you think are some of the things the pamphlet will say.

As you read through the article, keep the following questions in mind:

1. On page 1, what does the surgeon general's message urge readers? What is he trying to persuade us to do?

2. The headings grab our attention. Page 2 dispels some of the myths about catching AIDS, even using bold print to highlight ideas—for example, "You won't get AIDS from saliva, sweat, tears, urine or a bowel movement." Also on page 3 are lists of "Risky Behavior" and "Safe Behavior" that are easy to read and understand. Why does the pamphlet use so many different elements—boldface, italics, boxed text, different size headings—to make its points?

3. Half of page 4 is devoted to information about condoms. Why?

4. Much of page 6 is devoted to concerns for babies and kids. Why?

Understanding AIDS

A MESSAGE FROM THE SURGEON GENERAL

This brochure has been sent to you by the Government of the United States. In preparing it, we have consulted with the top health experts in the country.

I feel it is important that you have the best information now available for fighting the AIDS virus, a health problem that the President has called "Public Enemy Number One."

Stopping AIDS is up to you, your family and your loved ones.

Some of the issues involved in this brochure may not be things you are used to discussing openly. I can easily understand that. But now you must discuss them. We all must know about AIDS. Read this brochure and talk about it with those you love. Get involved. Many schools, churches, synagogues, and community groups offer AIDS education activities.

I encourage you to practice responsible behavior based on understanding and strong personal values. This is what you can do to stop AIDS.

WHAT AIDS MEANS TO YOU

AIDS is one of the most serious health problems that has ever faced the American public. It is important that we all, regardless of who we are, understand this disease.

AIDS stands for *acquired immu-*

nodeficiency syndrome. It is a disease caused by the Human Immunodeficiency Virus, HIV—the AIDS virus.

The AIDS virus may live in the human body for years before actual symptoms appear. It primarily affects you by making you unable to fight other diseases. These other diseases can kill you.

Many people feel that only certain "high risk groups" of people are infected by the AIDS virus. This is untrue. *Who you are has nothing to do with whether you are in danger of being infected with the AIDS virus. What matters is what you do.*

People are worried about getting AIDS. Some should be worried and need to take some serious precautions. But many are not in danger of contracting AIDS.

The purpose of this brochure is to tell you how you can, and just as important, how you can't become infected with the AIDS virus.

Your children need to know about AIDS. Discuss it with them as you would any health concern.

HOW DO YOU GET AIDS?

There are two main ways you can get AIDS. First you can become infected by having sex—oral, anal or vaginal—with someone who is infected with the AIDS virus.

Second, you can be infected by sharing drug needles and syringes with an infected person.

continued

continued

Babies of women who have been infected with the AIDS virus may be born with the infection because it can be transmitted from the mother to the baby before or during birth.

In addition, some persons with hemophilia and others have been infected by receiving blood.

Can You Become Infected?

Yes, if you engage in risky behavior.

The male homosexual population was the first in this country to feel the effects of the disease. But in spite of what you may have heard, the number of heterosexual cases is growing.

People who have died of AIDS in the U.S. have been male and female, rich and poor, white, Black, Hispanic, Asian and American Indian.

How Do You Get AIDS From Sex?

The AIDS virus can be spread by sexual intercourse whether you are male or female, heterosexual, bisexual or homosexual.

This happens because a person infected with the AIDS virus may have the virus in semen or vaginal fluids. The virus can enter the body through the vagina, penis, rectum or mouth.

Anal intercourse, with or without a condom, is risky. The rectum is easily injured during anal intercourse.

Remember, AIDS is sexually transmitted, and the AIDS virus is not the only infection that is passed through intimate sexual contact.

Other sexually transmitted diseases, such as gonorrhea, syphilis, herpes and chlamydia, can also be contracted through oral, anal and vaginal intercourse. If you

are infected with one of these diseases and engage in risky behavior you are at greater risk of getting AIDS.

YOU WON'T GET AIDS FROM INSECTS—OR A KISS

No matter what you may have heard, the AIDS virus is hard to get and is easily avoided.

You won't just "catch" AIDS like a cold or flu because the virus is a different type. The AIDS virus is transmitted through sexual intercourse, the sharing of drug needles, or to babies of infected mothers before or during birth.

You won't get the AIDS virus through everyday contact with the people around you in school, in the workplace, at parties, child care centers, or stores. You won't get it by swimming in a pool, even if someone in the pool is infected with the AIDS virus. Students attending school with someone infected with the AIDS virus are not in danger from casual contact.

You won't get AIDS from a mosquito bite. The AIDS virus is not transmitted through a mosquito's salivary glands like other diseases such as malaria or yellow fever. You won't get it from bed bugs, lice, flies or other insects, either.

You won't get AIDS from saliva, sweat, tears, urine or a bowel movement.

You won't get AIDS from a kiss.

You won't get AIDS from clothes, a telephone, or from a toilet seat. It can't be passed by using a glass or eating utensils that someone else has used. You won't get the virus by being on a bus, train or crowded elevator with a person who is infected with the virus, or who has AIDS.

The Difference Between Giving And Receiving Blood

1. **Giving blood.** You are not now, nor have you ever been in danger of getting AIDS from giving blood at a blood bank. The needles that are used for blood donations are brand-new. Once they are used, they are destroyed. There is no way you can come into contact with the AIDS virus by donating blood.

2. **Receiving blood.** The risk of getting AIDS from a blood transfusion has been greatly reduced. In the interest of making the blood supply as safe as possible, donors are screened for risk factors and donated blood is tested for the AIDS antibody. Call your local blood bank if you have questions.

WHAT BEHAVIOR PUTS YOU AT RISK?

You are at risk of being infected with the AIDS virus if you have sex with someone who is infected, or if you share drug needles and syringes with someone who is infected.

Since you can't be sure who is infected, your chances of coming into contact with the virus increase with the number of sex partners you have. Any exchange of infected blood, semen or vaginal fluids can spread the virus and place you at great risk.

The following behaviors are risky when performed with an infected person. You can't tell by looking if a person is infected.

Risky Behavior

Sharing drug needles and syringes.
Anal sex, with or without a condom.
Vaginal or oral sex with someone who shoots drugs or engages in anal sex.
Sex with someone you don't know well (a pickup or prostitute) or with someone you know has several sex partners.
Unprotected sex (without a condom) with an infected person.

Safe Behavior

Not having sex.
Sex with one mutually faithful, uninfected partner.
Not shooting drugs.

WHAT ABOUT DATING?

Dating and getting to know other people is a normal part of life. Dating doesn't mean the same thing as having sex. Sexual intercourse as a part of dating can be risky. One of the risks is AIDS.

How can you tell if someone you're dating or would like to date has been exposed to the AIDS virus? The bad news is, you can't. But the good news is, as long as sexual activity and sharing drug needles are avoided, it doesn't matter.

You are going to have to be careful about the person you become sexually involved with, making your own decision based on your own best judgment. That can be difficult.

Has this person had any sexually transmitted diseases? How many people have they been to bed with? Have they experimented with drugs? All these are sensitive, but important, questions. But you have a personal responsibility to ask.

Think of it this way. If you know someone well enough to have sex, then you should be able to talk about AIDS. If someone is unwilling to talk, you shouldn't have sex.

Do Married People Get AIDS?

Married people who are uninfected, faithful and don't shoot drugs are not at

continued

continued

risk. But if they engage in risky behavior, they can become infected with the AIDS virus and infect their partners. If you feel your spouse may be putting you at risk, talk to him or her. It's your life.

WHAT IS ALL THE TALK ABOUT CONDOMS?

Not so very long ago, condoms (rubbers or prophylactics) were things we didn't talk about very much.

Now, they're discussed on the evening news and on the front page of your newspaper, and displayed out in the open in your local drugstore, grocery, and convenience store.

For those who are sexually active and not limiting their sexual activity to one partner, condoms have been shown to help prevent the spread of sexually transmitted diseases. That is why the use of condoms is recommended to help reduce the spread of AIDS.

Condoms are the best preventive measure against AIDS besides not having sex and practicing safe behavior.

But condoms are far from being foolproof. You have to use them properly. And you have to use them every time you have sex, from start to finish. If you use a condom, you should remember these guidelines:

1. Use condoms made of latex rubber. Latex serves as a barrier to the virus. ''Lambskin'' or ''natural membrane'' condoms are not as good because of the pores in the material. Look for the word ''latex'' on the package.

2. A condom with a spermicide may provide additional protection. Spermicides have been shown in laboratory tests to kill the virus. Use the spermicide in the tip and outside the condom.

3. Condom use is safer with a lubricant. Check the list of ingredients on the back of the lubricant package to make sure the lubricant is water-based. Do not use petroleum-based jelly, cold cream, baby oil or cooking shortening. These can weaken the condom and cause it to break.

WHAT DOES SOMEONE WITH AIDS LOOK LIKE?

It is very important that everyone understands that a person can be infected with the AIDS virus without showing any symptoms at all.

It is possible to be infected for years, feel fine, look fine and have no way of knowing you are infected unless you have a test for the AIDS virus.

During this period, however, people infected with the AIDS virus can pass the virus to sexual partners, to people with whom drug needles are shared, and to children before or during birth. That is one of the most disturbing things about AIDS.

Once symptoms do appear, they are similar to the symptoms of some other diseases. As the disease progresses, they become more serious. That is because the AIDS virus keeps your body's natural defenses from operating correctly.

If you are concerned whether you might be infected, consider your own behavior and its effects on others. If you feel you need to be tested for the AIDS virus, talk to a doctor or an AIDS counselor for more information.

Is There A Cure For AIDS?

There is presently no cure for AIDS.

Medicines such as AZT have prolonged the lives of some people with AIDS. There is hope that additional treatments will be found.

There is also no vaccine to prevent uninfected people from getting the infection. Researchers believe it may take years for an effective, safe vaccine to be found.

The most effective way to prevent AIDS is avoiding exposure to the virus, which you can control by your own behavior.

SHOULD YOU GET AN AIDS TEST?

You have probably heard about the "AIDS Test." The test doesn't actually tell you if you have AIDS. It shows if you have been infected with the virus. It looks for changes in blood that occur after you have been infected.

The Public Health Service recommends you be confidentially counseled and tested if you have had any sexually transmitted disease or shared needles; if you are a man who has had sex with another man; or if you have had sex with a prostitute, male or female. You should be tested if you have had sex with anyone who has done any of these things.

If you are a woman who has been engaging in risky behavior, and you plan to have a baby or are not using birth control, you should be tested.

Your doctor may advise you to be counseled and tested if you are a hemophiliac, or have received a blood transfusion between 1978 and 1985.

If you test positive, and find you have been infected with the AIDS virus, you must take steps to protect your partner.

People who have always practiced safe behavior do not need to be tested.

There's been a great deal in the press about problems with the test. It is very reliable if it is done by a good laboratory and the results are checked by a physician or counselor.

If you have engaged in risky behavior, speak frankly to a doctor who understands the AIDS probelm, or to an AIDS counselor.

For more information, call your local public health agency. They're listed in the government section of your phone book. Or, call your local AIDS hotline. If you can't find the number, call 1-800-342-AIDS.

THE PROBLEM OF DRUGS AND AIDS

Today, in some cities, the sharing of drug needles and syringes by those who shoot drugs is the fastest growing way that the virus is being spread.

No one should shoot drugs. It can result in addiction, poor health, family disruptions, emotional disturbances and death. Many drug users are addicted and need to enter a drug treatment program as quickly as possible.

In the meantime, these people must avoid AIDS by not sharing any of the equipment used to prepare and inject illegal drugs.

Sharing drug needles, even once, is an extremely easy way to be infected with the AIDS virus. Blood from an infected person can be trapped in the needle or syringe, and then injected directly into the bloodstream of the next person who uses the needle.

Other kinds of drugs, including alcohol, can also cause problems. Under their influence, your judgment becomes impaired. You could be exposed to the AIDS virus while doing things you wouldn't otherwise do.

Teenagers are at an age when trying different things is especially inviting. They must understand how serious the drug problem is and how to avoid it.

Drugs are also one of the main ways in which prostitutes become infected. They may share needles themselves or have sex with people who do. They then can pass the AIDS virus to others.

For information about drug abuse treatment programs, contact your physician, local public health agency or community AIDS or drug assistance group.

continued

continued

AIDS AND BABIES

An infected woman can give the AIDS virus to her baby before it is born, or during birth. If a woman is infected, her child has about one chance in two of being born with the virus.

If you are considering having a baby, and think you might have been at risk of being infected with the AIDS virus, even if it was years ago, you should receive counseling and be tested before you get pregnant.

You must have a long talk with the person with whom you're planning to have a child. Even if you have known this person for a long time, there's no way to be sure he or she hasn't been infected in the past, possibly without realizing it. That person needs to think hard and decide if an AIDS test might be a good idea. So should you.

TALKING WITH KIDS ABOUT AIDS

Children hear about AIDS, just as we all do. But they don't understand it, so they become frightened. They are worried they or their friends might get sick and die.

Children need to be told they can't get AIDS from everyday contact in the classroom, cafeteria or bathrooms. They don't have to worry about getting AIDS even if one of their schoolmates is infected.

Basic health education should be started as early as possible, in keeping with parental and community standards. Local schools have the responsibility to see that their students know the facts about AIDS. It is very important that middle school students—those entering their teens—learn to protect themselves from the AIDS virus.

Children must also be taught values and responsibility, as well as skills to help them resist peer pressure that might lead to risky behavior. These skills can be reinforced by religious and community groups. However, final responsibility rests with the parents. As a parent, you should read and discuss this brochure with your children.

HELPING A PERSON WITH AIDS

If you are one of the growing number of people who know someone who is infected, you need to have a special understanding of the problem.

No one will require more support and more love than your friend with AIDS. Feel free to offer what you can, without fear of becoming infected.

Don't worry about getting AIDS from everyday contact with a person with AIDS. You need to take precautions such as wearing rubber gloves only when blood is present.

If you don't know anyone with AIDS, but you'd still like to offer a helping hand, become a volunteer. You can be sure your help will be appreciated by a person with AIDS.

This might mean dropping by the supermarket to pick up groceries, sitting with the person a while, or just being there to talk. You may even want to enroll in a support group for caregivers. These are available around the country. If you are interested, contact any local AIDS-related organization.

Above all, keep an upbeat attitude. It will help you and everyone face the disease more comfortably.

DO YOU KNOW ENOUGH TO TALK ABOUT AIDS? TRY THIS QUIZ

It's important for each of us to share what we know about AIDS with family members and others we love. Knowledge and understanding are the best weapons we have against the disease. Check the boxes. Answers below.

1. If you are not in a "high risk group," you still need to be concerned about AIDS.
   ☐ True   ☐ False
2. The AIDS virus is not spread through
   ☐ A. insect bites.
   ☐ B. casual contact.
   ☐ C. sharing drug needles.
   ☐ D. sexual intercourse.
3. Condoms are an effective, but not foolproof, way to prevent the spread of the AIDS virus.
   ☐ True   ☐ False
4. You can't tell by looking that someone has the AIDS virus.
   ☐ True   ☐ False
5. If you think you've been exposed to the AIDS virus, you should get an AIDS test.
   ☐ True   ☐ False
6. People who provide help for someone with AIDS are not personally at risk for getting the disease.
   ☐ True   ☐ False

Answers

1. **True.** It is risky *behavior* that puts you at risk for AIDS, regardless of any "group" you belong to.

2. **A & B.** The AIDS virus is not spread by insects, kissing, tears, or casual contact.

3. **True.** However, the most effective preventive measure against AIDS is not having sex or shooting drugs.

4. **True.** You cannot tell by looking if someone is infected. The virus by itself is completely invisible. Symptoms may first appear years after you have been infected.

5. **True.** You should be counseled about getting an AIDS test if you have been engaging in risky behavior or think you have been exposed to the virus. There is no reason to be tested if you don't engage in this behavior.

6. **True.** You won't get AIDS by helping someone who has the disease.

Reading for Meaning

After carefully reading the pamphlet, write down the answers to the following questions.

1. What is AIDS?
2. How do people get AIDS?
3. How can you tell who has AIDS?
4. Exactly how is AIDS trasmitted through sex?

5. What are some ways that people incorrectly fear catching AIDS?

6. As a young person dating, what worries about AIDS should you have?

7. How do condoms help prevent AIDS?

8. Can people who have no symptoms give you AIDS?

9. If you and your partner want to have a baby, what is the safest thing to do?

10. What people should get tested for AIDS?

11. Some states, New York for instance, have used pictures of very sick AIDS patients in commercials to warn the public about the disease. This practice is not followed in *Understanding AIDS*. Do you think that the document would have been more powerful if such pictures had been included?

Writing from Reading

For each of the following assignments, remember to consider your *subject*, *purpose*, and *audience*.

1. Now that you've read the brochure on AIDS and answered questions about it, try to think how you could write a summary of the material in it for children, ages 10–13, in grades 5 to 8. You are going to have to be very clear in explaining some sensitive points to people who are not yet adults. Follow these steps:
   a. Brainstorm for ten minutes and make a list of the points you want to include in your summary.
   b. Go back over your list and give it some order, some pattern of organization.
   c. Using the revised list above, write your summary.

2. Some religious groups find the discussion of AIDS very distasteful, especially the emphasis on using condoms. They feel that since all premarital and extramarital sex is wrong, persuading people to use condoms implies consent or approval of sex outside marriage. Also, some Catholics hold that *all* artificial methods of birth control are immoral, and they are opposed to the use of condoms for that reason. Brainstorm or freewrite about your thoughts on this subject, trying also to anticipate the arguments against your viewpoint. Write a rough draft of your argument and then a revised draft.

READING: "KILLER ILLNESSES OF HISTORY"

The following article in *U.S. News & World Report* by Stacy Wells has the subtitle "AIDS will be added to the dishonor roll," and a picture (not shown) depicting people of the Middle Ages fearful of the Black Death. On a piece of paper, predict what the article will say.

Now read the first and last paragraphs:

> With cases doubling every 13 months, AIDS will soon take its place in the rogues' gallery of the world's major scourges. The Black Death killed a quarter to a half of Europe's population—25 million to 50 million people—in one three-year spasm from 1347 to 1350. At its height in the 18th century, smallpox killed about 400,000 Europeans a year, including such heads of state as Queen Ulrika Eleonora of Sweden in 1741. Some 22 million people died in the influenza outbreak of 1917–18. Even as many people fought off the flu, a louse-borne typhus devastated Russia and eastern Poland.
>
> •   •   •
>
> But that's about the only positive thing about AIDS. It is the first sexually transmitted disease of pandemic proportions—an epidemic that ranges beyond one or two countries. While syphilis and its ilk ravaged humankind for many centuries until the advent and wide use of penicillin in the 1940s—and still bedevil Third World countries—they never decimated entire populations. If a vaccine does not appear until the turn of the century, the death toll could be in the tens of millions. And so far there's no evidence that AIDS will die out on its own.

Write down a further prediction.

In reading the entire article, notice how the writer uses facts and figures and comparison/contrast to explain what AIDS *is* and what it *is not*.

AIDS will be added to the dishonor roll
Killer illnesses of history

With cases doubling every 13 months, AIDS will soon take its place in the rogues' gallery of the world's major scourges. The Black Death killed a quarter to a half of Europe's population—25 million to 50 million people—in one three-year spasm from 1347 to 1350. At its height in the 18th century, smallpox killed about 400,000 Europeans a year, including such heads of state as Queen Ulrika Eleonora of Sweden in 1741. Some 22 million people died in the influenza outbreak of 1917–18. Even as many people fought off the flu, a louse-borne typhus devastated Russia and eastern Poland.

The germ that caused the Black Death, or bubonic plague, was spread through the air and through flea bites. The fleas picked up the germs from the hordes of black rats that made their homes in the filth-ridden city streets. The Black Death killed more people in less time than any other disease, until some of those who became sick developed immunity and recovered. As the immune population grew, fewer people became infected, and the plague eventually ran out of steam.

Smallpox, on the other hand, racked Europe for centuries, a major killer until Edward Jenner found a vaccine in 1796. After a successful inoculation campaign in Asia during the 1970s, the World Health Organization announced in 1979 that smallpox had been wiped out.

continued

continued

A Massachusetts killer

Deaths from the flu epidemic of 1917–18 included half a million Americans. In Massachusetts alone, it killed 15,000 people in four months. At the pace it was spreading, the virus would have wiped out civilization in weeks, but, like the Black Death, people recovered from it and became immune.

Typhus spread quickly from 1918 to 1922 because of overcrowding and unsanitary conditions in prison camps and refugee homes. Some 3 million people died before the disease ran its course.

The polio epidemic infected some 400,000 Americans during its peak from 1943 to 1956 and killed about 22,000 of them by paralysis and respiratory failure. Panicky parents wouldn't let their children swim in public pools, and ineffectual quarantines were imposed on entire towns. After the Salk and Sabin vaccines were introduced in 1955 and 1961, polio all but vanished in the United States. Brazil has wiped it out over the past five years by immunizing 20 million children across the country. It remains a problem in less developed nations.

Compared with plagues of the past, AIDS is relatively difficult to contract. Unlike the Black Death, it is not spread by insect bites. Unlike smallpox, it is not spread by casual skin contact. Unlike influenza, it is not spread through coughs and sneezes. And unlike typhoid, it is not spread through contaminated water.

But that's about the only positive thing about AIDS. It is the first sexually transmitted disease of pandemic proportions—an epidemic that ranges beyond one or two countries. While syphilis and its ilk ravaged humankind for many centuries until the advent and wide use of penicillin in the 1940s—and still bedevil Third World countries—they never decimated entire populations. If a vaccine does not appear until the turn of the century, the death toll could be in the tens of millions. And so far there's no evidence that AIDS will die out on its own.

By Stacy Wells

Reading for Meaning

1. What is the main idea of the article?

2. How does the writer support the main idea?

3. Wells uses both comparison/contrast and chronological order in her article. In what ways does Wells claim that AIDS is different from other major epidemics?

4. What are some of the serious differences between AIDS and the other "killer illnesses of history" that Wells points to in the concluding paragraph?

5. Do you think that there will always be some terrible disease present to ravage mankind? Much of the research in genetic engineering being done now has caused scientists to worry that new and dangerous bacteria could be accidentally loosed upon the environment by incautious experiments. What is man's responsibility for widespread diseases like bubonic plague and AIDS?

Vocabulary in Context

Write down the definition of the italicized words below taken from the article. Try to guess the meaning from the context. Use a dictionary only if you have to.

1. "With cases doubling every 13 months, AIDS will soon take its place in the [a.] *rogue's gallery* as one of the world's major [b.] *scourges*."

2. "While syphilis and its [a.] *ilk* ravaged humankind for many centuries until the advent and wide use of penicillin in the 1940s—and still bedevil Third World countries—they never [b.] *decimated* entire populations."

Writing from Reading

For each of the following assignments, remember to consider your *subject, purpose,* and *audience.*

1. Using the information from the article, compare AIDS with other "killer illnesses." Use either the side-by-side method or the one-at-a-time method. Begin with freewriting or brainstorming and write at least one revised draft.

2. Write a short essay in which you describe the future spread of AIDS— for example, what groups of people and what geographical areas do you think will be hit hardest? Do your prewriting, write one rough draft, and write a final draft.

3. *Peer reading assignment.* Do either of the assignments above, sharing your work at each stage of the writing process with the other students in your group.

READING: "AIDS: A CRISIS IGNORED"

Before reading the following *U.S. News & World Report* editorial by Mortimer B. Zuckerman, try to turn the title into a question—for example, Why has AIDS been ignored? Using your answer, predict on a piece of paper the content of the article.

Now read the first and last paragraphs of the essay:

You have a friend or an employee with AIDS who remains sexually active with various women. What is your moral obligation to this person? To the women whose health he is jeopardizing? To the community or to other employees? Is silence an act of omission— the moral equivalent of being accessory to an assault or even to murder? Or is disclosure of his condition a betrayal? Certainly it is a violation of privacy, and it probably also threatens his livelihood.

• • •

At the heart of the innumerable individual tragedies of the AIDS epidemic, there are fundamental tensions between the rights of the individual to civil liberty and the role of the state in assuring the public welfare. How we reconcile these values will say much about our nation as we confront what may be the gravest public-health crisis in our history.

Make a new prediction.

AIDS: A CRISIS IGNORED

by MORTIMER B. ZUCKERMAN
Chairman and Editor-in-Chief of *U.S. News & World Report*

You have a friend or an employee with AIDS who remains sexually active with various women. What is your moral obligation to this person? To the women whose health he is jeopardizing? To the community or to other employees? Is silence an act of omission—the moral equivalent of being accessory to an assault or even to murder? Or is disclosure of his condition a betrayal? Certainly it is a violation of privacy, and it probably also threatens his livelihood.

These new questions will become an everyday concern for all of us. For AIDS isn't just a gay disease or a drug users' disease. It's everybody's disease. There are at least 1.5 million people in the U.S. who carry the AIDS virus. Each one puts his or her sexual partners at risk. No wonder there is concern that AIDS may be on the verge of "breaking out." Even the most conservative estimates agree that by 1991 AIDS will be one of the worst epidemics in U.S. history. There may well be panic. Now, when the public mood is anxious but rational, is the time for political leadership to form public policy.

Our government has been too passive in the face of this terrible disease. Even more alarming is the complacency of individuals. Behavior that spreads the virus is hardly changing, at least among heterosexuals. People still engage in casual sex without using a condom, which shields against the virus. Drug users still share contaminated needles. Recently a sensitive and powerful Phil Donahue show on AIDS got unimpressive ratings. Massive public education is overdue. Britain is years behind the U.S. in the incidence of AIDS, but its Conservative government has embarked on a major campaign advocating condom use.

We have to go further than education, but how much further is a sensitive question. There is a serious case for blood testing to identify carriers of the AIDS virus.

Blood screening has one enormous advantage. It is the only way, given the disease's long latency period, that someone can determine if he or she is a virus carrier. But most people shun voluntary testing. They fear a breach of confidentiality and the risk of blood-testing errors—understandable given the social stigma that accompanies AIDS and the risks to one's job, housing and friendships.

What about mandatory testing? Does government responsibility for the public welfare carry with it an obligation to alert the infected and the uninfected populations about the presence of the disease? There is precedence for mandatory testing to detect venereal disease that is nowhere near as deadly as AIDS—for example, to secure marriage licenses. Opponents would argue that mandatory testing carries with it Orwellian overtones of government intrusion into an individual's most intimate privacy. So it does. But consider the opposite position: Has anyone a right to a privacy that menaces public health?

Before public fears slip into public furor, there must be a forum for the debate that is constructive and reasoned. We have to find a way to protect the rights of the victim without at the same time victimizing the public. The issues are explosive and controversial. Even simple sex education for children has long been opposed by certain parents. Many would deplore pro-viding free sterile needles to drug users when we are in the middle of a campaign to stamp out drugs altogether. Beyond that, there are complex issues of the legal obligations of employers, landlords and insurers to guarantee that AIDS victims do not become economic and social untouchables, and we have not even begun to think about the enormous financial burdens of medical treatment, or the rights of victims to determine the time and manner of their own death. No moral issues of our times have had such profound implications for social policy.

The President should take the initiative. He should form a national commission on AIDS. Its members should be so authoritative that their report will serve as a catalyst for public debate.

At the heart of the innumerable individual tragedies of the AIDS epidemic, there are fundamental tensions between the rights of the individual to civil liberty and the role of the state in assuring the public welfare. How we reconcile these values will say much about our nation as we confront what may be the gravest public-health crisis in our history.

Reading for Meaning

1. What is the thesis of the editorial?
2. How does Zuckerman support his thesis?
3. In the first paragraph, Zuckerman raises questions about "moral obligations." Give some examples of the kinds of questions he raises.
4. Zuckerman predicts that because people may be in a panic about the AIDS epidemic by 1991, now is a good time for national leadership. Why?
5. What examples does Zuckerman give to suggest that heterosexuals are too complacent about AIDS?
6. What is one great advantage of blood testing for AIDS?
7. Why are people afraid of voluntary blood testing for AIDS?
8. What are the two sides to the question of mandatory blood testing?

9. According to Zuckerman, there are "two fundamental tensions" caused by the AIDS question. What are they?

Vocabulary in Context

Write down the definition of each of the italicized words below taken from the article. Try to guess the meaning from the context. Use a dictionary only if you have to.

1. "Our government has been too passive in the face of this terrible disease. Even more alarming is the *complacency* of individuals."

2. "Blood screening has one enormous advantage. It is the only way, given the disease's long *latency* period, that someone can determine if he or she is a virus carrier."

3. "Opponents would argue that mandatory testing carries with it *Orwellian* overtones of government intrusion into an individual's most intimate privacy."

4. "No moral issues of our times have had such *profound implications* for social policy."

Writing from Reading

For each of the following assignments, remember to consider your *subject, purpose,* and *audience.*

1. Freewrite or brainstorm about the reasons for AIDS being a "crisis ignored." Then write a rough draft and a revised draft on the topic.

2. Write an essay about whether or not we should be doing more about AIDS in America right now. Use prewriting and revision techniques.

3. *Peer reading assignment.* Do either of the assignments above, sharing your work at each stage in the writing process with the other students in your group.

READING: "MUSCLING IN"

We'll now turn from AIDS to another public-health concern—the increasing use of steroids, drugs that bulk up the body at the cost of putting the user's long-term health at grave risk. This first of three articles in the *Wall Street Journal* on the physical and psychological dangers of steroids to both the individual user and society focuses on the growing demand for steroids and the drug trafficking trade that has grown to satisfy it. Before reading the piece, by Stanley Penn, look at the title and subtitles:

Muscling In

As Ever More People Try Anabolic Steroids, Traffickers Take Over

Dope Dealers Smuggle Drugs From Mexico for Athletes And for the Merely Vain

Sideline Business of the Gym

Write down what you think the article will say.
Now read the first two and last two paragraphs:

The Seoul Olympic Games may be best remembered for their still-unfolding doping scandals. But the uproar over steroid use by Canadian sprinter Ben Johnson and other world-class athletes overshadows an even more ominous trend: a growing appetite for the muscle-building drugs among fitness buffs, student athletes and skinny youths yearning to bench-press like an Arnold Schwarzenegger.

"Bulging muscles are in," says Don Leggett, an official of the federal Food and Drug Administration. "Guys want to look good at the beach. High-school kids think steroids may enhance their ability to get an athletic scholarship, play pro sports or win the girl of their heart. Steroid use in this country has spread down to general people."

• • •

As such use suggests, convincing users that anabolic steroids are bad remains a serious obstacle. It is undeniable that steroids build strength. "The temptation is powerful," says Mr. Ventura, the former pro wrestler. "I took oral steroids, 15 milligrams per day. In 30 days, my bench press went from 315 pounds to 390 pounds. Normally, it takes six months."

Mr. Ventura, 37, says he quit anabolic steroids in 1981, because "I didn't want to tear my body apart." Today, he is a commentator on a weekly wrestling TV show. His photo appears on posters the FDA is shipping to the nation's high schools this month. The fierce-looking, hairy-chested Mr. Ventura, a ring dangling from one ear, is shown saying, "Don't pump trouble. Stay away from steroids."

Write down a further prediction.

As you read the entire article, note what facts the writer uses to persuade you that his position is correct.

Muscling In

As Ever More People Try Anabolic Steroids, Traffickers Take Over

---

Dope Dealers Smuggle Drugs From Mexico for Athletes And for the Merely Vain

---

Sideline Business of the Gym

BY STANLEY PENN

Staff Reporter of THE WALL STREET JOURNAL

The Seoul Olympic Games may be best remembered for their still-unfolding doping scandals. But the uproar over steroid use by Canadian sprinter Ben Johnson and other world-class athletes overshadows an even more ominous trend: a growing appetite for the muscle-building drugs among fitness buffs, student athletes and skinny youths yearning to bench-press like an Arnold Schwarzenegger.

"Bulging muscles are in," says Don Leggett, an official of the federal Food and Drug Administration. "Guys want to look good at the beach. High-school kids think steroids may enhance their ability to get an athletic scholarship, play pro sports or win the girl of their heart. Steroid use in this country has spread down to general people."

The Johnson case, some people have hoped, may take some of the shine off steroids. After all, the runner's positive test has cost him a gold medal, adulation, a new 100-meter-dash world record, and millions in endorsement money. But the reverse may be happening. "Since the Ben Johnson episode, kids are coming into gyms asking for steroids because they want to run faster," says Bob Goldman, chief physician and chairman of the drug testing committee of the International Federation of Body Builders.

The Big Boys

Now illicit steroids are a $100 million-a-year market, federal authorities say. And now, supplanting the doctors who have improperly given athletes the drugs, the real experts of the dope-supply business are getting involved: gangs of narcotics traffickers. "Steroids constitute a growing threat to our national health and safety," warned Gene Haislip, a Drug Enforcement Administration official, in House testimony recently.

Steroids are not, however, on the list of substances the DEA goes after. And, reflecting the drugs' ambiguous image, the effort to suppress them faces an unusual problem: Steroids are also used by some iron-pumping police officers.

Anabolic steroids are synthetic hormones developed to prevent the wasting away of muscle in debilitating illnesses. In healthy people, they promote muscle strength and mass. But prolonged use can also lead to stunted growth in youngsters, high blood cholesterol, kidney disease and even fatal liver cancer. Because anabolic steroids are similar to the male hormone testosterone, they can prompt a male's body to make less of its own testosterone, resulting in shrunken testicles and feminized breasts.

The drug, either oral or injected, is approved for only a few disorders, among them certain cases of anemia and breast cancer.

We Deliver

Increasingly, steroids now are smuggled into the U.S. from Mexico or Europe, then dispensed by mail or through health clubs and gyms. Gyms "are a hotbed" for steroid sales, says Dr. Goldman of the body-builders federation. "Kids who work in these gyms make $4, $5 an hour," he says. "Now some are making $1,000 a week in cash selling steroids. Membership in some gyms isn't going that well, so they start a steroid business. They make a lot more from that than from memberships."

Jesse Ventura, a former professional wrestler, says a steroid dealer pays almost daily visits to the suburban Minneapolis gym he goes to. "He stays for an hour or two. He claims he only makes $10,000 a year on steroids. Yet he drives a $70,000 Turbo Porsche."

The markup certainly is attractive. A steroid advertised as Dianabol retails for $5 a bottle in Tijuana, Mexico (no prescription is needed). Traffickers peddle it for $18 a bottle to U.S. dealers, who sell it to users for about $50 a bottle. And the merchandise moves. Some big-time traffickers have notified their dealers that they won't accept orders under $100,000.

Price Lists and Codes

Traffickers typically store the steroids in stash houses, "then rent an office and do a mail-order business," says William Gately, a Customs agent in Phoenix. "They send out price lists to people with access to major health clubs. They take orders over the phone, then send the steroids through U.S. mail or overnight delivery. Payments are sent in cash."

Dealers speak in code when ordering. Two bottles of injectable Dianabol may be "D-2," for instance, says narcotics investigator Steven Stogsdill, of Grand Junction, Colo. A multi-state team he is part of is investigating a California-based network suspected of shipping steroids in Texas, Kansas, Oklahoma, Nevada, Ohio, Missouri, and Louisiana.

To the traffickers, this is serious business. According to criminal charges filed in San Diego federal court last year, when a man in Phoenix reneged on a steroid deal, his supplier sent an emissary named Leonard T. Swirda. Mr. Swirda took along an accomplice carrying a 12-inch club, a double-edged knife and leather gloves weighted with metal, says the indictment, which accuses Mr. Swirda of beating and cutting the dealer. In a separate action, Mr. Swirda last May was indicted for cocaine trafficking in a Spokane, Wash., federal court. He has pleaded innocent in both cases.

More than half the steroids smuggled into the U.S. are counterfeit, bearing the names of reputable manufacturers. Most supplies come from Mexico. While often just as effective, some of the counterfeits are produced in makeshift, unsanitary labs and are of dubious purity, lawmen say.

Mexican-made steroids might have had tragic consequences at a small college in Rangely, Colo. A student at Colorado Northwestern Community College was arrested in April for peddling steroids to fellow students. The 19-year-old bought them in Juarez, Mexico, for $400 and resold them for 10 times that, to 10 to 25 students at the school in Rangely, Colo.

continued

continued

"These were men and women interested in amateur athletics, basketball and weight-lifting," says the Rangely police chief, Alan Pfeuffer.

When chemists tested the steroids, they found high concentrations of cortisone, a different kind of steroid that is a byproduct of anabolic-steroid manufacture and is supposed to be removed. When injected, it could kill a person who was allergic to it, and in any case cortisone use needs to be cut gradually to avoid severe side effects. The Rangely police chief hurriedly offered students a doctor's aid in getting off cortisone, and several took him up on it.

The Mexican sources of steroids are quite handy. It is a mere 20-minute drive from San Diego to the Hotel Fiesta Americana in Tijuana, where, in Suite 408, United Pharmaceuticals of Mexico offers "unlimited quantities" of steroids at "unbeatable prices," according to a sales brochure. On a wall is a poster of a woman pumping iron.

The receptionist hands a reporter a price list. "Tell your friends there is no prescription necessary to obtain steroids," the list says. And: "We happily accept American Express and Master Cards."

Three bottles said to be steroids cost $58.89 in U.S. cash. One contains tablets, the other two an injectable liquid. The labels suggest the drugs come from prominent pharmaceutical makers. The bottle of Dianabol, for example, bears the name "Ciba Geigy" of Colon, Panama. But the Swiss-based drug giant never made Dianabol in Panama, halted all production world-wide in 1982 and destroyed its inventory, according to a U.S. Ciba-Geigy spokeswoman.

The firm in Suite 408, United Pharmaceuticals of Mexico, is a leader in the illicit steroid market, according to a U.S. indictment filed in San Diego last year. It also names the firm's affiliate, Laboratorios Milano de Mexico, and its owner, Juan Macklis. Neither Mr. Macklis—a Mexican citizen also known as John Fontana—nor his companies have answered the criminal charges. He is considered a fugitive, a prosecutor says.

Traffickers ship Mexican steroids to the U.S. concealed in vehicles, says Kenneth Ingleby, a U.S. Customs official in San Diego. Delivery people, called "mules," get $600 to $1,500 a shipment. A mule typically deposits his shipment in a motel room inside the U.S. border. Then the purchaser, after paying cash to the Mexican supplier, receives motel-room keys, collects the order and is gone.

Dozens of Convictions

U.S. Justice officials claim some success against steroid traffickers: They have obtained federal convictions or guilty pleas from 60 individuals in the past 30 months, and 120 more people face charges. Rising prices suggest that the arrests have caused some shortages, says Philip L.B. Halpern, an assistant U.S. attorney in San Diego.

Mr. Macklis's operation was badly hurt last year with the arrest of "numerous individuals" he had hired to smuggle steroids, according to the indictment. Turning to free-lancers, Mr. Macklis asked Eric F. Kelly to smuggle "approximately $100,000 worth of steroids each week" into the U.S. for a single customer, according to federal charges against Messrs. Macklis and Kelly. Mr. Kelly pleaded guilty to a conspiracy-fraud charge last November.

But despite Justice Department claims, many steroid traffickers seem to stay one step ahead of the law. To avoid border risks, some traffickers have begun manufacturing in the U.S. At least one clandestine lab has been shut down: Fountain Valley Research Laboratories Inc., 35 miles south of Los Angeles. Operated by Jeffrey Feliciano, the lab produced what were billed as East German steroids. The labels read: *Eigentum Der DDR—Versen-*

den Gesetzlich Verboten—"Property of GDR, export prohibited."

The steroids fetched a premium $180 per bottle. "East German steroids are rated the best," says a California lawman. "Their athletes have the reputation of being better, bigger and stronger."

Earlier this year, Mr. Feliciano pleaded guilty in a Westminster, Calif., state court to conspiracy to make steroids illegally, drawing a one-year jail sentence. He also faces a federal charge, to which he has pleaded innocent.

The Drug Enforcement Administration's 2,800 agents aren't apt to be on the trail of steroid dealers anytime soon. A bill in the House would give the DEA jurisdiction, but the drug agency itself opposes the bill. It says it doesn't have the resources. Unauthorized steroid sale now is a misdemeanor, though legislation moving through Congress would make it a felony.

Off the Scent

Another problem is that dogs used by U.S. Customs agents to sniff out concealed heroin and cocaine so far haven't been able to detect steroids.

Then there's the matter of local police departments. Some policemen—how many, nobody knows—themselves use illicit steroids to increase physical strength. "It's a macho thing," says a U.S. prosecutor. "This is a matter of concern. A cop buying steroids from somebody isn't out to see that guy get busted."

As such use suggests, convincing users that anabolic steroids are bad remains a serious obstacle. It is undeniable that steroids build strength. "The temptation is powerful," says Mr. Ventura, the former pro wrestler. "I took oral steroids, 15 milligrams per day. In 30 days, my bench press went from 315 pounds to 390 pounds. Normally, it takes six months."

Mr. Ventura, 37, says he quit anabolic steroids in 1981, because "I didn't want to tear my body apart." Today, he is a commentator on a weekly wrestling TV show. His photo appears on posters the FDA is shipping to the nation's high schools this month. The fierce-looking, hairy-chested Mr. Ventura, a ring dangling from one ear, is shown saying, "Don't pump trouble. Stay away from steroids."

Reading for Meaning

1. What is the main idea of the article?

2. How does the writer support his main idea?

3. What warning does the writer give about the effect of Ben Johnson's being forced to relinquish his Olympic gold medal?

4. What are the physical dangers of steroid use?

5. What is the author's purpose in describing in such detail the "Mexican connection" for steroids and hidden drug factories in the United States?

6. What are some of the problems of detecting and arresting drug dealers?

7. Why has Jesse Ventura been chosen as spokesperson against the use of steroids?

8. Do you think that if more information about the dangers of steroids were available, young people would be scared off? Should a public document like *Understanding AIDS* be disseminated about the evils of steroid use?

Vocabulary in Context

Write down the definition of each of the italicized words below taken from the article. Try to guess the meaning from the context. Use a dictionary only if you have to.

1. "... the runner's positive test has cost him a gold medal, *adulation*, a new 100-meter-dash world record, and millions in endorsement money."
2. "... synthetic *hormones* ..."
3. "... to prevent the wasting away of muscle in *debilitating* illnesses."
4. "... *testosterone* ..."
5. "... his supplier sent an *emissary* named Leonard T. Swirda."
6. "... *cortisone* ..."
7. "... *Messrs.* Macklis and Kelly."
8. "... *clandestine* lab ..."
9. "... *misdemeanor* ..."
10. "... *felony*."

READING: "FOR TEENS, STEROIDS MAY BE BIGGER ISSUE THAN COCAINE USE"

This article by Marj Charlier appeared side-by-side in the *Wall Street Journal* with Stanley Penn's piece. First preread the title, first two paragraphs, and last two paragraphs:

For Teens, Steroids May Be Bigger Issue Than Cocaine Use

Aaron Henry wanted to play football in the worst way, but he felt he wasn't big enough or fast enough. So, at 13, he started taking anabolic steroids.

Soon it seemed his dream would come true. His first year in high school, he was a linebacker and a nose guard on a winning St. Charles, Mo., football team. As a sophomore, he had bulked up to 175 pounds.

• • •

Michelle Robins, an 18-year-old working out at The Gym in North Dallas, is frightened by her boyfriend's behavior shifts when he takes steroids. "One minute he's real nice and the next minute he's nasty," she says. And a student at Stephen F. Austin College in Nagadoches, Texas, says when he was on steroids, he would react to a traffic dispute by running the other car off the road.

Virtually no high-school steroid testing is done. A youngster can take steroids throughout his career and win a college sports scholarship before ever submitting to testing. Says Lyle Micheli, sports-medicine director at Children's Hospital in Boston, "This is something the medical community is going to have to address."

Write down your prediction about what the article will say.

Notice how effective *personal examples* are in this second article. In your writing, too, personal examples can be very powerful.

For Teens, Steroids May Be Bigger Issue Than Cocaine Use

* * *

BY MARJ CHARLIER

Staff Reporter of THE WALL STREET JOURNAL

Aaron Henry wanted to play football in the worst way, but he felt he wasn't big enough or fast enough. So, at 13, he started taking anabolic steroids.

Soon it seemed his dream would come true. His first year in high school, he was a linebacker and a nose guard on a winning St. Charles, Mo., football team. As a sophomore, he had bulked up to 175 pounds.

But he had also become aggressive, so testy that he didn't want to be with others, and he quit playing football. He turned violent, beating his girlfriend, threatening to kill his sister, and attempting suicide. Finally, as a senior in high school, he was hospitalized for drug addiction.

Today, Aaron is off steroids, but his football dream is dead. Though he rejoined the team as a high-school senior, no college would sign him because of his addiction. "I ended up destroying my dream," he says.

Hundreds of thousands of American teen-agers are taking anabolic steroids, orally or by injection, to play better or to simply look better. As many as 7% of American high-school males have taken or are taking steroids, according to a survey of 3,400 boys by Pennsylvania State University professor Charles Yesalis. In Portland, Ore., 38% of high-school football players surveyed by Oregon Health Sciences University researchers said they knew where to get the drugs.

"People think the cocaine issue is big," says Pat Croce, a Philadelphia physical therapist who works with athletes. "It's not as big as anabolic steroids. Among kids, it's epidemic."

In interviews at health clubs around Dallas, teen-agers all denied using steroids, but most said they knew someone who did. Daryl Simonetti, who worked at a recently closed gym, says 25% to 30% of the youths working out there took steroids—most simply to look good. "I'd tell them they were going to impress the women one day and be dead the next," he says.

Young people know that steroids build muscle mass and strength. "Our entire defensive line was on steroids, and they were the division champs," says one Dallas high-school student working out in a suburban health club.

Even those who know the risks may use the drugs. "I'm going to see how big I can get naturally before I decide whether to use them," says 16-year-old Jimmy Kaleta of North Dallas, who wants to be a professional wrestler. His trainer, a

continued

continued

380-pound pro, says he has taken steroids for seven years and considers the risks overblown.

Steroid use by youngsters can cause problems that last a lifetime: liver tumors, jaundice, blood disorders, sterility. The drugs can shut down bone growth plates. "You may have a kid who's genetically gifted to be 6-foot-5 and 235 pounds, but with steroids you may end up with a 5-foot-10 obese teen on your hands," asserts Keith Wheeler, a bio chemist at Ross Laboratories in Columbus, Ohio.

But doctors are equally worried about psychological effects. Aggressive behavior is almost universal among anabolic-steroid users. Harvard psychologist Harrison Pope has documented cases of full-blown psychosis, including paranoia and delusions, that followed steroid use. One steroid-pumped youngster told Prof. Pope he bought a car for $25 and had a friend videotape him as he ran it into a tree at 35 miles an hour.

Michelle Robins, an 18-year-old working out at The Gym in North Dallas, is frightened by her boyfriend's behavior shifts when he takes steroids. "One minute he's real nice and the next minute he's nasty," she says. And a student at Stephen F. Austin College in Nagadoches, Texas, says when he was on steroids, he would react to a traffic dispute by running the other car off the road.

Virtually no high-school steroid testing is done. A youngster can take steroids throughout his career and win a college sports scholarship before ever submitting to testing. Says Lyle Micheli, sportsmedicine director at Children's Hospital in Boston, "This is something the medical community is going to have to address."

Reading for Meaning

1. What is the thesis of the article?
2. How does the writer support his thesis?
3. Why does the writer use both the results of surveys about steroids as well as "case studies" of youths who take them?
4. Describe the psychological risks of steroids.

Vocabulary in Context

Write down the definition of each of the words below taken from the article.

1. "... *jaundice* ..."
2. "... *psychosis* ..."
3. "... *paranoia* ..."

Writing from Reading

For each of the following assignments, remember to consider your *subject*, *purpose*, and *audience*.

1. You are the high-school football coach of a young team that appears to be getting better. On occasion, however, you wonder how so many of

your sophomores seem to be getting bigger and stronger so fast. Worried about steroids, you write to Aaron Henry, the young man described in Charlier's article, and invite him to come speak to your team. Assume the role of Aaron Henry and write four or five paragraphs to use in your speech.

2. Jim Mitchell is a first-year wrestling coach at Deaver High. After talking with kids about the dangers of steroids, he is surprised about how vehemently the kids defend their reasons for taking them. Take on the role of a sophomore wrestler at Deaver, just beginning to acquire strength and speed from steroids, and write an organized letter to Coach Mitchell explaining your position.

3. *Simulation game.* High-school sophomore Jim Hughes is told by the football coach, Ben Fast, that he can be first string as a junior—if he can bulk up and gain some weight. The oldest child in a family of seven kids, Jim knows that the only way he can go to a four-year college is on a football scholarship. A friend of Jim's, Norb Hueller, also a football player, assures Jim that he can get steroids fairly cheaply at his health club. Bob and Mary Hughes, Jim's parents, sitting quietly in their living room, accidentally overhear the two boys discussing how they will purchase steroids. The parents decide to discuss the matter with the two boys immediately.

In small groups take one of the five roles—Jim Hughes, Ben Fast, Norb Hueller, Bob Hughes, and Mary Hughes—and write out an explanation of what you think Jim should do. Read your papers to each other, then polish and refine them at home for class next day. Several students should be chosen from the different groups to read his or her point of view to the rest of the class; the teacher and students can decide which papers are the most convincing.

READING: "CANTALOUPE FOR THE N.F.L."

The following *New York Times* piece by George Vecsey is about steroid use in the National Football League. First read the title, heading, and the first two and last two paragraphs:

Cantaloupe for the N.F.L.

All right, let's step on the scales of justice. Fess up. How many of us, unwilling or unable to exercise outdoors in the past month of rain, heat and humidity, have slouched in air-conditioned lethargy in front of the tube?

While watching The Singing Detective, the Hugging Democrats and the Self-Destructing Mets, haven't we all been hitting a bit too hard on the ice cream, the chips and the dips, the midnight sandwiches and liquid refreshment that may taste great but are not totally less filling? Pants don't fit you, Bunkie? Is that what's troubling you?

Gluttony is an honored tradition in pro football.

Then there are the so-called recreational drugs. The recent reinstatement of Michael Ray Richardson is a positive sign that the National Basketball Association will honor the two-year review process rather than the technical lifetime ban in its drug policy. Two years is quite serious enough for a first-time offender who is caught and then stays clean.

There are enough drug problems without the N.F.L. encouraging athletes to be artificially big and strong. Instead of publicity releases, how about passing the carrot sticks?

Make your prediction about what the article says (how, for example, is "cantaloupe" associated with "gluttony"?).

As you read the entire editorial, pay close attention to how different in *tone* it is from the other two articles on steroids. Is this approach more *persuasive*?

George Vecsey/Sports of The Times

Cantaloupe for the N.F.L.

All right, let's step on the scales of justice. Fess up. How many of us, unwilling or unable to exercise outdoors in the past month of rain, heat and humidity, have slouched in air-conditioned lethargy in front of the tube?

While watching The Singing Detective, the Hugging Democrats and the Self-Destructing Mets, haven't we all been hitting a bit too hard on the ice cream, the chips and the dips, the midnight sandwiches and liquid refreshment that may taste great but are not totally less filling? Pants don't fit you, Bunkie? Is that what's troubling you?

While we civilians stock up on the cantaloupe and the cottage cheese, it is also time for the National Football League to go on a diet. In a desperate attempt to be as massive as the drug-crazed lunatics on the other side of the line of scrimmage, football players have been gobbling their anabolic steroids at escalating rates in recent years.

Anabolic steroids by males can cause muscle spasms, excessive hair growth, edema, acne, headache and dizziness, prostate enlargement, breast enlargement as well as damage to the reproductive organs.

The dependence on steroids can also lead to something called "roid rage," according to Dr. Robert Voy, the director of

Gluttony is an honored tradition in pro football.

sports medicine and science of the United States Olympic Committee, in a recent article in Medical Tribune. And the N.F.L.'s own expert, Dr. Forrest Tennant, recently said steroids are now being seen as addictive.

The league is so disturbed by the medical evidence—which has merely been coming out over the past decade— that any player who tests positive for steroids may be disciplined. If he is caught twice. Sometime in the future. Maybe.

The bold new policy was unveiled last week as Commissioner Pete Rozelle issued his annual memo on drug abuses, this one a 15-page manifesto.

●   ●   ●

In the recent past, only a few enlightened linemen with irreplaceable skills like Fred Dryer and Alan Page have declined to balloon themselves up toward 300 pounds. As pointed out in these pages yesterday, Page, who will be inducted into the pro Hall of Fame on Saturday, angered Coach Bud Grant of the Minnesota Vikings by keeping his frame lean and healthy.

The average big boy coming out of college, in a desperate bid to play a game or two in the N.F.L., has gone out and found steroids wherever he could. Coaches never urge their players to do anything illegal. As long as most of the bulk is muscle, coaches don't want to know what laboratory it came from.

Now it is time for the N.F.L. to put its money where its publicity machine is. The league should encourage good health by putting in a weight limit for every 11-man unit that takes the field.

An arbitrary glance at last year's Giants roster yielded an average of 235 pounds for the starting offensive unit and 233 pounds for the defense. Let's limit each unit to an average of 220 pounds per player.

How would it work? The league could surely afford some of those giant truck scales that are used to weigh 16-wheel rigs along the interstates.

Picture it. Giants have third-and-2 on the Jets' 9-yard-line. Joe Walton waves in his short-yardage unit. All 11 Jets crowd together on the truck scale. The crowd grows quiet. But one of the Jets' linebackers ate a double helping of steak and fries at the Sunday morning meatfest. Suddenly, lights go off and sirens start wailing. Jets overweight. Penalty of 5 yards.

Frankly, the suspense of the weigh-in before every play could eliminate the dull spots of football, where nothing much happens for 30 seconds at a time. Imagine the tension late in the game as the coaches huddle with hand-held computers, debating whether their 260-pound nose guard will tip the scales. Picture the graphics television could use.

Or they could go with weight classes, like boxing and amateur wrestling. You could use three heavyweights, five middleweights and three lightweights at all times. Color their helmets red, white and blue.

Either way, this would encourage more jogger physiques like that of Alan Page and fewer appliance physiques like that of William (Refrigerator) Perry. The Bears have tried to bring the talented and athletic Mr. Perry close to 300 pounds, but he is now apparently taking treatment for an "eating disorder."

●   ●   ●

continued

continued

One does not like to joke about a possible addiction to food, but gluttony is an honored tradition in pro football. The former lineman Art Donovan is making a living out of his wit, his nickname—Fatso—and his obsessive diet of hot dogs and beer.

Just as Donovan needed the billowing fat to push around his opponent in less scientific times, so today's football players need bulk and power just to keep a job.

It would be unfair to single out football as the only sport—or the only occupation—with health and drug problems. Boxing rewards athletes for hitting each other in the brain pan. Many athletes are tempted to play with pain, not knowing if they can really trust the team doctor, who is paid by management.

Testing for drugs has its own problems with complicated laws and questionable technology. Pedro Delgado of Spain kept the maillot jaune, the yellow jersey of the Tour de France champion, only because he tested positive for a drug that will not become illegal until next week. Eric Griffin tested positive for a banned substance and was dismissed from the United States Olympic boxing squad without an appeal, despite his protestations that he was innocent.

Then there are the so-called recreational drugs. The recent reinstatement of Michael Ray Richardson is a positive sign that the National Basketball Association will honor the two-year review process rather than the technical lifetime ban in its drug policy. Two years is quite serious enough for a first-time offender who is caught and then stays clean.

There are enough drug problems without the N.F.L. encouraging athletes to be artificially big and strong. Instead of publicity releases, how about passing the carrot sticks?

Reading for Meaning

1. What is the main idea of the editorial?
2. How does the author support the main idea?
3. Why does the author contrast "we civilians" with the "drug-crazed lunatics" of football?
4. What does the writer think about the N.F.L.'s current policy regarding steroid use?
5. Why does Vecsey present his "weight-limit" solution to the steroid problem?
6. Does Vecsey's humor work in this piece about a serious problem?

Vocabulary in Context

Write down the definition of each of the italicized words below taken from the article. Try to guess the meaning from the context. Use a dictionary only if you have to.

1. "How many of us . . . have slouched in air-conditioned *lethargy* in front of the tube"
2. ". . . *edema* . . ."
3. ". . . a 15-page *manifesto*."

Writing from Reading

For each of the following assignments, remember to consider your *subject*, *purpose*, and *audience*.

1. Although this editorial examines the same subject—steroids—as the other two pieces, the writer's tone is quite different. Give some examples of Vecsey's humor.

2. Compare Vecsey's article with the two pieces on steroids from the *Wall Street Journal*.

3. *Simulation game*. Todd Pierce is a senior football player at a major university. At 6-2 and 190 pounds, Pierce is told by the pro scout, Jim Winters, that he must get bigger and stronger if he wants to play in the N.F.L. Winters makes his comments to Todd, his fiancée Mary, and his college coach, Bob Johnson, in a quiet dinner at a local restaurant. Divide into groups of four and take one of the four roles—Todd Pierce, Jim Winters, Mary, or Bob Johnson—and write an explanation of what you would say at dinner that night. Share your writing with the rest of your group, and make a revised version for the next class.

CHAPTER
13

Argument Writing

Most college writing argues for a point of view; it demands from the writer clarity and strong evidence, not the impulsive display of emotion and impromptu reasoning associated with oral arguments. It must also be fair, weighing both sides of an issue and presenting opposing views justly. The persuasive writer steers the reader toward his or her way of thinking by logically arguing in such a way that the reader accepts the writer's conclusion as his or her own. Arguing well is more than an academic skill; it is necessary in daily life, too—whether trying to convince the boss of your plan, a client of your product, or a policeman of your innocence.

The pattern for argument writing is very similar to that for the essay exam:

1. Introductory paragraph ending with a thesis
2. Paragraph on opposing point of view, perhaps with supporting reason(s)
3. Paragraph refuting the opposing point of view and establishing your own
4. Paragraph(s) giving supporting reasons for your point of view
5. Conclusion

READING: "VALUES, OPPORTUNITIES AND UNWED PARENTHOOD"

The following article by David Blankenhorn follows the classic pattern of argument writing: introduction, refutation of opposing points of view, and presentation of the author's own views. First do your prereading. On a piece of paper predict the content of the article from the title and biographical note:

Values, opportunities and unwed parenthood

• • •

David Blankenhorn is codirector of the Institute for American Values, a public policy organization in New York that does research on family issues and is sponsoring a national Commission on the American Family.

Now read the first and last two paragraphs:

Unwed teenage parents have become one of our most intractable social dilemmas. A recent Harris poll found that more than 80 percent of Americans regard teen pregnancies as "a serious national problem" requiring new efforts by schools, parents and the media. In the last year, a spirited debate has erupted over the wisdom of allowing school-based health clinics to prescribe or dispense contraceptives to teenagers. Even presidential aspirants, looking to 1988, are staking claims to the issue, often as part of a broader "profamily" program.

Despite this flurry of attention, there has been little progress in reaching a national consensus about even the definition of the problem, much less the proper response. Why is this the case?

• • •

Better education also means teaching values. For example, sex education should not only do a better and earlier job of imparting biological knowledge but should be combined with what some school curriculums now call "family life education" designed to reinforce family values, encourage sexual responsibility and promote communication between students and their parents.

These ideas suggest an approach that is neither liberal nor conservative, Republican nor Democratic. They seek to address the causes, not just the symptoms, of unwed parenthood. They reflect the belief that strong values and greater opportunities can work together, not against one another in some false political antagonism. Perhaps, as we look ahead to the post-Reagan era of social policy, it is a program whose time has come.

Write down a further prediction.

As you read the whole article, try to see *how* and *where* the writer divides his argument into three parts: introduction, refutation of opposing arguments, and presentation of his own point of view.

Values, opportunities and unwed parenthood

By David Blankenhorn

Unwed teenage parents have become one of our most intractable social dilemmas. A recent Harris poll found that more than 80 percent of Americans regard teen pregnancies as "a serious national problem" requiring new efforts by schools, parents and the media. In the last year, a spirited debate has erupted over the wisdom of allowing school-based health clinics to prescribe or dispense contraceptives to teenagers. Even presidential aspirants, looking to 1988, are staking claims to the issue, often as part of a broader "pro-family" program.

Despite this flurry of attention, there has been little progress in reaching a national consensus about even the definition of the problem, much less the proper response. Why is this the case?

The key facts are simple enough: About one million teenagers become pregnant each year. After abortions and miscarriages, this results in about 500,000 births. Contrary to what many people believe, the rate of teenage childbearing has been declining for years; due to contraception, abortion and delays in marriage, it is much lower than it was in 1960.

The crux of today's crisis is unwed parenthood. The percentage of teenage mothers who are unmarried has more than tripled in the last 25 years, from 15 percent in 1960 to 56 percent in 1984. Four out of 10 white teen mothers are unwed, compared to fewer than one in 10 in 1960. Today nine out of 10 black teen mothers are unmarried, up from four in 10 in 1960. Indeed, while minority teens make up only 27 percent of the adolescent popula-tion, they account for nearly 60 percent of all births to unwed teens.

These statistics define the heart of the issue. All the social science evidence available points to an inextricable link between unwed parenthood and a host of evil: poverty, infant mortality, joblessness, long-term welfare dependency, school failure, crime and family breakdown. In 1985, births to teenage mothers cost taxpayers more than $16 billion in welfare outlays alone. The complete costs, of course—the individual and social costs of broken lives—cannot be calculated.

The National Research Council's recently released study, "Risking the Future," illustrates, unfortunately, how many liberals approach this crisis. Their central policy recommendation is to increase the use and availability of contraceptives, especially through school-based clinics. Contraceptive services, they urge, should be inexpensive or free, should be advertised to teens through the media and should not require parental consent. In addition, they endorse a wide range of services and programs—from sex education to health care—for teenage mothers and their children.

The flaw in this approach is that it reduces the problem of unwed parenthood to one of contraceptive ignorance. But neither common sense nor the report's own evidence supports such a notion. About 85 percent of sexually active teenagers report using contraceptives, though some are irregular users. Yet what mainly determines teenagers' sexual behavior is not what they know about birth control, but what their world is like and what they believe about themselves. Do they come from strong, intact families? Do they do well in school? Do they feel good about themselves? Do they believe that unwed parenthood is morally wrong? Do they believe the future holds opportunity for them?

The determinant questions, in short, are not about the mechanics of contraception but about opportunity, self-perception and values. To avoid unwed parenthood, teenagers must have more than the means; they also must have the motive. No strategy which avoids these facts will be effective.

The authors of "Risking the Future" are especially weak on the question of values. They present their findings as objective, scientific research, undistorted by moral judgments. But don't they see that moral behavior goes to the heart of the teen parenthood dilemma? Don't they see that values is what this fuss is all about?

Conservatives usually choose different issues to dodge. While they are eager to frame the problem of unwed parenthood in moral terms, their acute myopia regarding its social sources can only be understood as the product of an ideology that is impervious to evidence. This ideology holds that government never solves social problems, but always makes them worse. Thus a recently released White House report on the family blames unwed parenthood and family breakdown on "an antifamily agenda" that pursues "a government solution to every problem government caused in the first place."

This is a dangerous fantasy, which does violence not only to social reality but to the conservatives' own campaign for moral values. For by pretending that public policy can do nothing about the social conditions which foster unwed parenthood, the conservatives expose their moral arguments to charges of hypocrisy. Indeed, moral exhortation without public policies to expand opportunity will not solve the unwed parenthood crisis, and may, as conservatives like to say, make it worse.

What will work? Here are a few ideas that suggest the outlines of a fresh, bipartisan approach.

Public policies should foster stronger families and greater sexual responsibility. One idea, now being tried in Wisconsin, is to require teenage fathers, whether married or not, to assume some financial responsibility for their children. These stricter child support payments not only help mothers and their children, but also create strong reasons for boys not to make babies before they are ready to become fathers.

A serious effort to combat unwed parenthood must include an employment strategy, especially for poor and minority youth, for whom joblessness and unwed parenthood are closely intertwined. One place to start is the welfare system. Welfare payments, whenever possible, should be replaced with guaranteed jobs, including child care. Initially, such a program would be more costly than the current system, but in the long run it would offer recipients a genuine ladder out of poverty. Moreover, it would curtail the subsidies for unwed parenthood that plague the current system, replacing them with the same incentives for family formation that operate in the larger society.

The evidence is also clear that better education and stronger schools would reduce unwed parenthood. A Children's Defense Fund study found that girls with poor academic skills are five times more likely to become mothers before age 16 than are girls with even average skills. Numerous initiatives, some involving partnerships between the public and private sectors, offer at-risk teens better job skills, academic remediation and work experience leading to full-time jobs.

Better education also means teaching values. For example, sex education

continued

continued

should not only do a better and earlier job of imparting biological knowledge but should be combined with what some school curriculums now call "family life education" designed to reinforce family values, encourage sexual responsibility and promote communication between students and their parents.

These ideas suggest an approach that is neither liberal nor conservative, Republican nor Democratic. They seek to address the causes, not just the symptoms, of unwed parenthood. They reflect the belief that strong values and greater opportunities can work together, not against one another in some false political antago-nism. Perhaps, as we look ahead to the post-Reagan era of social policy, it is a program whose time has come.

David Blankenhorn is co-director of the Institute for American Values, a public policy organization in New York that does research on family issues and is sponsoring a national Commission on the American Family.

Reading for Meaning

1. What is Blankenhorn's thesis?
2. How does he support his thesis?
3. Where does Blankenhorn announce the topic of his essay?
4. How does Blankenhorn convince the reader of the seriousness of unwed motherhood?
5. Blankenhorn points out the failures of both liberals and conservatives to resolve the problems he describes. List his criticisms of each side.
6. In the last six paragraphs, Blankenhorn presents solutions to the problems he raises. Explain each of his proposed solutions.

Vocabulary in Context

Write down the definition of each of the italicized words below taken from the article. Try to guess the meaning from the context. Use a dictionary only if you have to.

1. "... *intractable* social dilemmas."
2. "... presidential *aspirants* ..."
3. "... *inextricable* link between unwed parenthood and a host of evil ..."
4. "... their acute *myopia* regarding its social causes ..."
5. "... product of an [a.] *ideology* that is [b.] *impervious* to evidence."
6. "... joblessness and unwed parenthood are closely *intertwined.*"

Writing from Reading

For each of the following assignments, remember to consider your *subject, purpose,* and *audience*; in some cases the purpose and audience call for special attention.

1. Evaluate the solutions Blankenhorn gives. Are they realistic? Why or why not?
2. Some large inner-city high schools now sponsor sex education clinics that distribute contraceptives and provide information about sex. Compare *your* opinion of such clinics with that of Blankenhorn.
3. *Simulation game.* Using Blankenhorn's ideas and your own, consider the following scenario:

   Public High is thinking of opening a new sex education clinic providing contraceptive information and devices. At a school board hearing considering the matter, a parent and a student for the clinic will present their views to be followed by a parent and student who will argue against the establishment of such a clinic.

   Assume one of the four roles—parent for, student for, parent against, student against—and construct the arguments you would use at the hearing. Use freewriting or brainstorming in composing your paragraphs.

READING: "THEY'RE PAYING THROUGH THE NOSE"

The following *Sports Illustrated* article by Douglas S. Looney is a long, complicated argument, involving facts, judgments, and the opinions of experts. First look at the title:

THEY'RE PAYING THROUGH THE NOSE

Try to turn it into a question: *Who* is paying "through the nose"? *What* are "they" paying? Now read the first two and last two paragraphs:

There's trouble in Paradise, a/k/a [also known as] the Meadowlands racetrack. Since this temple to people's insatiable quest for a no-sweat buck opened 16 months ago in a New Jersey swamp, all manner of betting, racing, attendance and purse records have been set.

But a new and unenviable record also has been established at Meadowlands, where both standardbreds and thoroughbreds race year round: most horses getting sick.

• • •

Dr. Leroy Coggins of Cornell is seeking to get horsemen to use a flu vaccine more than they have been. But the vaccine can make a horse sick for a day or two. For this reason, many horsemen shun it. So what's the answer to controlling upper respiratory illness? Says Coggins, ''Don't race as much, certainly don't race in the winter and never let horses get together." Vaporizer-like medication may help. Allergic horses may be aided by being bedded down on peat moss instead of straw and eating prepared feed instead of hay and oats. A horse can be cured by not racing him too soon after a throat ailment. But because the recommended recovery period usually is about a month, that is advice trainers find difficult to swallow. They think in terms of at least three races a month and those big numbers of Meadowlands are a strong temptation.

So all these factors—polluted air, poor weather, too much money at stake, too frequent racing (sometimes as many as three races in 10 days for a horse), too much movement of horses —are converging at the Meadowlands. And there apparently is no cure. Except moving the nation's No. 1 harness track.

On a piece of paper, predict what the article will say.

As you read the entire piece and see how Looney introduces argument after argument, try to determine what his thesis is.

THEY'RE PAYING THROUGH THE NOSE

by DOUGLAS S. LOONEY

There's trouble in Paradise, a/k/a the Meadowlands racetrack. Since this temple to people's insatiable quest for a no-sweat buck opened 16 months ago in a New Jersey swamp, all manner of betting, racing, attendance and purse records have been set.

But a new and unenviable record also has been established at Meadowlands, where both standardbreds and thoroughbreds race year round: most horses getting sick.

The track denies it. Executive Director Jack Krumpe said, "If there were such a problem, the horsemen would have come to us and told us. They haven't." Then Krumpe quietly dispatched an underling to check the story out. What Krumpe presumably is hearing back is that respiratory maladies—ailments such as coughs, sore throats and breathing problems that keep horses out of races or make them perform poorly—are rampant at the track. While this type of sickness is a growing problem around the country,

Meadowlands leads other tracks by open lengths.

For months there has been talk along the backstretch. Veterinarians and trainers say—anonymously or in very low voices—that, for sure, there is a problem. Horsemen are reluctant to knock the goose that has laid racing's largest golden egg, for Meadowlands' reputation for excellence, smart management and largess is unmatched (SI, Sept. 12).

From the day it opened, the East Rutherford track was a winner. In 181 nights of harness racing in 1977, for example, bettors pushed more than $338 million through the windows. Meadowlands became the showpiece of standardbred racing. Across the Hudson, Yonkers and Roosevelt raceways fumed as they were displaced as the ranking harness tracks in the land. Business at Yonkers nosedived so much that there is talk of letting it go to the dogs. Almost as significantly, Meadowlands is just completing a highly successful four-month thoroughbred operation—run at night, contrary to tradition and the wishes of most horsemen. Across the Hudson, Aqueduct and Belmont are uneasy. They have resorted to thousand-dollar giveaways and have hired big bands to keep bettors two-stepping to the windows.

Meadowlands has become so important and so influential that when it sneezes, tracks elsewhere tend to come down with colds—which may be more fact than hyperbole. On January 18, Meadowlands opens its second harness season, and there is apprehension, for the track can do little about most of the causes of the respiratory ailments that afflict the horses. Part of the problem is the location of the track, part that it offers such big money.

Proof of the Meadowlands malady comes from many sources. Dr. Kenneth P. Seeber, a local veterinarian, says he normally uses his fiberoptic endoscope—a flexible, $5,000 device for looking down horses' throats and around corners—eight to 10 times a week. In 1977 at Meadowlands he used it that many times a *day*. The view was not pretty. When asked if upper respiratory problems are worse at Meadowlands than anywhere else, another vet, Dr. Jim Mitchell, says, "There's no denying that." Dr. Allan Wise agrees: "Yes, absolutely." Further, says Wise, "If a horse didn't have respiratory problems at, say, Monmouth [another Jersey track], he does here; if he had problems at Monmouth, they are worse here."

Why?

A primary theory, and the one favored by many horsemen, is air pollution. Dr. Fred Adams says, "Meadowlands is a victim of its environment." Thoroughbred Trainer Don Combs says, "It's more difficult for a horse to breathe here. That's fact." And this leads to throat problems, including bleeding. One of harness racing's leading figures, Billy Haughton, says, "Sometimes the odor is so bad at Meadowlands you can hardly stand it." Son Peter chimes in, "It's a horrible place for a racetrack, animals and humans."

Horsemen get medical backing on this point. Dr. Jill Beech is an assistant professor of medicine at the University of Pennsylvania's New Bolton Center, the Mayo Clinic for horses. "I'm getting a lot of calls from Meadowlands," she says. "People are saying their horses didn't have respiratory problems elsewhere but they do there. I say, 'You're not the only one,' and they say, 'Right, I know lots of other horses here with the same problems.'" Beech tells horsemen she thinks the air pollution could be the reason and that if their animals are susceptible to respiratory difficulties, they had better take them elsewhere. "But," says Beech, "Meadowlands is where the money is."

So what does she suggest? "Well, some trainers are smart enough to race there but also smart enough not to stable there." One who will follow this course is Don Galbraith, who helped train ABC Freight, a prominent 3-year-old trotter. "We had eight horses at Meadowlands last spring," says Galbraith, "and five got sick with bad throats." This time around, he says, if he races at Meadowlands he will ship in a horse from Monticello, N.Y. and send it right back afterward. John Chapman, who is one of the nation's leading harness drivers, plans similar strategy. "There's so much of this respiratory stuff at Meadowlands," he says. "Something's wrong there."

William D. McDowell, head of the Hackensack Meadowlands Development Commission, is defensive. "I'd be hard pressed to think the air has anything to do with the health of the horses," he says. "If you go by smell alone, you can conclude that everything is rotten."

Rotten is how things frequently smell around Meadowlands. The surrounding industrial mishmash has been abused for 200 years. Every day more

continued

continued

than 16 million pounds of garbage are brought to the area from 140 or so New Jersey communities. Methane gas from the garbage sometimes catches fire and burns uncontrollably. Nearby chemical plants, including a company that makes perfume fragrances, contribute to the pollution. Heavy traffic on the adjacent New Jersey Turnpike further fouls the air. State authorities insist the carbon monoxide is within federal limits but concede that hydrocarbons, substances that are mainly emitted from vehicles and which can't be seen and are seldom smelled, are way above federal standards. Hydrocarbons create ozone, which hampers breathing. Finally, the moss in the swamps smells like rotten eggs.

McDowell does admit that "If I were a horseman, I would blame my problems on things I can see and smell. That's normal." Herb Paley, a thoroughbred trainer at Meadowlands, says, "I don't care how clean the government tells me the air is. I know it's unhealthy. I can feel it in my lungs." With that he pulls from his pockets handfuls of pills and decongestants. Veterinarian Wise says, "The quality of the air is so irritating. I feel good when I leave my home in South Jersey and awful when I get here." Byron Sullivan, supervisor of the Newark field office at the New Jersey Bureau of Air Pollution Control, confesses, "There's no way the air around Meadowlands can be beneficial to plants and animals." He suggests a return to bicycles. Regardless, Krumpe says, "The air is cleaner now than when we got here."

One firm loudly criticized by horsemen for emitting odors is Scientific Chemical Processing, Inc., right across the street from the stable area. However, Herbert Case, a vice-president, says his plant emits nothing, and he sniffs, "Our problem is those horrible odors from the racetrack." Another suspect is U.O.P., the company that makes fragrances. Daren Chenkin, a company engineer, says, "Eighty-five to 95% of the time it's not us. I tell you, we're fussy." The Air Pollution Control people say they talk to both companies, and Sullivan says U.O.P. promises to outline a program of pollution control at a meeting this month. Bob Grant, a spokesman for the Hackensack Meadowlands Commission, says, "Maybe the problem is that man is not good for his environment and the brain is an evolutionary mistake."

A major problem with horses is chronic pharyngitis, which is comparable to adenoid difficulties in children. New Bolton Center's Charles W. Raker, an expert on upper respiratory ailments, thinks that "environmental pollutants may be a significant factor" in aggravating pharyngitis. He points out that sucking in huge volumes of dirty air (a horse normally exchanges 40 liters of air a minute at rest, at least 250 under stress) can irritate the throat and lungs, which often results in bleeding.

New Jersey keeps tightening its regulations regarding use of the main antibleeding drug, Lasix. The state racing commission thinks that Lasix may mask other illegal drugs, although evidence seems to suggest that's not why the horsemen at Meadowlands are so eager to use it. Most veterinarians say Lasix lowers horses' blood pressure, which eases pressure on fragile blood vessels, which in turn lessens their chances of breaking and bleeding. "Racing with a mouth full of blood," says Seeber, "is like running with a throat full of water." About 8% of the horses at Meadowlands are injected with Lasix. Seeber, like many veterinarians, considers Lasix valuable because it enables a horse to race closer to his form, thus making him a fairer bet. An anti-Lasix vet, Jim Mitchell, says, "I don't give a damn about the $2 bettor. I care about the horse." He thinks sick animals should be rested. In his opinion the drug definitely aids breathing and this is a big competitive advantage to any horse that is injected with it, whether he's a bleeder or not.

The greenback lure of Meadowlands may cause as many problems as air pollution. Horses race at the track for around $110,000 a night. Keystone, a nearby Philadelphia thoroughbred track, averages $62,000 a day in purse money. Freehold, N.J., a harness track, averages around $25,000 a day and Philadelphia's Liberty Bell $33,000. With so much money at stake, owners—who pay up to $1,000 a month to keep a horse in training—have their heads turned by the size of the Meadowlands pots. They are not anxious to turn a horse out at the first sniffle. Again, Seeber makes a pitch for permissive medication. "It's like GM," he says. "They don't say, 'Ah, nuts, we can't seem to correct all the defects, so we're going to stop making cars.' They work on the problems."

The money attracts horses to Meadowlands from all over the country, and, naturally, they arrive with viral bugs from back home. In world-record time these germs then pass through the barns, especially those occupied by 2- and 3-year-olds. Often, horses on the verge of sickness are shipped anyway, because a Meadowlands race offers too much money to pass up. Some 5,000 horses were shipped in and out of Meadowlands in 1977. In contrast, at Roosevelt and Yonkers raceways essentially the same group of horses race all year.

In the Meadowlands barns the horses face each other. Thus, one coughing horse can ruin a lot of days for everyone else. At most tracks horses are stabled back to back, with partitions in between. Meadowlands *can* do something about its barn design, but compared to the other factors involved, this one is minor.

Year-round racing is hard on horses. Seeber says, "If you drive a car only 5,000 miles a year, it doesn't take much care. But if you drive it 50,000, it takes a lot." Still, states insist their tracks stay open year-round because they need the money. Meadowlands will contribute close to $8 million to New Jersey on a 1977 handle of approximately $500 million. Trotting's Stanley Dancer is one who doesn't think horses are getting sicker more often at Meadowlands. Rather, he believes that 12-month racing is not conducive to a horse's health.

Trainers are under pressure at Meadowlands—as elsewhere—to enter horses to fill out a field, especially in bad weather. If a horseman complies, he can expect the racing secretary to make a race especially designed for his horse at a later, more advantageous time. So everyone's back gets scratched except the horse's. Without doubt, racing in the cold seems to bother some horses. One theory is that the wintry air the horse sucks in is insufficiently warmed before reaching the lungs.

Dr. Leroy Coggins of Cornell is seeking to get horsemen to use a flu vaccine more than they have been. But the vaccine can make a horse sick for a day or two. For this reason, many horsemen shun it. So what's the answer to controlling upper respiratory illness? Says Coggins, "Don't race as much, certainly don't race in the winter and never let horses get together." Vaporizer-like medication may help. Allergic horses may be aided by being bedded down on peat moss instead of straw and eating prepared feed instead of hay and oats. A horse can be cured by not racing him too soon after a throat ailment. But because the recommended recovery period usually is about a month, that is advice trainers find difficult to swallow. They think in terms of at least three races a month and those big numbers of Meadowlands are a strong temptation.

So all these factors—polluted air, poor weather, too much money at stake, too frequent racing (sometimes as many as three races in 10 days for a horse), too much movement of horses —are converging at the Meadowlands. And there apparently is no cure—except moving the nation's No. 1 harness track.

Reading for Meaning

1. What is the main idea of the article?
2. How does Looney support his point of view?
3. Why is the title of the article appropriate?
4. Explain some of the causes of the pollution at Meadowlands.
5. Explain the physical ills the horses may sustain because of the polluted environment.
6. Even with all the problems there, why is Meadowlands so attractive to horsemen?
7. Why does New Jersey restrict the use of Lasix for race horses?
8. Does the writer cite any defenders of Meadowlands to balance his argument?
9. What suggestions does Dr. Coggins have about the problems at Meadowlands?
10. Do you agree with the author's solution for the problems at Meadowlands?

Vocabulary in Context

Write down the definition of each of the italicized words below taken from the article. Try to guess the meaning from the context. Use a dictionary only if you have to.

1. ". . . people's *insatiable* quest . . ."
2. ". . . Meadowlands' reputation for excellence, smart management, and *largess* . . ."
3. "Which may be more fact than *hyperbole*."
4. ". . . *fiberoptic endoscope* . . ."
5. ". . . chronic *pharyngitis* . . ."
6. ". . . *adenoid* difficulties . . ."

Writing from Reading

The following exercises examine several paragraphs from Looney's article in detail. First read the paragraphs and then answer the following questions.

1. From the day it opened, the East Rutherford track was a winner. In 181 nights of harness racing in 1977, for example, bettors pushed more than $338 million through the windows. Meadowlands became the showpiece of standardbred racing. Across the Hudson, Yonkers and Roosevelt raceways fumed as they were displaced as the ranking harness tracks in the land. Business at Yonkers nosedived so much that there is talk of letting it go to the dogs. Almost as significantly, Meadowlands is just completing a

highly successful four-month thoroughbred operation—run at night, contrary to tradition and the wishes of most horsemen. Across the Hudson, Aqueduct and Belmont are uneasy. They have resorted to thousand-dollar giveaways and have hired big bands to keep bettors two-stepping to the windows.

a. What is Looney's claim, the topic sentence of this paragraph?

b. List the arguments he uses to support his claim.

c. As proof that Meadowlands is a "winner," what does Looney assert has been its effect on other racetracks?

2. Proof of the Meadowlands malady comes from many sources. Dr. Kenneth P. Seeber, a local veterinarian, says he normally uses his fiberoptic endoscope—a flexible, $5,000 device for looking down horses' throats and around corners—eight to 10 times a week. In 1977 at Meadowlands he used it that many times a *day*. The view was not pretty. When asked if upper respiratory problems are worse at Meadowlands than anywhere else, another vet, Dr. Jim Mitchell, says, "There's no denying that." Dr. Allan Wise agrees: "Yes, absolutely." Further, says Wise, "If a horse didn't have respiratory problems at, say, Monmouth [another Jersey track], he does here; if he had problems at Monmouth, they are worse here."

a. What is Looney's claim, the topic sentence of this paragraph?

b. List the arguments he uses to support his claim.

c. Why does Looney use the opinions of veterinarians?

3. Which is how things frequently smell around Meadowlands. The surrounding industrial mishmash has been abused for 200 years. Every day more than 16 million pounds of garbage are brought to the area from 140 or so New Jersey communities. Methane gas from the garbage sometimes catches fire and burns uncontrollably. Nearby chemical plants, including a company that makes perfume fragrances, contribute to the pollution. Heavy traffic on the adjacent New Jersey Turnpike further fouls the air. State authorities insist the carbon monoxide is within federal limits but concede that hydrocarbons, substances that are mainly emitted from vehicles and which can't be seen and are seldom smelled, are way above federal standards. Hydrocarbons create ozone, which hampers breathing. Finally, the moss in the swamps smells like rotten eggs.

a. What is Looney's claim, the topic sentence of this paragraph? What word does he use to qualify or limit it?

b. List the arguments he uses to support his claim.

c. Why does Looney refer to state authorities on pollution?

4. . . . Seeber says, "If you drive a car only 5,000 miles a year, it doesn't take much care. But if you drive it 50,000, it takes a lot." Still, states insist their tracks stay open year-round because they need the money. Meadowlands will contribute close to $8 million to New Jersey on a 1977 handle of approximately $500 million. Trotting's Stanley Dancer is one who doesn't think horses are getting sicker more often at Meadowlands. Rather, he believes that 12-month racing is not conducive to a horse's health.

Part of the topic sentence has been deleted from this paragraph. Write down an appropriate claim based on the evidence presented in the rest of the paragraph.

5. So all these factors—polluted air, poor weather, too much money at stake, too frequent racing (sometimes as many as three races in 10 days for a horse), too much movement of horses—are converging at the Meadowlands. And there apparently is no cure. Except moving the nation's No. 1 harness track.

   a. What is Looney's claim, the topic sentence of this paragraph?

   b. List the evidence he uses to support his claim.

6. *Simulation game.* We have seen that the author of the article, Douglas Looney, believes there is no solution to the problems at Meadowlands racetrack—except to move the track, which is a serious step. In this simulation, the class has the opportunity to come up with some alternatives to Looney's proposal. Imagine that the state of New Jersey is going to hold a hearing about the fate of the racetrack, and all interested factions will be allowed to present their views in a fifteen-minute speech and a short paper. Here are the various groups that will make presentations at the hearing:

   ▲ *Owners of the racetrack.* This group of wealthy civic leaders and businessmen has invested a great deal of time and money in the racetrack, which is widely acknowledged to be one of the best run in the country. If the track were to move, it would be a disaster for them.

   ▲ *State revenue officials.* Meadowlands brings in millions of tax dollars to the state every year. This money is used primarily to fund the state school system already struggling for survival. If the track were to be closed or moved to a different state, the loss of funds would be serious.

   ▲ *Racehorse owners and trainers.* These people have a real dilemma because their horses are getting sick, yet they have always been treated fairly by the management of Meadowlands racetrack, who simply refuse to believe there is any problem with the environment at the track.

   ▲ *Veterinarians.* Almost all the local veterinarians will testify that horses are being harmed by being forced to run in the polluted air of the racetrack.

   ▲ *Fans.* They like the racetrack. It is convenient for fans both in New York and New Jersey, and the place is very well run.

     Form a group with three or four other students and choose one of the positions above to represent. Consider the different options your party has, and the arguments for and against each one. Brainstorm about this for ten minutes, and combine your list with those of the other members of the group into one master list. Next, choose a spokesperson for your group who will read its full list of arguments to the entire class. As each group in turn makes its brief presentation, write down any points you can think of to rebut those arguments opposed to your own group's interests. For homework, each student writes the best possible argument for his or her group in a four- or five-paragraph essay.

Get together in your groups again the following class and read your papers out loud to one another. Then work together to compile a master paper, a consensus of your group. Have your spokesperson read the arguments to the whole class. The teacher serves as hearing officer, keeping track on the blackboard of the facts used by each group to argue its point of view and then picking a "winner."

READING: "STUDIES LINK SUBTLE SEX BIAS IN SCHOOLS WITH WOMEN'S BEHAVIOR IN THE WORKPLACE"

Here is another piece, by Sharon E. Epperson of the *Wall Street Journal*, that is primarily argumentative. First read the title:

Studies Link Subtle Sex Bias in Schools With Women's Behavior in the Workplace

What questions can you derive from the title? For example, what *types* of women's behavior? Write down what you think the article will say.

Now read the first two and last two paragraphs:

What's holding women back as they climb the success ladder?
Classrooms may be partly to blame.

• • •

For example, the Sadkers' study included a math teacher who was active in the National Organization for Women. She told the Sadkers she probably wouldn't benefit from their training sessions on sexism in the classroom because she had been concerned about the issue for years. After viewing videotapes of her classroom interaction, however, she said she was "stunned" to find that she was talking to boys more than twice as much as to girls, and praising them four times as much.

Such disparities are the reason some educators stress the usefulness of single-sex schools, which are nonetheless on the decline. All-girl schools and women's colleges "create a more positive learning environment for females, who don't have to fear failing in front of males," maintains the University of Wisconsin's Ms. Ayer. She says she believes the schools help females get away from traditional social conditioning and give them freedom "to show what they can do."

Write down a further prediction.

As you read the entire article, look carefully at the arguments the writer uses to persuade the reader to accept her thesis.

Studies Link Subtle Sex Bias in Schools With Women's Behavior in the Workplace

By SHARON E. EPPERSON
Staff Reporter of THE WALL STREET JOURNAL

What's holding women back as they climb the success ladder?

Classrooms may be partly to blame.

Overt discrimination it isn't, for schools are increasingly offering equal opportunities to girls and boys in both formal courses and extracurricular activities, including sports. But several studies suggest that, from first grade through college, female students are the victims of subtle biases. As a result, they are often given less nurturing attention than males.

Consider these findings from studies at schools in the U.S. and Britain. Compared with girls, boys are:

—Five times as likely to receive the most attention from teachers.

—Eight times as likely to call out in class, which helps to explain why they out-talk girls there by a ratio of 3 to 1.

(When the teacher is female and the majority of the class is male, boys are 12 times as likely to speak up.)

—Twice as likely to demand help or attention from the teacher, to be seen as model students or to be called on or praised by teachers.

Researchers maintain that a chilly climate for women in the classroom undermines self-esteem and damages morale. They believe, too, that some of these patterns of student-teacher interaction may help set the stage for expectations and interactions later in the workplace.

Emotional Baggage

"Females aren't taught to be risk takers; they don't have the same autonomy as males," asserts Jane Ayer, associate dean of education and professor of counseling psychology at the University of Wisconsin, Madison. "And you take what you've learned about yourself in the classroom into the workplace."

In coed schools, researchers find that girls receive considerably less direct attention than boys. For instance, a study of teachers' interactions with pupils in more than a hundred fourth-, sixth- and eighth-grade math and language-arts classes found that boys receive significantly more praise, criticism and remedial help.

Reactions of both male and female teachers to their female students "aren't that great," says David Sadker, an American University professor of education who conducted the four-year study with his wife, Myra, also an education professor at American. Teachers often accept the girls' responses without offering constructive comment, Mr. Sadker explains.

"In the workplace," he argues, "women are less likely to present themselves as effective managers. A lot of it deals with passive roles" they assume at school.

In lower grades, other researchers have found, boys often also receive more attention through disciplinary action. These scoldings for disruptive activity can make boys "less sensitive to negative feedback from teachers" and may further their aggressive behavior, says Marlaine Lockheed, a senior research scientist for the World Bank who studied the matter while working for the Educational Testing Service in Princeton, N.J.

Yet another study, begun in 1981 by two researchers at the University of Illinois, has measured the self-confidence of 80 high-school valedictorians, salutatorians and honor students. The study found that, upon graduation, 23% of the men and 21% of the women believed they were "far above average" in intelligence. As college sophomores, only 4% of the women said they felt far above average, while 22% of the men rated themselves that way. By senior year in college, none

of the women reported feeling far above average, compared with 25% of the men.

This apparent lack of self-esteem on the part of the women appears to be rooted in classroom interaction, says Bernice Sandler, executive director of the Association of American Colleges' project on the status and education of women. Researchers, she notes, have found that even in college classes "men receive more eye contact from their professors than women, are called on more often and receive informal coaching from their instructors."

Racial prejudice can make the situation even worse. "Minority women in higher education frequently face double discrimination—once for being female and once for being racially or ethnically different," noted a 1986 report by the college association's project on women. "For example, intellectual competence and leadership ability, along with other primary academic qualities, are associated not only with males but with white males."

A More Comfortable Setting

Researchers say sexual bias leads some women to opt for courses with a large female enrollment, where they will feel more comfortable voicing their opinions. Bertha French, a junior at the University of Virginia, Charlottesville, agrees. She notes that women usually dominate discussions in her mostly female French classes; the two or three male students don't speak up so much. "I think it's because it's not considered a masculine major," she says. In her male-dominated government classes, she adds, she and other female students sometimes feel intimidated.

At many schools, students, teachers and administrators often seem unaware of everyday inequities in the classroom. Fac-

continued

continued

ulty members may consider themselves too evenhanded to discriminate.

For example, the Sadkers' study included a math teacher who was active in the National Organization for Women. She told the Sadkers she probably wouldn't benefit from their training sessions on sexism in the classroom because she had been concerned about the issue for years. After viewing videotapes of her classroom interaction, however, she said she was "stunned" to find that she was talking to boys more than twice as much as to girls, and praising them four times as much.

Such disparities are the reason some educators stress the usefulness of single-sex schools, which are nonetheless on the decline. All-girl schools and women's colleges "create a more positive learning environment for females, who don't have to fear failing in front of males," maintains the University of Wisconsin's Ms. Ayer. She says she believes the schools help females to get away from traditional social conditioning and give them freedom "to show what they can do."

Reading for Meaning

1. What is the writer's thesis?
2. How does she support her thesis?
3. What different kinds of evidence does the writer use in her article?
4. According to the article, how does racial prejudice affect discrimination against women?
5. Explain how much of the writer's argument is based on "a cause and effect" relationship.
6. Why do some educators recommend single-sex schools?

Vocabulary in Context

Write down the definition of each of the italicized words below taken from the article. Try to guess the meaning from the context. Use a dictionary only if you have to.

1. "*Overt* discrimination it isn't, for schools are increasingly offering equal opportunities to girls and boys in both formal courses and extracurricular activities, including sports."
2. "As a result, they are often given less *nurturing* attention than males."
3. ". . . *valedictorians* . . ."
4. ". . . *salutatorians* . . ."
5. "Such *disparities* are the reason some educators stress the usefulness of single-sex schools . . ."

Writing from Reading

For each of the following assignments, remember to consider your *subject*, *purpose*, and *audience*.

1. Pretend you are a grammar-school or high-school teacher in a coeducational school. What might you do to change your classroom teaching practices after reading this article? Explain your answer in an essay.
2. In a fully developed essay, state why you agree or disagree with the thesis of the article.
3. A question not raised in the article is *why* girls are given less attention than boys. If the bias exists as the article states, what is the reason for it? Explain your answer in an essay.

READING: "A RAT-INFESTED GYM IN PANAMA BREEDS PACK OF CHAMPIONS"

We'll now turn to two different viewpoints on the ethics of professional boxing. In this first article, Jose De Cordoba of the *Wall Street Journal* shows tolerance, if not outright approval, of a bloody sport. By revealing a world where boxing is a way of life, he gives the reader a unique perspective on its merits. He must thus argue with subtlety, rather than merely cite supporting facts, to persuade a less than sympathetic audience of what in this society is a controversial point of view.

First read the title and subtitle:

A Rat-Infested Gym in Panama Breeds Pack of Champions

* * *

Boxers Train There Seeking A Way Out of the Slums; Curing Ills With Red Ants

On a piece of paper write down what you think the article is about.
Next read the first two and last two paragraphs:

PANAMA CITY, Panama—The slums of this tiny nation breed fighters. The Maranon gym turns them into champions.

Panama may be able to boast more boxing champions per capita than any other country. It has had 16 world title holders, from "Panama" Al Brown in the 1930s to Roberto "Hands of Stone" Duran in the 1980s. Most of them learned how to fight at the Maranon, a rat-infested, tin-roofed converted trolley terminal.

• • •

The youngsters learn those tricks by hanging around at the Maranon. One recent day, among the usual crowd of amateurs and professionals, two 11-year-old brothers, bobbed and weaved, looking more experienced than their years. Such fighters are called *abrebocas*, which means curtain raisers.

Even the youngest contenders get a few minutes in the ring before the crowd. At the Maranon, boys as young as 11 years old sometimes open Friday night amateur matches with two-round bouts. The purse is small—the fighters collect coins thrown into the ring by spectators—but dreams of glory are enough to bring them back. "I'd like to be a world champion, like Duran," says one of the brothers, Santos Gasces, sweat streaming down his pint-sized body.

Make a new prediction.

As you read the entire article, consider the author's tone and the reasons he gives for his point of view.

A Rat-Infested Gym in Panama Breeds Pack of Champions

* * *

Boxers Train There Seeking A Way Out of the Slums; Curing Ills With Red Ants

---

By JOSE DE CORDOBA
Staff Reporter of THE WALL STREET JOURNAL

PANAMA CITY, Panama—The slums of this tiny nation breed fighters. The Maranon gym turns them into champions.

Panama may be able to boast more boxing champions per capita than any other country. It has had 16 world title holders, from "Panama" Al Brown in the 1930s to Roberto "Hands of Stone" Duran in the 1980s. Most of them learned how to fight at the Maranon, a rat-infested, tin-roofed converted trolley terminal.

Eusebio "Scorpion" Pedrosa, a former world lightweight champion who started his training here as a ragged boy of 11, calls the gym "a cradle of champions . . . a lucky place." Jose Ferrer, a former fighter who now referees amateur bouts, says, "It's everybody's alma mater."

Factory of Dreams

The Maranon is a dingy dream factory, as squalid as the slums its young boxers are fighting to leave. The roof leaks. The floor is riddled with holes and, in places, is rotted by rain. Rusty, exposed nails trip and gouge the careless. A stench of sweat, old leather, mildew and urine hangs heavy in the tropical heat.

The ring in the middle of the gym has ropes that are frayed and drooping. A few weeks ago, during an amateur fight, both boxers hit the ropes and fell out of the ring. One sprained his hand, but still managed to win the bout.

Yet the gym is an irresistible lure for boxers—amateur and professional. That is partly because the gym usually provides them a full house of admiring spectators, and "boxers love to be seen," says one promoter. Dozens of unemployed men spend hours watching the near-great and the still-unknown work out at the Maranon. Every now and then, the fans are rewarded for their loyalty. Recently, Mr. Duran, a demigod in Panama, returned to the gym for a workout.

Every weekday, dozens of boxers come here to skip rope, hit boxing bags and spar a few practice rounds. For all of them, it is a chance to pummel their way out of a life of poverty. There are no heavyweights at the Maranon. Panamanian boxers typically are underfed and scrawny, and they usually compete in weight classes below 150 pounds. But they are street-tough and hungry to win.

'Criminal Instincts'

"You need to be hungry to get into boxing," says Saul "Little Lead" Espinosa, a former boxer. A grimy towel wrapped around his neck, he watches a young boxer he is training pound a bag in the crowded gym. "You have to destroy another human being," Mr. Espinosa says. "If you don't have the heart for it, you will be destroyed. If you don't have a criminal instinct, you won't survive."

"This one," he mumbles through a toothless mouth, "has criminal instincts."

The fighter, Eduardo "Tarzan" Lopez, says he once had hopes of being a jockey, but a trainer lured him to the ring after seeing him fight at a country fair when he was 14. He is 19 now, with 30 bouts under his belt, all of which he won. A country boy, Mr. Lopez has to take a two-hour bus ride every morning to get to the gym.

A sense of obligation propels him. He says he fights in order to help support his family, which his father abandoned. His dream: "To become a world champion," he says.

Mr. Espinosa, who once helped train Mr. Duran, the three-time world champion, has a lot riding on Mr. Lopez. If the fighter makes it big, Mr. Espinosa stands to collect as much as 10% of a sizable purse, the standard trainer's fee. For now, however, the trainer lives on the few dollars he collects from the boxer's manager, a rich local businessman, and support from his sons.

Mr. Espinosa doesn't let Mr. Lopez forget how much his trainer has invested in him, though. The trainer says he has told the youth that he will "shoot him in both legs" if the boxer abandons him after making it big.

Red Ants and Spider Webs

Boxing is more a religion than a sport in Panama. In the 1970s, the country's military-controlled government promoted boxing in order to foster national pride. The late Gen. Omar Torrijos, a big boxing fan, would pay big-time U.S. promoters to give his country's top boxers shots at title bouts, a former cabinet member recalls.

Boxers who make it to the top are national heroes, held in greater esteem than most of the country's leaders, including the embattled Gen. Manuel A. Noriega. People here still talk about the day in 1980 that Mr. Duran beat Sugar Ray Leonard for the welterweight (under 147 pounds) crown. Panama erupted into a day-long fiesta. Until three years ago, Panama also rewarded its retired world champions with a pension of $300 a month.

The hazards are many, though. The Maranon doesn't have a doctor on staff, and injuries rarely get adequate medical attention. Mr. Pedrosa, the former champ, recalls how one of his trainers once used burnt spider web to treat a cut, which later

continued

continued

got infected. Another favorite remedy was a concoction of crushed red ants mixed with rubbing alcohol, which was rubbed on tired muscles.

Heart of the Slum

Jose Marmolejo, featherweight crown contender, is at the top of the gym's pecking order at the moment. Decked out in a bright red jumpsuit, a headband bending his frizzy hair into the shape of a turnip, he carves out a small practice area from the crush of spectators by jogging backwards and jabbing into the air as if fending off a swarm of bees.

He has a choice spot at the Maranon. There aren't as many holes in the floor as elsewhere in the gym. "This is my corner," he glares. "If there are other people when I come, I say 'Get out.'"

The Maranon (Spanish for cashew tree) is the heart of the neighborhood, an aging, densely-packed slum built at the turn of the century to warehouse workers digging the nearby Panama Canal. The government has demolished many derelict houses, but half-naked children still swarm around unpainted and rotting wooden houses that list like punch-drunk boxers. Wraparound porches with iron railings give the area the feel of a down-and-out New Orleans.

The Way of Life

Fighting is a way of life on these streets, and the young boys who duke it out often seem professionally trained. "You will see kids jabbing and throwing upper-cuts like professionals," says Mr. Ferrer, the referee.

The youngsters learn those tricks by hanging around at the Maranon. One recent day, among the usual crowd of amateurs and professionals, two 11-year-old brothers, bobbed and weaved, looking more experienced than their years. Such fighters are called *abrebocas*, which means curtain raisers.

Even the youngest contenders get a few minutes in the ring before the crowd. At the Maranon, boys as young as 11 years old sometimes open Friday night amateur matches with two-round bouts. The purse is small—the fighters collect coins thrown into the ring by spectators—but dreams of glory are enough to bring them back. "I'd like to be a world champion, like Duran," says one of the brothers, Santos Gasces, sweat streaming down his pint-sized body.

Reading for Meaning

1. What is the main idea of the article?
2. How does the author support his main idea?
3. Why is boxing so important in Panama?
4. What does the tone of the article reveal about the author's attitude toward boxing?
5. Why does the author call the Maranon a *"dingy* dream factory"?
6. De Cordoba emphasizes the fact that there are no heavyweight boxers at the Maranon. Why are all the boxers in lower weight classes?
7. According to Saul Espinosa, why must all good fighters have "criminal instincts"?
8. Why did the Panamanian government reward boxing heroes?

Vocabulary in Context

Write down the definition of each of the italicized words below taken from the article. Try to guess the meaning from the context. Use a dictionary only if you have to.

1. "Recently, Mr. Duran, a *demigod* in Panama, returned to the gym for a workout."
2. "The government has demolished many [a.] *derelict* houses, but half-naked children still swarm around unpainted and rotting wooden houses that [b.] *list* like punch-drunk boxers."

READING: "LET'S COUNT BOXING OUT"

This *Sports Illustrated* editorial by Frank Deford is harshly critical of boxing. Note that because Deford is advocating a popular belief (except to boxing enthusiasts) he can afford to be judgmental and satirical without alienating most of his readers.

Using your prereading techniques, read the title and subtitle:

LET'S COUNT BOXING OUT
What's sporting about men pummeling each other?

Write down what you think the article will say.
Now read the first and last paragraph:

> Now that the Super Bowl is behind us, we can turn our attention to the bout between Sugar Ray Leonard and Marvin Hagler, Fight of the Century for this year. With luck, it will also be the last boxing extravaganza to hinder the lurching progress of mankind.
>
> • • •
>
> Fortunately, those who profess these beliefs are a dying breed. Boxing has effectively choked off its future. However much attention the Leonard-Hagler fight might attract, if it is a Fight of the Century, it is not of this century but just some grim vestige of a time long gone.

Make a new prediction.
Before reading the editorial in its entirety, you should know that prior to the fight in question between Marvin Hagler and Sugar Ray Leonard, Leonard suffered a detached retina during a previous fight. Even though Leonard's eye had healed, there was some question as to whether or not he should expose himself to further possible eye damage. (The fight went ahead as scheduled, and Leonard fortunately sustained no injury to his eye during his victory over Hagler.)

LET'S COUNT BOXING OUT
What's sporting about men pummeling each other?

BY FRANK DEFORD ■

Now that the Super Bowl is behind us, we can turn our attention to the bout between Sugar Ray Leonard and Marvin Hagler, Fight of the Century for this year. With luck, it will also be the last boxing extravaganza to hinder the lurching progress of mankind.

It says a great deal about the enfeebled state of boxing that no fight of broad interest can be concocted with existing pugilists. This one is being forced on us only by bringing back the fetching Mr. Leonard from retirement and then tantalizing our most sordid instincts with the gruesome proposition that he might come away from the proceedings no longer able to make out light and form.

Sadly, it is clear to me now that boxing is never going to be banned—not in the official way that bearbaiting and lynching are outlawed. Of course, any activity whose express purpose is to amuse customers with the ''sport'' of having human beings pummel one another is patently immoral and has no place in a society that aspires to being civilized, even one that embraces Rambo. But given the prevalence of such everyday crimes against humanity as starvation, homelessness and prejudice, not even a sympathetic Congress is going to waste its time trying to proscribe an activity that physically does harm to a relatively small number of poor people.

Nevertheless, boxing's greatest sin is not that a Sugar Ray may lose his sight, a Muhammed Ali his verbal skills, a Duk Koo Kim his life. The larger damage is that boxing poisons all who are exposed to its baseness. A child watching on television who sees one man rattle another

man's brain while bystanders cheer wildly cannot help but come away with the conclusion that society approves of such amusement.

Boxing was bound to suffer its current decline, for it is simply too transparently mean to have escaped forever the harsh scrutiny it deserves. The regular and altogether ludicrous argument that you can't ban boxing and deny fans their blood, lest you deny indigent black and Hispanic boys an avenue to success, doesn't wash with any more logic than claiming that we must leave the Mafia alone rather than close off employment opportunities for industrious Sicilian tykes. The development of other professional sports, notably football, baseball and basketball, answers that labored defense in an even more direct way.

Still, it has always tickled me that boxing has done so much to destroy itself. The sport is so corrupt, so grasping, that for 30 years or more it has displayed all of its major attraction only for top dollar in theaters, while *all* other major sporting events have been seen on home TV. The result has been to remove boxing from the mainstream, sending it back to the time when bouts were forced onto barges. So now a whole generation of sports fans has grown up without having seen a live showcase boxing event.

In continuing this policy, the Blinding of Sugar Ray will be shown only on closed circuit. But it is my contention that when lesser bouts are displayed on weekend afternoons on the networks, or on ESPN or HBO in prime time, the cigarette-pack model must be followed. That is, for every hour of televised boxing, one minute must be set aside for Ali or some other poor wretched graduate of the sweet science to be duly exhibited, to mumble and shuffle and reveal how dangerous boxing can be to your health.

Gratefully, the removal of boxing to Vegasianna and to the barges-cum-theaters has also served to rob the sport of much of its literary allure. Because boxing is so primeval and dramatic, it has always attracted some superb writers, who have glamorized its cruelty and sentimentalized its nefarious ways and the scoundrels who plot its schemes. A.J. Liebling's accounts, which titillated the swells who subscribed to *The New Yorker*, epitomized this slumming genre.

Many people in boxing are indeed colorful characters. They sort of remind me of some of my old southern relatives, who always confounded me as I was growing up. Although they were among the most dear and charming humans I ever encountered, they had this one cuckoo notion—about nigras, in their case. They would give me all this mumbo jumbo about how it really had nothing to do with race (for goodness' sake!) but was all just state's rights and stuff like that. Similarly, with straight faces, boxing's defenders will claim that brutality is not the issue, that boxing is a noble exercise, equal parts art and a job bank for the disadvantaged.

Fortunately, those who profess these beliefs are a dying breed. Boxing has effectively choked off its future. However much attention the Leonard-Hagler fight might attract, if it is a Fight of the Century, it is not of this century but just some grim vestige of a time long gone.

Reading for Meaning

1. What is the thesis of Deford's editorial?
2. How does Deford support his thesis?
3. According to Deford, what damage done especially to children is "boxing's greatest sin"?
4. How has boxing "destroyed" itself?
5. Deford outlines a "cigarette-pack model" to counter the effects of boxing on network TV. Explain what the plan calls for. Do you think it would work?

Vocabulary in Context

Write down the definition of each of the italicized words below taken from the article. Try to guess the meaning from the context. Use a dictionary if you have to.

1. "... *bearbaiting* and lynching are outlawed."
2. "Of course, any activity whose express purpose is to amuse customers with the 'sport' of having human beings pummel one another is *patently* immoral . . ."

3. "... not even a sympathetic Congress is going to waste its time trying to *proscribe* an activity that physically does harm to a relatively small number of poor people."

4. "Because boxing is so [a.] *primeval* and dramatic, it has always attracted some superb writers, who have glamorized its cruelty and [b.] *sentimentalized* its [c.] *nefarious* ways and the scoundrels who plot its schemes."

5. "A. J. Leibling's accounts, which [a.] *titillated* the [b.] *swells* who subscribed to *The New Yorker* [c.] *epitomized* this slumming [d.] *genre.*"

6. "However much attention the Leonard-Hagler fight might attract, if it is a Fight of the Century, it is not of this century but just some grim *vestige* of a time long gone."

Writing from Reading

For each of the following assignments, remember to consider your *subject*, *purpose*, and *audience*.

1. Compare De Cordoba's and Deford's views on whether or not boxing provides some poor, disadvantaged youth with a chance to get out of the slums.

2. Do you think the dreams of aspiring young fighters in Panama are realistic in America? Can you think of a similar sport, like professional football or basketball, that young Americans might aspire to? In an essay, compare its advantages and disadvantages to those of boxing.

3. What is your opinion of professional boxing? Choose a thesis and then write an argument essay on your position.

4. If Deford were to examine boxing in Panama, do you think his views would be changed at all? Explain your answer in an argument essay with a clear thesis.

PART FIVE

Handling Sources

▲▲▲

CHAPTER
14

Using and Documenting
Sources Correctly

In writing essays it is important to take facts and opinions from other sources to provide evidence for your arguments or point of view. You must, however, be careful when using the words and ideas of "experts" or authorities in your writing. You must learn to correctly use and document your sources—books, newspapers, magazine articles, and so on—adapting borrowed material for your own purposes without simply copying or plagiarizing someone else's work. As a general principle, you should credit the source of *every* idea or quote you use with a footnote or some other means of documentation. In this chapter we'll examine four ways to employ source material: the direct quotation, the paraphrase, the summary, and some combination of these three methods. We will study examples from Douglas S. Looney's *Sports Illustrated* article, "They're Paying Through the Nose" (see pp. 224–27), throughout the chapter for illustrations of the correct use and documentation of sources.

THE DIRECT QUOTATION

The Direct Quotation Set Off by Itself

The simplest way to use the words and ideas of another is through direct quotation, identifying the writer or speaker and repeating his or her exact words. In arguing that conditions at Meadowlands racetrack are very harmful to horses, for example, Looney directly quotes various knowledgeable figures in Paragraph 9:

Dr. Fred Adams says, "Meadowlands is a victim of its environment." Thoroughbred Trainer Don Combs says, "It's more difficult for a horse to breathe here. That's a fact."

Notice how the direct quotation in this case is set off by itself. Looney first identifies his sources—Dr. Fred Adams and Thoroughbred Trainer Dan Combs—and then uses the word "says" to indicate the sources' actual spoken words:

Dr. Fred Adams says,

(Introduction of first source followed by a comma)

"Meadowlands is a victim of its environment."

(Actual words of speaker enclosed in quotes)

Thoroughbred Trainer Don Combs says,

(Introduction of second source followed by a comma)

"It's more difficult for a horse to breathe here. That's a fact."

(Actual words of speaker enclosed in quotes)

The Interrupted Direct Quotation

Another way to use a direct quotation is to interrupt it with the introduction of the source. Here is an example from paragraph 17:

"Racing with a mouth full of blood," says Seeber, "is like running with a throat full of water."

"Racing with a mouth full of blood,"

(First part of quote followed by a comma)

says Seeber,

(Introduction of source followed by a comma)

"is like running with a throat full of water."

(Rest of quotation with a period inside quotes)

Direct Quotation as Part of a Sentence

Another way to use a direct quotation is to incorporate it into a sentence without any punctuation. Look at this example from paragraph 16 of Looney's article:

> New Bolton Center's Charles W. Raker, an expert on upper respiratory ailments, thinks that "environmental pollutants may be a significant factor" in aggravating pharyngitis.

New Bolton Center's Charles W. Raker, an expert on upper respiratory ailments, thinks that
↑
(Beginning of Looney's own sentence)

"environmental pollutants may be a significant factor"
↑
(Direct quotation)

in aggravating pharyngitis.
↑
(End of Looney's sentence)

Plagiarism

Plagiarism is copying someone else's words or ideas and using them as your own. Students often fall victim to plagiarism when they have a long paper with many sources and try to take the easy way out—copying material without taking the trouble to document their sources. A dead giveaway that a student has plagiarized is use of vocabulary words out of character with his or her writing style, especially highly advanced or technical words. You must be scrupulous to avoid the original wording of another work when writing a summary of or paraphrasing something from it. That is why a thesaurus, which lists synonyms of words, can be helpful and keep you out of trouble.

Let's construct some phony examples of plagiarism from Looney's article. Here again is the last sentence we studied:

> New Bolton Center's Charles W. Raker, an expert on upper respiratory ailments, thinks that "environmental pollutants may be a significant factor" in aggravating pharyngitis.

Now suppose Looney had written the sentence this way:

> Environmental pollutants may be a significant factor in aggravating pharyngitis.

Because there are no quotation marks and no source is given, we must assume that the idea and words are Looney's. This would be plagiarism, Looney having copied the words and/or ideas of someone else and claimed them as his own.

Now let's construct a more subtle type of plagiarism. Imagine that Looney had written the following:

New Bolton Center's Charles W. Raker, an expert on upper respiratory ailments, thinks that environmental pollutants may be a significant factor in aggravating pharyngitis.

Even though this would have Looney acknowledging Raker as the source of this idea, it would still be plagiarism because Raker's exact words are not set off with quotation marks. A paraphrase or a summary must be in *your* words, not those of the original source.

Writing Practice

Let's now practice the three ways of using direct quotations. Review the examples on the preceding pages for each exercise.

1. In the following exercise merge the source and the direct quotation into one sentence, setting the quotation off by itself.

   EXAMPLE   Dr. Leroy Coggins of Cornell; "Don't race as much, certainly don't race in the winter, and never let horses get together."

   ANSWER   Dr. Leroy Coggins of Cornell advises, "Don't race as much, certainly don't race in the winter, and never let horses get together."

   a. Don Galbraith, who helped train ABC Freight; "We had eight horses at Meadowlands last spring and five got sick with bad throats."
   b. Herb Paley, a thoroughbred trainer at Meadowlands; "I don't care how clean the government tells me the air is. I know it's unhealthy. I can feel it in my lungs."
   c. Anti-Lasix vet Jim Mitchell; "I don't give a damn about the $2 bettor. I care about the horse."
   d. Executive Director Jack Krumpe; "The air is cleaner now than when we got here."

2. In the following exercises merge the source and the direct quotation into one sentence, interrupting the quotation with the introduction of the source.

   EXAMPLE   Dr. Leroy Coggins of Cornell; "Don't race as much, certainly don't race in the winter, and never let horses get together."

   ANSWER   "Don't race as much," advises Dr. Leroy Coggins of Cornell, "certainly don't race in the winter, and never let horses get together."

   a. Don Galbraith, who helped train ABC Freight; "We had eight horses at Meadowlands last spring and five got sick with bad throats."
   b. Herb Paley, a thoroughbred trainer at Meadowlands; "I don't care how clean the government tells me the air is. I know it's unhealthy. I can feel it in my lungs."

    c. Anti-Lasix vet Jim Mitchell; "I don't give a damn about the $2 bettor. I care about the horse."

    d. Executive Director Jack Krumpe; "The air is cleaner now than when we got here."

3. In the following exercises merge the source and the direct quotation into one sentence, incorporating the quotation into the sentence without any punctuation.

    EXAMPLE   Dr. Leroy Coggins of Cornell; "Don't race as much, certainly don't race in the winter, and never let horses get together."

    ANSWER   Dr. Leroy Coggins of Cornell advises horsemen not to "race as much, certainly don't race in the winter, and never let horses get together."

    a. Don Galbraith, who helped train ABC Freight; "We had eight horses at Meadowlands last spring and five got sick with bad throats."

    b. Herb Paley, a thoroughbred trainer at Meadowlands; "I don't care how clean the government tells me the air is. I know it's unhealthy. I can feel it in my lungs."

    c. Anti-Lasix vet Jim Mitchell; "I don't give a damn about the $2 bettor. I care about the horse."

    d. Executive Director Jack Krumpe; "The air is cleaner now than when we got here."

Capitalization and Punctuation

Below are some helpful hints about capitalization and punctuation to keep in mind when using direct quotations in your writing.

Capitalization

1. If the quotation is set off by itself and is a complete sentence, it begins with a capital letter:

> Thoroughbred Trainer Don Combs says, "*It's* more difficult for a horse to breathe here. That's a fact."

2. If the quotation is interrupted, begin the second part of it with a small letter:

> "Racing with a mouth full of blood," says Seeber, "*is* like running with a mouth full of water."

3. If the quotation is incorporated into the structure of the sentence, begin it with a small letter:

> New Bolton Center's Charles W. Raker, an expert on upper respiratory ailments, thinks that "*environmental* pollutants may be a significant factor" in aggravating pharyngitis.

Punctuation

1. Commas and periods always go *inside* end quotation marks:

    An anti-Lasix vet, Jim Mitchell, says, ''I don't care about the $2 bettor.''

2. Colons and semicolons *not part of the quotation* always go *outside* end quotation marks:

    Douglas S. Looney quotes many veterinarians in his article, ''They're Paying Through the Nose'': Doctors Kenneth Seeber, Jim Mitchell, and Alan Wise, among others.

3. An ellipsis, or omission, at the beginning or in the middle of a quotation is shown by three evenly spaced periods:

    At the end of his article, Looney summarizes the problems at Meadowlands race-track: ''. . . polluted air, poor weather, too much money at stake, too frequent racing (sometimes as many as three races in 10 days for a horse), too much movement of horses—are converging at the Meadowlands.''

    At the end of his article, Looney summarizes the problems at Meadowlands racetrack: ''So all these factors—polluted air, poor weather, too much money at stake, too frequent racing . . . , too much movement of horses—are converging at the Meadowlands.''

4. An ellipsis at the end of a quoted sentence is indicated by four periods, the first one ending the sentence:

    At the end of his article, Looney summarizes the problems at Meadowlands race-track ''. . . polluted air, poor weather, too much money at stake, too frequent racing (sometimes as many as three races in 10 days for a horse), too much movement of horses. . . .''

THE PARAPHRASE AND THE SUMMARY

An alternative to directly quoting sources in your writing is to paraphrase or summarize them. A paraphrase is an *almost word-for-word* restatement of something spoken or written, while a summary is a *concise* restatement with far fewer words. As a reader it is often difficult to distinguish a paraphrase from a summary of a source, because they are both restatements of words or ideas without the use of quotations. For the writer, especially the student writer, the summary is more difficult to compose because it involves condensing material into fewer words. It is important that you learn how to paraphrase and summarize sources correctly.

There are two guiding principles you should keep in mind when using either method: first, *always* tell your reader where the ideas you are using originated; and second, be careful not to use any of the exact words of the original source. This second rule can be very difficult to follow, but don't let it discourage you from paraphrasing and summarizing. Remember that good writing has *variety*, and that includes how sources are used. Use a thesaurus, or dictionary of synonyms, if you are having trouble rewording an idea. If a source's wording is particularly forceful or eloquent, go ahead and use it as a direct quote. On the whole, though, *don't lean too much on direct quotes* in your writing. Remember that *you* are the one writing the paper. Simply quoting each source is repetitious and boring to the reader.

The Paraphrase

For some examples of the paraphrase, let's return to Douglas Looney's article on Meadowlands racetrack. Here is a sentence from paragraph 17:

> Seeber, like many veterinarians, considers Lasix valuable because it enables a horse to race closer to his form, thus making him a fairer bet.

(Seeber's idea, Looney's words)

Here is another, longer paraphrase from paragraph 21:

> Trotting's Stanley Dancer is one who doesn't think horses are getting sicker more often at Meadowlands. Rather, he believes that 12-month racing is not conducive to a horse's health.

(Dancer's idea, Looney's words)

Let's see if we can now paraphrase one of Looney's *own* sentences from paragraph 18:

> The greenback lure of Meadowlands may cause as many problems as air pollution.

Here is how you might paraphrase Looney's sentence, expressing the same idea in roughly the same number of words, but in *different* words:

> The greed for money at Meadowlands is the source for as many of its troubles as the bad air.

Looney's Words	New Words
"greenback"	"money"
"lure"	"greed"
"cause"	"is the source for"
"problems"	"troubles"
"air pollution"	"bad air"

Now try it. Write a paraphrase of Looney's sentence, using as many of your own words as possible.

Let's try paraphrasing another of Looney's sentences, this one from paragraph 21:

> Year-round racing is hard on horses.

> Running for the whole calendar year puts enormous pressure on horses.

Looney's Words	New Words
"Year-round"	"the whole calendar year"
"racing"	"running"
"is hard"	"puts enormous pressure"

Again, you give it a try, expressing Looney's idea in your own words. Note that you can't always find synonyms for some words in the original source like "horses."

Writing Practice

Rewrite each of the following quotations in your own words.

1. "Proof of the Meadowlands malady comes from many sources."

2. "Meadowlands has become so important and so influential that when it sneezes, tracks elsewhere tend to come down with colds."

3. "From the day it opened, the East Rutherford track was a winner."

4. "The surrounding industrial mishmash has been abused for 200 years."

5. "Heavy traffic on the adjacent New Jersey Turnpike further fouls the air."

The Summary

Summarizing a source is more difficult than paraphrasing because it requires you to retain the ideas of the original while reducing the number of words. Here is how you might summarize a paragraph from Looney's article:

> In the Meadowlands barns the horses face each other. Thus, one coughing horse can ruin a lot of days for everyone else. At most tracks horses are stabled back to back, with partitions in between. Meadowlands *can* do something about its barn design, but compared to the other factors involved, this one is minor.

↓

> Meadowlands stables are arranged so that coughing horses spread germs face-to-face. Meadowlands can fix this problem, but not the other more serious ones.

Looney uses more than fifty words in his paragraph; the summary, less than half as many. The phrase "coughing horses," and the idea that Meadowlands can fix the less serious problem of horses spreading germs, have been retained. The mention of "partitions" has been omitted because "face-to-face" explains the problem. Notice also that "barns" has been replaced by "stables" and "are arranged" has been substituted for "are stabled."

Now you try to summarize Looney's paragraph in your own words. See if you can condense his words into one or two sentences:

> For months there has been talk along the backstretch. Veterinarians and trainers say—anonymously or in very low voices—that, for sure, there is a problem. Horsemen are reluctant to knock the goose that has laid racing's largest golden egg, for Meadowlands reputation for excellence, smart management and largess is unmatched.

↓

> For a long time horsemen have privately acknowledged that there are troubles at Meadowlands, but they are slow to criticize openly such an intelligent, well-run, generous operation.

Looney's fifty-one words have been condensed to twenty-seven. The ideas of the horsemen speaking secretly about the problems and their wanting to avoid being openly critical of a well-run organization have been kept, but the references to "backstretch" and the "goose with the golden egg" have been omitted. Also consider the word substitutions:

Looney's Words	New Words
"months"	"time"
"veterinarians and trainers"	"horsemen"
"say—anonymously or in very low voices"	"have privately acknowledged"
"reputation for excellence, smart management and largess"	"intelligent, well-run, generous operation"

Now it's your turn. Condense Looney's paragraph into one sentence using your own words. Take your time and allow for mistakes.

Writing Practice

Condense each of the following passages from Looney's article. Use your own words while retaining the original idea.

1. "On Jan. 18, Meadowlands opens its second harness season, and there is apprehension, for the track can do little about most of the causes of the respiratory ailments that afflict the horses. Part of the problem is the location of the track, part that it offers such big money."

2. "Trainers are under pressure at Meadowlands—as elsewhere—to enter horses to fill out a field, especially in bad weather. If a horseman complies, he can expect the racing secretary to make a race especially designed for his horse at a later, more advantageous time."

3. "So all these factors—polluted air, too much money at stake, too frequent racing (sometimes as many as three races in 10 days for a horse), too much movement of horses—are converging at the Meadowlands."

Using the Direct Quotation with the Paraphrase or the Summary

A third way of using sources is to combine the direct quotation with a summary or paraphrase. Because Looney's article is really an extended argument for the closing of Meadowlands racetrack, he uses many sources—veterinarians, horse trainers and owners, and environmental officials. For the sake of variety, he uses quotations, paraphrases, and summaries of those sources. In some cases, Looney also *combines* use of the direct quotation and the summary, as in this example:

> An anti-Lasix vet, Jim Mitchell, says, "I don't give a damn about the $2 bettor. I care about the horse." He thinks sick animals should be rested. In his opinion the drug definitely aids breathing and this is a big competitive advantage to any horse that is injected with it, whether he's a bleeder or not.

Notice that Looney first identifies the speaker, then quotes him, and finally summarizes his point of view.

Sometimes Looney employs direct quotations with fairly lengthy paraphrases:

> New Bolton Center's Charles W. Raker, an expert on upper respiratory ailments, thinks that "environmental pollutants may be a significant factor" in aggravating pharyngitis. He points out that sucking in huge volumes of dirty air (a horse normally exchanges 40 liters of air a minute at rest, at least 250 under stress) can irritate the throat and lungs, which often results in bleeding.

Again, analyze Looney's method. He identifies Raker as an expert, quotes him, and then summarizes his views.

A final caution on word choice in introducing direct quotations. When Looney introduces a direct quotation in his article, in most cases he does so with the word "says": "Jim Mitchell *says*"; "Seeber *says*"; "*Says* Coggins." As a student, however, you should get in the habit of using a variety of words other than "says" when introducing direct quotations. Here is a sample of words that you can substitute for "says": "declares," "asserts," "states," "comments," "remarks," "affirms," and "conjectures." Perhaps you can look up or think of some more. Some of these words have different shades of meaning from the bland "says," so you must be careful to see that your choice makes sense in the context of the sentence.

Writing Practice

1. Rewrite each of the following passages from Looney's article, combining a direct quotation with a paraphrase.
    a. An anti-Lasix vet, Jim Mitchell, says, "I don't give a damn about the $2 bettor. I care about the horse."

    b. Veterinarian Wise says, "The quality of the air is so irritating. I feel good when I leave my home in South Jersey and awful when I get here."

    c. Daren Chenkin, a company engineer, says, "Eighty-five to 95% of the time it's not us."

    d. Bob Grant, a spokesman for the Hackensack Meadowlands Commission, says, "Maybe the problem is that man is not good for his environment and the brain is an evolutionary mistake."

    e. Says Coggins, "Don't race as much, certainly don't race in winter, and never let horses get together."

2. Rewrite each of the following passages from Looney's article, combining a direct quotation with a summary.

    a. An anti-Lasix vet, Jim Mitchell, says, "I don't give a damn about the $2 bettor. I care about the horse." He thinks sick animals should be rested. In his opinion the drug definitely aids breathing and this is a big competitive advantage to any horse that is injected with it, whether he's a bleeder or not.

    b. New Bolton Center's Charles W. Raker, an expert on upper respiratory ailments, thinks that "environmental pollutants may be a significant factor" in aggravating pharyngitis. He points out that sucking in huge volumes of dirty air (a horse normally exchanges 40 liters of air a minute at rest, at least 250 under stress) can irritate the throat and lungs, which often results in bleeding.

    c. Year-round racing is hard on horses. Seeber says, "If you drive a car only 5,000 miles a year, it doesn't take much care. But if you drive it 50,000, it takes a lot." Still, states insist their tracks stay open year-round because they need the money. Meadowlands will contribute close to $8 million to New Jersey on a 1977 handle of approximately $500 million.

    d. Beech tells horsemen she thinks that air pollution could be the reason and that if their animals are susceptible to respiratory difficulties, they had better take them elsewhere. "But," says Beech, "Meadowlands is where the money is."

    e. One who will follow this course is Don Galbraith, who helped train ABC Freight, a prominent 3-year-old trotter. "We had eight horses at Meadowlands last spring," says Galbraith, "and five got sick with bad throats." This time around, he says, if he races at Meadowlands, he will ship in a horse from Monticello, N.Y. and send it right back afterward.

DOCUMENTING SOURCES

Any writer that uses words or ideas from books, newspaper articles, or any other sources must document those sources. Providing correct documentation allows the reader to consult the original book or article cited for more information or to see how the writer used the outside source. There are three main types of material that must be documented:

▲ Direct quotations

▲ Summaries or paraphrases

▲ Drawings, maps, and illustrations

A writer who *incompletely* documents sources, or who takes someone else's words or ideas and falsely represents them as his or her own, is commiting plagiarism. Students often neglect to document the source of a summary or paraphrase, so remember that you cannot use the *ideas* of another writer as your own—*even if you rewrite them in your own words.* You must always indicate the original source.

Parenthetical Documentation

One of the groups that sets guidelines for research papers is the Modern Language Association, or MLA. Since 1984 the MLA has recommended the use of parenthetical documentation, that is, indicating in parentheses a shorthand reference—name of author and page number—to a direct quotation, paraphrase, or summary in a sentence. For the sake of clarity parenthetical references should be placed as close as possible to the words or ideas from the source, and at a natural pause, usually at the end of a sentence. At the end of the paper on a separate page titled "Works Cited," the writer provides more complete information about the sources.

Here is an example of parenthetical documentation in a sentence:

```
Meadowlands Racetrack has quickly grown in stature:
"Meadowlands has become so important and so influential that
when it sneezes, tracks elsewhere tend to come down with
colds" (Looney 21).
```

The source of the quotation is in parentheses: "Looney" is the author, "21" is page 21 of his article.

If you use the author's name in your sentence, indicate only the page number:

```
According to Douglas Looney, Meadowlands Racetrack has
quickly grown in stature: "Meadowlands has become so impor-
tant and so influential that when it sneezes, tracks else-
where tend to come down with colds" (21).
```

In parenthetical documentation, the parentheses always comes *before* the period unless the quotation is four lines or more, in which case the quotation is indented. In an indented quotation, the parentheses comes *after* the period, as in the following example:

The writer finds no easy solutions to the dilemmas surrounding Meadowlands:

> So all these factors—polluted air, poor weather, too
> much money at stake, too frequent racing (sometimes as
> many as three races in 10 days for a horse), too much
> movement of horses—are converging at the Meadowlands. And
> there apparently is no cure—except moving the nation's
> No. 1 harness track. (Looney 21)

"Works Cited" Section

For each parenthetical reference in the text of his or her paper, the writer
gives more complete information of the source on a separate page at the
end of the paper, called "Works Cited." The word "cited" means "referred
to, used." All the articles or books "referred to" or "used" in the paper are
listed in alphabetical order of the authors' last names. If no author is given,
as is the case with some magazine and newspaper articles, use the first
letter of the first word of the title (excluding the articles "A," "An," and
"The") to put the list in order.

Capitalize the first word, last word, and all important words of each
title. Do not capitalize the articles "a," "an," and "the" unless they are the
first or last words in a title; the same rule holds for prepositions like "to,"
"for," and "on" and conjunctions like "and" and "or."

Use this format when listing sources in the "Works Cited" section of
your paper:

1. The author's last name is followed by his or her first name and a period:

Looney, Douglas S.

2. The name of the article, followed by a period, is inside quotation marks:

"They're Paying through the Nose."

3. The title of the book, magazine, newspaper is underlined and followed
by a period:

Sports Illustrated.

4. The date of the source is followed by a colon and the page numbers,
followed by a period (abbreviate all months except May, June, and July):

2 Jan. 1978: 18–21.

Here is the complete listing of the source:

Looney, Douglas S. "They're Paying through the Nose."
Sports Illustrated 2 Jan. 1978: 18–21.

Examine two more sample parenthetical references from the text of a paper side-by-side with the corresponding listing of the source in the "Works Cited" section:

Book

Text	"Works Cited"
"The tragedy of lameness seems so unfair to children that they are embarrassed in its presence" (Angelou 8).	Angelou, Maya. I Know Why the Caged Bird Sings. New York: Bantam, 1969.

or

According to Maya Angelou, "The tragedy of lameness seems so unfair to children that they are embarrassed in its presence" (8).

Newspaper Article

Text	"Works Cited"
"For most two-household children, each home has a different personality and rules" (Ansberry 1).	Ansberry, Clare. "Kids Are Often Losers in Joint Custody." Wall Street Journal. 9 Sept. 1988, sec. 2: 1.

PART SIX

Doing Special
Writing Tasks

▲▲▲

Chapter

15

Writing for Other Subjects

The need for good writing skills is not limited to English composition class. No matter what subject you are writing about, you will need to express yourself well and clarify your ideas for the reader. This is as true for math, science, and computer science as it is for the liberal arts or social studies.

Writing helps you to learn more about your subject. If you can write clearly about an idea, you know that you understand it. To reassure themselves before a test, some anxious students simply write out, without notes or textbook, all that they know about the topic. The principles you have learned in this book about the writing and reading processes apply to *all* types of writing and reading. Prewriting, such as brainstorming or freewriting, is important to all writing; so is revising and proofreading. Many instructors, not just those who teach English, reward good, clear writing. Also, since all readings are essentially organized in the same way, your skills of prereading and predicting should help you to decipher articles about highly specialized or unfamiliar topics.

In this chapter we'll study articles from several disciplines—natural science, sociology, psychology, and the humanities—to find ways of writing clearly and capably about them. Even if you are not an expert on these topics, you should be able to write intelligently about them.

READING: "HYBRID PROTEIN TO FIGHT CANCER IS CREATED IN LAB"

This first article, by Jerry Bishop of the *Wall Street Journal,* is about genetic engineering. First read the title:

Hybrid Protein to Fight Cancer Is Created in Lab

What questions can we make of the title? We might wonder *how* the protein is made. What is a "hybrid" protein? ("A composite or combination of two parts.") Write down what you think the article will say.

Now read the first and last paragraphs:

> Genetic engineers welded two human genes together, transferred them to bacteria that produced a hybrid protein with enhanced cancer-fighting activity.
>
> • • •
>
> However, Dr. Taylor said, it's not known how the human immune system would react to such a strange, unnatural protein as the hybrid. Thus, extensive animal tests need to be done before it's known whether the hybrid would be useful in treating human cancer.

Make a further prediction.

Now read the entire article.

Hybrid Protein to Fight Cancer Is Created in Lab

By Jerry E. Bishop

Staff Reporter of The Wall Street Journal

1   Genetic engineers welded two human genes together, transferred them to bacteria that produced a hybrid protein with enhanced cancer-fighting activity.

Thesis.

2   The hybrid protein was the product of the gene for interferon, a protein the body naturally produces to fight viruses and cancer, and the gene for tumor necrosis factor, or TNF, another natural human protein that has anti-cancer effects.

Description of both parts of hybrid.

---

continued

continued

³ The genetic engineering trick was pulled off by researchers at Genentech Inc. in San Francisco, and at Indiana University in Bloomington.

Who did the genetic engineering and where.

⁴ In human cancer patients, genetically engineered versions of the proteins each have shown some benefits in some patients but the results have been far short of expectations. One type of genetically engineered interferon, called alpha interferon, is marketed by Schering-Plough Corp., Madison, N.J., and Hoffmann-La Roche Inc. for a certain type of leukemia. TNF, which is being produced by several biotechnology companies including Genentech, is still considered experimental. Hoffmann is the U.S. unit of F. Hoffmann-La Roche & Co. of Switzerland.

More information on the two parts of the hybrid.

⁵ The Indiana scientists asked Genentech researchers to try to fuse the two proteins into a hybrid after experiments showed that when used in combination the two proteins seemed synergistic. That is, they had a greater effect on test-tube grown cancer cells than would be expected from simply adding the effects seen when each protein was used alone.

Why the experiment was done.

⁶ To get the hybrid protein the Genentech scientists trimmed a nonactive end off both the human interferon and TNF genes and spliced them into adjacent spots in a bacterium's genetic apparatus. The hybrid interferon-TNF protein churned out by the bacterium was just as effective against viruses as interferon alone, showing the hybrid retained its interferon activity, the scientists reported in a recent issue of Science, the weekly scientific journal.

How the experiment was conducted.

⁷ The hybrid protein had even greater effects on laboratory cancer cells than was expected from the earlier experiments using the proteins in combination. This suggests the hybrid is affecting the cancer cells in a way different than the proteins normally act.

Results of the genetic engineering.

⁸ The enhanced anti-cancer effect was seen at very low dosages of the hybrid,

noted Indiana biologist Milton Taylor. This suggests the hybrid may be useful in humans, particularly since the use in humans of both interferon and TNF is limited by severe side effects.

Possible usefulness of the project for humans.

9   However, Dr. Taylor said, it's not known how the human immune system would react to such a strange, unnatural protein as the hybrid. Thus, extensive animal tests need to be done before it's known whether the hybrid would be useful in treating human cancer.

Reservations about the potential for humans and the necessity of further testing on animals.

Look again at the first paragraph of the article, which tells *what happened*:

Genetic engineers welded two human genes together, transferred them to bacteria that produced a hybrid protein with enhanced cancer-fighting activity.

The paragraph, actually one sentence, functions like the introduction to a student essay, stating the topic in the form of a main idea or thesis. The rest of the piece elaborates on this paragraph.

In paragraph 2 the author describes each of the two parts of the hybrid—interferon and tumor necrosis factor, or TNF.

Paragraph 3 explains *who* conducted the research and *where* it was done.

Paragraph 4 describes interferon and TNF in more detail.

Paragraph 5 explains *why* the project was carried out—because the two proteins seemed synergistic when used in combination.

Paragraph 6 tells *how* the project was carried out, describing the process by which the hybrid protein is constructed in chronological order: "To get the hybrid protein the Genentech scientists trimmed a nonactive end off both the human interferon and TNF genes and spliced them into adjacent spots in a bacterium's genetic apparatus." Note the step-by-step pattern of the description:

1. The scientists trimmed a nonactive end off the interferon gene.

2. The scientists trimmed a nonactive end off the TNF gene.

3. The scientists spliced both ends into adjacent spots in a bacterium's genetic apparatus.

All processes, whether in science or some other field, can be described in this chronological, step-by-step pattern.

Paragraph 7 gives the results of the genetic engineering: "The hybrid protein had even greater effects on laboratory cancer than was expected from the earlier experiments using the proteins in combination."

The results of the project as they pertain to humans are described in paragraph 8: "The enhanced anti-cancer effect was seen at very low dosages of the hybrid. . . . This suggests the hybrid may be useful in humans. . . ."

The concluding paragraph offers reservations about the results: more testing of the protein must be done on animals because "it's not known how the human immune system would react to such a strange, unnatural protein such as the hybrid."

The article clearly follows the pattern of answering the reporters' questions: the first part tells us *what*; the second part, *who* and *where* with more on *what*; the third section, *how*; and the last part new *what*— that is, the results of the experiment and what they might mean for mankind. *When* the experiment was conducted is explained briefly at the end of paragraph 6: ". . . the scientists reported in a recent issue of *Science*, the weekly scientific journal." The writer has taken a complex topic—genetic engineering—and used the reporter's questions to present information clearly to the reader.

Reading for Meaning

1. What is the thesis of the article?
2. How does the writer support his thesis?
3. Why is the hybrid cancer-fighting protein used only in low dosages?
4. Although results of experimenting with the new protein look very promising, what reservations do scientists have in regard to humans?
5. Before using the new hybrid protein in fighting human cancer, what must scientists do?

Vocabulary in Context

One of the problems in reading about a field like biology or biochemistry is learning terminology or vocabulary peculiar to that subject. To understand readings from one of these specialized fields, it is necessary to learn words with precise, often complex meanings. This *Wall Street Journal* article helps the reader a great deal by defining scientific terms right in their context—for example, "interferon, a protein the body naturally produces to fight viruses and cancer" and "TNF, another natural human protein that has anti-cancer effects." The writer also defines for the reader the key term "synergistic"; ". . . when used in combination the two proteins seemed synergistic. That is, they had a greater effect on test-tube grown cancer cells than would be expected from simply adding the effects seen when each protein was used alone."

Writing from Reading

For each of the following assignments, remember to consider your *subject, purpose,* and *audience.* The audience and purpose will be somewhat different from those of most college writing topics. Consider these two aspects of writing carefully because they will influence what you say.

1. If you were a doctor trying to give hope to a patient just diagnosed with cancer, what might you tell him or her about the new hybrid protein. Put your thoughts in the form of a letter to the patient.

2. Pretend that you are a recently diagnosed cancer patient who has just read this article. Write a letter to your doctor explaining your thoughts.

3. Role play as one of the researchers involved in the development of the hybrid protein who has read the article in the *Wall Street Journal* and been offended by the paragraph that says, "The genetic engineering *trick was pulled off* by researchers at Genentech Inc. in San Francisco, and at Indiana University in Bloomington." Write a letter to the editor of the newspaper explaining why, as a scientist, you are disturbed at having your work described as a "trick" you have "pulled off."

READING: "FOR MANY KIDS, PLAYTIME ISN'T FREE TIME"

This *Wall Street Journal* piece by Carol Hymowitz touches on several specialized disciplines—psychology, education, and sociology. Using your prereading techniques, read the title and subtitle first:

For Many Kids, Playtime Isn't Free Time

Educators Say Rigid Schedules Kill Spontaneity

Write down what you think the article is about.

Now read the first two and last two paragraphs:

Five-year-old Elizabeth Bush became fast friends with Aliza during day camp this summer. Naturally she wanted her new friend to visit her home in Manhattan and play—but that invitation took on the complexities of a business negotiation.

Elizabeth's nanny called Aliza's mother to schedule a "play date." The mother balked, insisting that she first become acquainted with Elizabeth's parents. A phone interview between the children's mothers ensued, with both exchanging information about their professions and child-rearing practices. Finally a two-hour play date was agreed upon—for 10 days later.

• • •

But some kids are beginning to demand less structure—and more freedom. Nine-year-old Kate Iger of Manhattan, for example, recently won permission to visit on her own a friend in an apartment building across the street. "My husband's frightened to death to let her out of our sight, but she's straining at the bit for more physical freedom," says her mother.

Similarly, Mrs. Knapp's nine-year-old daughter and her daughter's friends are requesting "quiet, much smaller birthday parties, with do-it-yourself craftsy things," she says. "They've been burned out by all the big groups and lavish entertainment, and they're saying 'Mommy, no more.'"

Write down a further prediction about the content of the article.

As you read the entire article, compare the backgrounds of these children with your own. Are there any similarities?

For Many Kids, Playtime Isn't Free Time

Educators Say Rigid Schedules Kill Spontaneity

By CAROL HYMOWITZ

Staff Reporter of THE WALL STREET JOURNAL

[1] Five-year-old Elizabeth Bush became fast friends with Aliza during day camp this summer. Naturally she wanted her new friend to visit her home in Manhattan and play—but that invitation took on the complexities of a business negotiation.

2   Elizabeth's nanny called Aliza's mother to schedule a "play date." The mother balked, insisting that she first become acquainted with Elizabeth's parents. A phone interview between the children's mothers ensued, with both exchanging information about their professions and child-rearing practices. Finally a two-hour play date was agreed upon—for 10 days later.

3   "When I was a kid and wanted to play, I walked out of my house and knocked on a neighbor's door—but those days are gone," says Elizabeth's mother, Pat. Now, she says "my friends' kids carry executive Day-Timer calendars" to keep track of dozens of activities and formal dates with friends.

4   This is today's play for more and more children. Schedules and supervision replace spontaneity and freedom. Lessons, not make-believe, are the rule. Indeed, if Mark Twain penned "The Adventures of Tom Sawyer" today, his barefoot hero would be shuttling between tennis camp and piano lessons instead of dreaming up pranks with his pal Huck Finn.

Producing Passivity

5   Educators and psychologists worry that such rigid regimens are producing passive—and pressured—kids. "I'm seeing seven, eight and nine-year-olds who are anxious and angry because they're over-programmed with activities that don't meet their needs," says Charles Clegg, a Los Angeles psychologist. "They're being told what they should like—which teaches them passivity—and also told to perform."

6   Jane Healy, a learning specialist at the private Hathaway Brown School in Cleveland, agrees that scheduled play often isn't play at all. "Play is spontaneous and self-initiated by definition," she says. Children who are used to constant direc-tion in lessons and team sports "are terrified to take risks"—from climbing a tree to tackling a difficult math problem, she maintains.

7   What's contributing to the orchestrated play? The return of women to the work force has required them to secure supervision for their children after school and in the summer—and often the only option is organized classes. "We're seeing a lot of lessons used for caretaking," says Susan Brownlee, an administrator at the private Ellis School in Pittsburgh.

8   Another factor: fast-track couples eager for a fast track for their kids. They're pushing them sooner and more often into activities they believe will enhance their kids' chances to land at the best schools and later, the best jobs.

9   Concern about children's safety—even in suburban and rural areas—is yet another issue. The era of missing children's pictures on milk cartons has effectively eliminated Huck Finn-type adventures.

10   "When my kids visit a friend a few blocks away, I want them to call me the minute they arrive, and if they make a stop along the way, they have to call from there," says Carol Marchick, a working mother who lives in affluent Palo Alto, Calif. "I'm frightened by all the child kidnappings and stories of child abuse."

11   Whatever the reasons, "the days of most middle-class children are so filled . . . that they have hardly any time to simply be themselves," writes child psychologist Bruno Bettleheim. "They are deprived of those long hours and days of leisure to think their own thoughts, an essential element in the development of creativity."

12   Consider 10-year-old Lindsay Corbett of Summit, N.J. This summer she attended an "enrichment program" at a local high school to study word processing, woodworking, pottery and flute, and also enrolled in a tennis camp. Now that

continued

continued

school has started, she is even busier, with a different activity slated nearly every day after classes: flute lessons on Tuesday afternoons, Girl Scouts on Wednesdays, piano on Thursdays, tennis on Fridays and soccer on Saturdays and Sundays.

13   "She's a straight A student but very well-rounded," her mother says. And Lindsay insists "I can handle it all."

14   But some kids aren't so sure they can handle it all, or want to. Nine-year-old Max Gross of Brooklyn has begged his parents to let him quit an after-school program he attends. "I'd rather be home alone, playing a game that's meant for just one person," he says.

15   That's impossible at the program, where he's surrounded by dozens of active kids. And he says he's often lonelier there than at home. "The other kids aren't exactly nice to you. It's their free time—and they don't really want to be there, so they take it out on you." (His parents insist on the program because of an attempted burglary at their apartment last year.)

16   Other overprogrammed children experience burnout. Eight-year-old Lisa Sweet of Manhattan signed up for five after-school activities last year, including tennis, gymnastics and ceramics—but soon felt overwhelmed and unable to keep up with her homework. "I worried that it was going to be too much for her but knew the schedule would be easier for me, so I didn't discourage it," admits her mother, Ellen, a magazine editor. She scrambled to adjust her own work schedule when Lisa insisted she needed some free time after school.

17   Kids who resist the new scheduled play, however, may find themselves without playmates. Twelve-year-old Peter Reaves of Pittsburgh treasures "his free time to ride his bike, play ball and just hangout," says his mother Debby. But this summer "all his friends enrolled in camp, so there was no one for him to hang out

with. He's got peer pressure to structure his time, too,"—or be isolated.

No Time to Unwind

18   With fewer chances to choose their own activities with pals, children may be forgetting how to have fun. Without time to unwind, "they're nervous, scattered and anxious," says Mary Newman, head of the private Town School in Manhattan. "I understand parents who figure it's better to stick a kid in gymnastics class than let him spend the afternoon watching TV," she adds. "But what adult wants to spend 10 hours a day or more moving from one planned activity to the next?"

19   Children of young professionals also are accustomed to being entertained. By age two or three they're not only attending gymnastics classes and toddler swimming lessons but lavish birthday parties that feature professional clowns, jugglers and magicians. "For a simple, nothing party, you've got to figure $500—once you count food, favors and entertainment for 20 or 30 kids," says Ilanna Knapp, an executive at a New Jersey securities firm and mother of two children, ages five and nine. "You can't do less, because you don't want to see your kids ostracized."

20   But some kids are beginning to demand less structure—and more freedom. Nine-year-old Kate Iger of Manhattan, for example, recently won permission to visit on her own a friend in an apartment building across the street. "My husband's frightened to death to let her out of our sight, but she's straining at the bit for more physical freedom," says her mother.

21   Similarly, Mrs. Knapp's nine-year-old daughter and her daughter's friends are requesting "quiet, much smaller birthday parties, with do-it-yourself craftsy things," she says. "They've been burned out by all the big groups and lavish entertainment, and they're saying 'Mommy, no more.'"

The subtitle of the article would make a good thesis: "Educators Say Rigid Schedules Kill Spontaneity." This main point is repeated several times—for example, in paragraph 5: "Educators and psychologists worry that such rigid regimens are producing passive—and pressured—kids."

The writer supports her thesis by drawing on the thoughts of numerous sociologists and psychologists of different levels of experience. Her most authoritative source is famed child psychologist Bruno Bettleheim, quoted in paragraph 11: ". . . the days of middle-class children are so filled . . . that they have hardly any time to simply be themselves. . . . They are deprived of those long hours and days of leisure to think their own thoughts, an essential element in the development of creativity." In paragraph 5 she quotes Los Angeles psychologist Charles Clegg: "I'm seeing seven, eight, and nine-year-olds who are anxious and angry because they're overprogrammed with activities that don't meet their needs. They're being told what they should like—which teaches them passivity—and also to perform." In paragraph 6 the writer quotes learning specialist Jane Healey: "Play is spontaneous and self-initiated by definition." Healey feels that kids who spend too much time in instruction and supervised team sports "are terrified to take risks."

Through such examples, the writer makes her thesis more convincing to the reader.

Reading for Meaning

1. What is the main idea of the article?
2. How does the author support her main idea?
3. What does the author point to as the cause or causes for so much structured play?
4. What are some of the problems psychologists fear that overprogrammed kids might have?
5. Kids who resist a great deal of structured play may have problems, too. What are they?
6. What is the point of the comparison with Tom Sawyer?

Vocabulary in Context

Write down the definition of each of the italicized words below taken from the article. Try to guess the meaning from the context. Use a dictionary only if you have to.

1. "Educators and psychologists worry that such rigid *regimens* are producing passive—and pressured—kids."
2. "'. . . you don't want to see your kids *ostracized!*'"

Writing from Reading

For each of the following assignments, remember to consider your *subject*, *purpose*, and *audience*.

1. Do you agree with the writer's thesis, that so much structured play may cause serious problems for kids?

2. Think back to your childhood. Were you programmed for classes and activities like the kids in the article, or did you have a lot of free time? Was childhood a time of development for you?

3. *Simulation game.* Look again at paragraphs 12 and 13, and consider the situation of Lindsay Corbett. Her life certainly seems to be over-regimented. In a group of four or five students, each take one of the following roles: Lindsay, Lindsay's mother, Lindsay's father, or psychologist Charles Clegg (quoted in paragraph 5). Discuss Lindsay's schedule, writing out what you think your character might say in the meeting and deciding whose position is the strongest.

READING: "A NEW GENETIC TEST CAN FORETELL AGONIZING DEATH: WOULD YOU TAKE IT?"

This article, by Peter Gorner of the *Chicago Tribune*, cuts across several specialized fields—biology, medicine, psychology, and perhaps sociology. It is a long reading about a painful and frightening topic. First look at the title and highlighted sentence:

A new genetic test can foretell agonizing death: Would you take it?

The DNA test for Huntington's disease has abruptly shoved medical science to the edge of an ethical abyss.

Write down what you think the article will say.

Now read the first two and last two paragraphs:

BALTIMORE—Paul and Karen Sweeney, dressed in their finest, kissed in the parking lot and marched resolutely to psychologist Kimberly Quaid's office at the Johns Hopkins Hospital. A lot of lives were on the line.

The psychologist greeted the young Virginia couple, and Karen began pacing the room. Paul sat stiffly, breathing deeply, staring straight ahead.

• • •

And despite the emotional rollercoaster Kimberly Quaid has ridden the last two years, she will keep administering the test.

"I can only hope," she says, "that in the future—and I mean the immediate future—we as a society will show compassion to those who through no fault of their own are doomed to suffer."

Write down a further prediction about the content of the article.

Now read the entire selection, trying to keep track of the arguments for and against the test for Huntington's disease.

A new genetic test can foretell agonizing death: Would you take it?

By Peter Gorner
Chicago Tribune

1   BALTIMORE—Paul and Karen Sweeney, dressed in their finest, kissed in the parking lot and marched resolutely to psychologist Kimberly Quaid's office at the Johns Hopkins Hospital. A lot of lives were on the line.

2   The psychologist greeted the young Virginia couple, and Karen began pacing the room. Paul sat stiffly, breathing deeply, staring straight ahead.

3   "Are you sure you want to know?"

4   Quaid asked the *pro forma* question one last time, doing everything by the book. Maybe they wouldn't want to know, despite months of testing and counseling,

particularly about suicide and whether Karen could cope with bad news.

5   She reacted sharply to Quaid's question. She'd spent most of her life wondering and worrying. She never had enjoyed a childhood; never known her mother, except as a twitching, flailing, helpless and mute victim strapped into a hospital bed before she mercifully died 10 years later. Karen's mother had gotten sick at 33, while pregnant with her. Now Karen, 28, was running out of time. Her emotions welled up, choking her.

6   "Yes! Please!" she screamed. "Tell us. Please."

continued

continued

7   The news is good, Quaid quietly told them: You beat it.

8   The test showed that there was a 95 percent probability that Karen didn't carry the gene for Huntington's disease, a rare and always fatal hereditary brain disorder.

9   She and Paul had a future after all. And, in that instant, so did their children: Melissa, Jesse, Brenndan and Shawn. Not to mention *their* children someday.

10   All suddenly, wonderfully, free.

11   The deadly gene that had murdered her grandfather and her mother and had already begun the slow killing of her 40-year-old brother had spared Karen and her new family line.

12   Two years ago, predictive testing for the Huntington's gene began at Hopkins and at Massachusetts General Hospital in Boston, institutions with long histories of caring for Huntington's patients.

13   New centers are operating at Columbia Presbyterian Medical Center in New York and at the Universities of Michigan and Minnesota.

14   The new test has produced agonizing dilemmas for the pioneering testers, quandaries that will become increasingly common in coming years as discoveries are made of specific genetic defects that predispose people to future physical and mental illnesses.

15   The idea of a test that can tell a healthy person today that in 20 years he may die of a stroke, cancer or heart attack, or have his happiness suffocated by a major depressive illness, is altogether new to society.

16   Do people really want that information? Dare society keep it from them? Huntington's disease carries with it a suicide rate 4 to 7 times the national average. Yet the historic DNA test for the lethal gene means the future is already here. It has abruptly shoved medical science to the edge of an ethical abyss.

17   "We know we're all going to die, yes," says Kimberly Quaid. "But most of us don't know how or when.

18   "Many people who come to us don't want to know for themselves; they want to be able to tell their children whether they need to worry. Others, though, say they have an overwhelming need to end the agony of not knowing.

The DNA test for Huntington's disease has abruptly shoved medical science to the edge of an ethical abyss.

19   "Right now, those of us in this field are becoming the gypsy fortunetellers of technology. What I see in my job is merely the tip of the iceberg, but it's very distressing. Frankly, I don't think we're ready for this."

20   Karen Sweeney says she vividly remembers the scene last November, when she received the test results on which she had bet her life. Karen recalls the unbelievable high, the hugging, the tears in Kim Quaid's eyes.

21   But Quaid doubts that Karen really remembers. At the moment of truth, people always freeze, regardless of the news. So far, the Hopkins team has told 8 people they will get Huntington's disease, 28 people that they won't, and 7 people that the test has failed and the results are inconclusive.

22   No matter the news, the brain seizes up in self-defense, denying, refusing to compute. People may act normally; they may sob in grief, sob in relief or sob in the frustration of no answer. But they're not really processing what's happening to them.

23   That's why researchers insist on the buddy system. There must be an "advocate" present at the disclosure sessions,

when healthy young people find out whether they're going to die from a legacy so horrifying that many doctors consider it the worst thing that can happen to a human being.

24 "Escapees" is another term the researchers use. Karen Sweeney is an escapee. All those who come to Hopkins for presymptomatic testing for Huntington's want to be told that they're escapees.

25 But not everyone is. And many others, who could learn, don't want to find out. Some people want to know but don't want other people to know, including their spouses and children.

26 "Every family poses new problems," says Jason Brandt, the cheerful young psychologist who heads the Hopkins testing program.

27 "We thought we were real smart cookies. We thought we had anticipated every possible snafu when we started this. Then the first five patients in the door had us hollering for help."

28 Quaid says she longed for an ethics hot line, somebody she could call who could tell her what to do.

29 What would you do with identical twins, one of whom wanted the test and the other didn't? The Hopkins team was bewildered. Identical twins share the same genes. If one carries the fatal flaw, the other is doomed as well.

30 "We decided they should work it out," says Brandt, "and if push came to shove, we wouldn't test them. But before they could make a decision, one of them started to show symptoms of the disease. That settled that."

31 What would you do with a doctor (not at Hopkins) who wanted a leukemia victim tested for the Huntington's gene before he considered giving her a life-saving bone-marrow Huntington's transplant? The phone call made Quaid shudder. She icily deflected the doctor.

32 What would you do with the pitiful people—10 so far—who came to Hopkins to be tested and already were showing signs of Huntington's?

33 "They were coming in, ostensibly, to be told that in 10 to 20 years, they will get the disease," Quaid says. "They were not prepared to be told: 'I'm sorry, you already have it.'"

34 These are just a few of the issues that the Hopkins team confronts every day. About 25,000 Americans suffer from Huntington's disease, but another 150,000 people live in its shadow, knowing they have a 50-50 chance of getting it. Huntington's, best known as the disease that killed folksinger Woody Guthrie, has been called history's first example of genetically caused insanity. It lies dormant until you reach middle age. Then it strikes, slowly drives you mad and kills you.

35 The disease is genetic, without doubt. By the time a parent develops it, he or she may already have had children. On average, half of them will die of Huntington's, as well. A sick parent is condemned, but the children don't know if they are too. They oversee the lingering deaths of their parents. They realize what may be in store.

36 So for them, the wait is excruciating, the ambiguity torturous, the anguish almost unimaginable. "There's not one waking hour that you don't think about it," says Karen Sweeney. "It influences everything you do."

37 Should such people get married and have kids? Most of them do and take a chance, knowing that if the gene blazes into action, they've ensured that those they love the most may face the same fate. If they forgo marriage and parenthood and the gene never shows up, they've sacrificed in vain.

38 The first signs of Huntington's disease are diabolically subtle. A twitch. Fidgeting. Clumsiness. A sudden fall. Absent-mindedness. Irritability. Depression.

39 Normal people rarely worry about

continued

continued

such things, but when someone at risk for Huntington's drops a dish, forgets a name or trips on the sidewalk, the effect is chilling.

40 Is it starting?

41 Eventually, if someone has the gene, his body starts to work as if by remote control. It starts to move. He can't stop it or control it. The brain has begun to die. The victim develops the distinctive frenzy of aimless twitching, lurching and jerking. As uncontrolled writing (choreic movements) gradually increases, the patient must be confined to a bed or wheelchair. Facial expressions may become distorted and grotesque: The eyes roll, the tongue darts in and out, the eyebrows glide up and down. At worst, the entire body becomes a horror of grotesque, involuntary movements. Speech is slurred at first, then indistinct, then finally stops altogether as the victim stiffens like a board and loses the ability to swallow.

42 Mental functions similarly deteriorate, and eventually the ability to reason disappears. Huntington's can take 20 terrible years to reach full cry. No treatment can slow the inexorable course, let alone halt it. Every afflicted person and his family must engage in herculean battles against the inevitable, struggling day after day to maintain hope and keep fighting.

43 Usually, victims must be institutionalized. Infection generally ends the story. Families, grieving, say they are amazed to see their loved ones finally stilled. The devilish dancing finally has ceased. Ironically, victims look as they once did, before the long suffering began.

44 For 25 years, genetic engineers hoped to find a marker for this obscene disease, some signpost in the complement of 46 human chromosomes that would predict whether someone carried the gene. Then future victims could make plans for their care. They could do something active, not merely wait in horror. Escapees would be freed. Affected fetuses could be detected in the womb, and parents could decide whether to bring them into the world. The heartbreaking killer might even be wiped out in a generation. It was a possibility; something society could debate.

45 In 1983, Harvard researcher James Gusella found such a marker and electrified science. Nancy Wexler, a Columbia University psychologist who may herself carry the gene, had worked with huge families of rural Venezuelans—9,000 of them, as of last spring—who have the highest rate of Huntington's in the world. By examining the blood of victims and looking for genetic patterns that escapees didn't have, Gusella was able to isolate the marker.

46 He didn't find the gene. But he pinpointed other genes close to it on its chromosome. And suddenly all of science knew where to look for the Huntington's gene: It's out somewhere on the far tip of Chromosome 4. The race to nail it down continues in laboratories every day. "I'm sure they'll find it soon," says Brandt. "Then they can tear it apart and figure out what's wrong. Then they can fix it."

47 Since the breakthrough, 16 more Huntington's markers have been found, fine-tuning the predictive test to virtually 100 percent—in the right families.

48 Hopkins needs blood from both affected and unaffected relatives to do the test. Sometimes there's not enough material available. Sometimes those who want to be tested are afraid to approach relatives about this ugly family secret. Sometimes the markers, the snapshots themselves, are confusing.

49 But in many families, scientists now can identify future victims early, before they have children. No longer do people have to suffer 30 or 40 years before the real nightmare begins.

50 The testing procedure, however, is long and involved, requiring months of

counseling and psychological testing to evaluate inner strengths, family and religious supports, marital relationships, employment situations. (Hopkins advises those who come for testing to buy disability coverage *before* they do.)

51   About a third of those who apply to the program drop out after a few counseling sessions.

52   "The process gives us a unique chance to do research," says Quaid, "to assess the impact of this clinical test before some Dr. Bagodonuts starts using it without any knowledge of what may happen.

53   "We don't advocate that anyone take this test. If someone decides they need the information, we will help them in any way we can.

54   "But the social, financial and psychological burdens of this disease are staggering. Family breakups and divorce are common. One frightened woman who called me was an adoptee. She had tracked down her biological parents. She found her natural father. He was in a nursing home with the terminal stages of Huntington's disease."

55   Despite polls showing that most Huntington's families wanted to take the test, relatively few have actually applied at the research centers. Living with a 50-50 chance, after all, holds a certain measure of hope. "Regardless of the results," Quaid says, "this test can completely change someone's self-concept. A lot of people don't get the family support that they expect. "One husband told me he probably wouldn't be able to handle it if his wife tested positive. He might leave her and would have to live with the knowledge that he was a coward. When I asked another man what he would do if his test were positive, he said: 'Well, I wouldn't cheat on my wife.'"

56   Nancy Wexler, at Columbia Presbyterian, declines to say if she has taken the test. She offers it reluctantly.

57   "It's not a good test if you can't offer people treatment," she says. She has been struck by those who come in for testing and already are showing signs of the disease.

58   "It really indicates how ambivalent people are," she says.

59   "These people say they want to have this information. But they don't really want it, or they would deliver it to themselves. They don't need a fancy DNA test. If they just looked at their fingers and toes, they'd say: 'Well, that's it, all right.'"

60   Denial, she notes, is a crucial coping strategy for human beings. How else can those living under a threat like Huntington's be expected to get through the day? All of us have health fears that we deny all the time.

61   "But we're cracking people's healthiest defense by making them attend to the fact that they will actually get this disease," Wexler says. "We're opening deep wounds.

62   "We spend all our time trying to get them to cope, to come to grips with the fact that it could be really bad news, so they're prepared for the worst. Then, if the news really is terrible, we instantly have to do a complete turnaround!

63   "We quickly must tell them: 'Well, you know, the disease isn't really all that bad. It takes a long time to progress, and research is going on like crazy. Surely there'll be a cure. Now don't get depressed, and please don't go out and kill yourself.'"

64   No one who has taken the test has tried so far, the centers report.

65   "Jumping out the window is just the most dramatic aspect of it," Wexler says. "People can jump out the window inside. Those might be harder to identify."

66   Brandt, a fellow psychologist, views the patients differently. "I don't think those who test positive for the gene are dying inside. They are amazingly courageous and resilient people. These patients

continued

continued

who come for testing are unique, I think. They're highly motivated: They want to know. They're also highly educated: Three years of college is the norm. Once they learn they carry the gene, they get on with their lives. They don't come in for regular therapy. They've found out what they needed to know. They don't dwell on it."

67 Nor do the escapees show predictable patterns. "Among those who have tested clear so far," Brandt says, "one got engaged, another had a baby, a third left her husband. So we're seeing different things."

68 The Hopkins program ferociously protects its clients' identities. Yet Quaid worries that such information one day might be used to discriminate against those who carry the gene. Employers might demand screening. Insurers might deny coverage. Then only the wealthy could take the test and learn their futures.

69 Nancy Wexler believes that perhaps now is not the time to volunteer for such a landmark test.

70 "That may be the best outcome after all," she says. Quaid, though, feels that many people really want to know. "I think the potential of this test to do enormous good is there. Half the people will turn out negative. For them it's just an enormous, enormous benefit."

71 Karen Sweeney obviously concurs, "I can't tell anyone to take the test," she says. "But I think we faced death—looked it square in the eye—and are better people for it. I believe many others can find that inner strength, if they try. I know I couldn't have continued to live my life the way it was before.

72 "My family has a future, because of these scientists. Their work may help my brother as well. I feel tremendous guilt that I was spared and he wasn't."

73 And despite the emotional roller-coaster Kimberly Quaid has ridden the last two years, she will keep administering the test.

74 "I can only hope," she says, "that in the future—and I mean the immediate future—we as a society will show compassion to those who through no fault of their own are doomed to suffer."

The first section of the article, paragraphs 1–11, relates the Sweeneys' traumatic visit to psychologist Kim Quaid for the results of the genetic test.

The next portion of the article (paragraphs 12–33) gives background about the genetic testing centers and details the ethical dilemmas the test raises.

Paragraphs 34–43 provide a fuller explanation of the nature and extent of Huntington's disease, its symptoms, and its effects on victims.

Paragraphs 44–53 discuss the work of scientists to isolate the Huntington's gene, and describe the test more fully.

The next section (paragraphs 54–70) informs us about the effects of the test on those who have gone through it, and the difficulties psychologists have with counseling testees afterwards.

The last section of the article, paragraphs 71–74, relates to the first—Karen Sweeney tells of her feelings about the test, and psychologist Kim Quaid hopes the future will offer compassion for those with Huntington's disease.

The writer focuses on cases like the Sweeneys to furnish the human interest aspect of the story, while also providing information about the disease itself and the biologists' hunt for a cure. The article is a skillful blend of examples and information.

Reading for Meaning

1. What is the main idea of the article?
2. How does the writer support the main idea?
3. What are the symptoms of Huntington's disease?
4. What are the odds of a child inheriting Huntington's disease from his or her parents, one of whom carries the gene?
5. What is the suicide rate among victims of Huntington's disease?
6. Why is there so much concern for protecting the privacy of those tested?
7. What scientific work remains to be done on Huntington's disease?
8. Explain the reasons for the ambivalence of those tested for the disease.

Vocabulary in Context

Write down the definition of each of the italicized words below taken from the article. Try to guess the meaning from the context. Use a dictionary only if you have to.

1. "'Are you sure you want to know?' Quaid asked the *pro forma* question . . .'"
2. "The new test has produced agonizing dilemmas for the pioneering testers, *quandaries* that will become increasingly common in coming years . . .'"
3. "As uncontrolled writhing (*choreic* movements) gradually increases . . .'"
4. "Every afflicted person and his family must engage in *herculean* battles against the inevitable . . .'"

Writing from Reading

For each of the following assignments, remember to consider your *subject, purpose,* and *audience.*

1. Explain the pros and cons of testing for Huntington's disease.
2. Write about the ethical dilemmas surrounding genetic testing.
3. *Simulation game.* Imagine that one of your parents died of Huntington's disease and you and your spouse have entered Kim Quaid's counseling program. Take one of four roles: testee, spouse, advocate, and Kim Quaid. Write out arguments for your point of view about whether or not a patient should take the test.

READING: "THE CLOSING OF POWER MEMORIAL ACADEMY: LOSS OF THE POWER OF LOVE"

We will now turn from science, sociology, and psychology to another specialized discipline—the humanities. The following personal essay was published in a college literary magazine. Using your prereading techniques, first read the title:

The Closing of Power Memorial Academy: Loss of the Power of Love

Write down a prediction about the content of the essay.

Now read the first paragraph and the last two paragraphs:

> Power's junior varsity baseball coach got to school early to post the names of those who had made the team. He had been a pitcher with desire and no fast ball. He couldn't stand to see the students whose names didn't make the list walk away. As he started to take the list out of his pocket, he heard a noise behind him and turned.
>
> • • •
>
> I suppose it is true that the dusty old building finally had to come down, but at what a price—all those acts of love for poor kids done no more, no more place of refuge for the tough kids of Manhattan's West Side. Those who taught at Power and those who went to school there were the lucky ones, having been exposed to real Christianity and love.
>
> The media had it wrong. Although basketball and Jabbar had perhaps made Power famous, teachers and students will always treasure it not as a basketball school, but as the Power of love.

Write down a further prediction about the essay.

As you read the entire piece, pay attention to the author's tone.

The Closing of Power Memorial Academy: Loss of the Power of Love

Power's junior varsity baseball coach got to school early to post the names of those who had made the team. He had been a pitcher with desire and no fast ball. He couldn't stand to see the students whose names didn't make the list walk away. As he started to take the list out of his pocket, he heard a noise behind him and turned.

"Jim Murphy, I believe."

"Yeah, coach."

"From Queens, right?"

"Yes."

"Sleep here?"

"Nope. Got up early. Wanted to see if I made it."

"It's almost ready. 'bout half an hour."

The coach went down and typed a new list so Murphy wouldn't know his name was added.

The closing of Power Memorial Academy, a boys' Catholic high school in New York City founded in 1931, made the national news, perhaps because it had once been home to basketball giant Kareem Jabbar. But the fuss should have been over the loss of those things the Christian Brothers and a lay staff did well—work with poor, inner-city kids from a smorgasbord of nationalities. As a young teacher, I had learned my profession at Power almost twenty years earlier and had never forgotten the lessons that unique school had provided me. The news of the school's demise saddened me.

Power lacked almost all of the amenities of the new Catholic high schools built on Long Island and New Jersey to which former city dwellers had fled: no lush green ball fields, no assembly hall or theater, no pool—just the "new gym" built in the fifties behind the school.

Power baseball teams practiced out in Sheeps Meadow of Central Park with no backstop or diamond, just grass and rocks and indulgent mounted policemen. All games were "away," the coaches and kids traveling in full uniform on the subway. Only the Orthodox Jewish kids under their yarmulkes looked as conspicuous.

The red-brick school, built as a hospital in the last century, was never included in those visual "I Love New York" promos about Lincoln Center just to the north. In fact, Power embarrassed its elegant and affluent neighbors. What was an old inner-city school doing squeezed between the new Fordham University downtown campus and the opulence of the Metropolitan Opera House and the New York State Theater? The tall, thin smokestack with high ceilings and dark, narrow hallways was an aesthetic blight on the area. One central staircase wound around a greasy elevator shaft, and two rickety fire escapes clung tentatively to the sides of the building. Foot traffic was so congested inside Power that teachers, not students, switched class every period.

But, though kids ridiculed the building, they still chose Power because the school was filled with kindness. The Principal, Brother Robert McMullen, governed Power with love. Inheriting a lay staff inclined towards mutiny because of the harsh regime of his predecessor, Brother McMullen converted the faculty by trusting them, by delegating authority to them, and by being kind to them. Teachers once sullen and uncooperative blossomed when given new responsibilities, such as the leadership of academic departments and additional extracurricular activities.

One day while walking through the locker room, the hard-nosed athletic director, Brother Sirignano, noticed that frosh runner Anthony Longo was dressing himself with underwear little better than rags:

"Anthony, what are you doin' wearin' that old stuff? You'll catch a disease."

"Well, Brother, this is all I have. I save the good clothes for my two little brothers."

"Anthony, finish getting dressed and come with me."

While taking the short subway ride to Macy's, Anthony confided that he was largely responsible for raising his two younger brothers, his parents unable or unwilling to take charge of them. The athletic director bought several sets of underwear for Anthony and for his brothers.

When school finances became very tight, faculty jumped in to help. They organized themselves with many of the parents and established a weekly bingo—which meant setting up the gym with tables and chairs every Thursday afternoon, running the games from 7 o'clock to 10 o'clock, taking everything down, and cleaning up for Friday's gym classes. The

continued

continued

same parents and faculty trudged in week after week for the hard work, but the games caught on, furnishing the school with an extra $50,000 a year.

Many other small miracles grew under Brother McMullen's example. Faculty and students awoke one day to this headline in the *Daily News*: "Power Honor Student Shoots Father." William Devaney, a sophomore, tired of his father's weekly beatings and drunken rages, finally defended himself by grabbing the man's gun away and shooting him. When two of the teachers went down to see William, a shy fifteen-year-old, they were shocked to find him incarcerated with hardened adult criminals. The principal made some phone calls to Power's "old boy" network, eventually reaching a compassionate judge who had the boy remanded to the custody of the juvenile home and later to a foster family when the shooting was found to be in self defense.

Junior Stephen Huska had been paralyzed for years by a choking stutter that made school a nightmare. His English teacher asked the boy's mother to come to school for a meeting:

"Mrs. Huska, you have a very nice boy here, but this stutter is killing him."

"I know, Mr. O'Brien, but what can we do?"

"There is a speech therapy program sponsored by the city which may help him, but there is a fee for each visit. Also, we don't know how long he might have to go."

"We'll do anything to help him, Mr. O'Brien. But will this really make him better?"

"Mrs. Huska, I'll be honest—we don't know for sure. They will test him first and then set up a program for him. But I really wish you'd give it a try."

"Stephen means the world to us. If he needs this, we'll find a way to pay for it."

The speech therapy program, a combination of individual counseling and group sessions, worked wonders for Stephen. After a few months, Mr. O'Brien noticed the difference:

"Stephen, your speech has really improved. You're doing great."

"Yes, thanks to you."

"No, Stephen. You did this yourself. You had the courage to face the problem, and you licked it."

The devastating power blackout that darkened the East Coast for 24 hours in 1965 illustrated the fondness of the boys for the school. Striking at rush hour, the blackout trapped teachers and students in extracurricular activities because the subways were shut down. Teachers cooked huge pots of spaghetti on the gas stoves in the cafeteria and allowed students to ransack the ice cream freezers. Once they had reassured their parents by phone that they would be okay for the night, the kids loved the adventure, being part of a giant sleep-in on the gym floor.

The next morning a Power teacher discovered among the guests a freshman from the Amsterdam Avenue projects right across the street.

Like all places truly alive, Power seemed to breed wacky people and crazy stories. Brother King, the intense moderator of the sodality prayer group, hired a band for a fund-raising dance in the gym. On the night of the dance, along with four male members of the band and their manager, came an attractive, buxom female. When Brother King spotted her, he accosted the manager:

"Mr. Gonzalez, who is the girl? We contracted just for the band."

"Oh, not to worry, Brother. She's just here to sing a few pop songs. There's no extra charge."

Mollified, Brother King retreated to the back of the gym until some time later when the girl began to perform. She burst into a sultry bump and grind that stopped all the dancers—boys and girls. Enraged by what he deemed obscene, Brother King strode through the crowd like Moses parting the Red Sea. Screaming "Stop the music," he grabbed the microphone and then banished the girl and the band from the stage, much like the God of the Old Testament driving our first parents from Eden. The students were stunned. But though their dance ended early, the evening left them with a great story.

A school dance triggered yet another funny incident. One of the younger teachers serving as chaperon caught a man in his 20's from the projects across the street trying to sneak in. Full of righteousness and authority, the teacher rudely shoved the crasher outside into the night. When the door slammed behind them, the teacher and the culprit were all alone, cut off from the gym and help;

"Hey, what do you think you're doin'? This is a kids' dance."

"Say, man, I just wanted to get into the dance."

"I'm countin' from one to ten, and you better be outta here."

"You alone, man. How you goin' to force me out?"

After some more posturing on both sides, the man at last gave up and left, probably unaware of the lesson he had just given the chaperon—assert no more authority than that you can actually back up.

Power was a unique school in which learning of many different kinds took place. Both teachers and students were able to transcend the bleak physical environment. Like a furnace driving heat to all corners of that squalid, old building, the kindness and love of Brother McMullen enkindled the hearts of teachers and students in a variety of ways, large and small.

I suppose it is true that the dusty old building finally had to come down, but at what a price—all those acts of love for poor kids done no more, no more place of refuge for the tough kids of Manhattan's West Side. Those who taught at Power and those who went to school there were the lucky ones, having been exposed to real Christianity and love.

The media had it wrong. Although basketball and Jabbar had perhaps made Power famous, teachers and students will always treasure it not as a basketball school, but as the Power of love.

This essay is written in the format of a magazine article; that is, it begins with an anecdote, or story, to catch the reader's interest, followed by the delayed "lead" about the background of the school's closing, and concludes with a succession of anecdotes describing Power.

Reading for Meaning

1. What is the main idea of the essay?

2. How does the writer support the main idea?

3. Why was Power Memorial Academy closed?

4. How does the narrator, the one who tells the story, know so much about the school?

5. What examples does the writer give of the kindness practiced in the school?

6. What contrasts does the author point to between Power and the newer suburban schools?

7. Point out specific places in the essay where the writer has answered the reporters' questions of *who, what, when, where, how* and/or *why*.

Vocabulary in Context

Write down the definition of each of the italicized words below taken from the essay. Try to guess the meaning from the context. Use a dictionary only if you have to.

1. "Power lacked almost all of the *amenities* of the new Catholic high schools . . ."

2. "Only the [a.] *Orthodox* Jewish kids under their [b.] *yarmulkes* looked as [c.] *conspicuous*."

3. "The tall, thin smokestack with high ceilings and dark, narrow hallways as an [a.] *aesthetic* [b.]. *blight* on the area."

4. "Brother King, the intense *moderator* of the *sodality* prayer group . . ."

Writing from Reading

For each of the following assignments, remember to consider your *subject, purpose,* and *audience*.

1. The writer claims that lively places are often the source of funny stories. Was your high school such a place? What humorous stories can you tell about your school?

2. Power Academy presents a contrast between an old, dilapidated exterior and a young, life-filled interior. Is there a building or place that you know of whose appearance hides what goes on inside or that surprises people when they go inside?

3. Have you ever been saddened by the loss of an old home or building that once meant much to you, like an old vacation home, school, or stadium? Using the reporters' questions of *who, what, when, where, how* and/or *why*, explain what you lost and how you feel now looking back on it.

READING AND WRITING ABOUT POETRY

Poetry is a special kind of literature, one that demands more careful, analytical reading than most prose. But the extra work is often rewarding. Read once through the following poem by Martha M. Vertreace:

MUSE
▲▲▲

My father carries me on his back,
my runny nose behind his ear
as I whisper secrets only for him;
his response, that silly, shy grin.
⁵In this snapshot, time stops to lie
as if smiles were ever that bright
or my pinafore starched and pressed,
its airy ruffle nearly over my head.
Now he follows me, just beyond reach
¹⁰at the corner of my eye, a shade
with no outline. Through him, I
watch lambent streetlights
melt snow off their metal caps,
water dripping, then freezing
¹⁵into fringe at night. A classic
northeaster hugs the seaboard.
Tidal Basin greys into anonymity,
ground too warm to hold late season
snow. If I look quickly, if I try
²⁰to catch him, he fades as if
by seeing I would return him
to shadows he escaped to
twenty years past. Instead, he
recites snatches of poetry, stories
²⁵he once told, songs he never wrote
but thinks I could.

When reading poetry, keep these points in mind:

1. *Punctuation.* Don't stop at the end of a line unless there is a period or semicolon there:

> . . . Through him, I
> watch lambent streetlights
> melt snow off their metal caps, . . .

In line 11 the subject "I" is separated from its verb "watch" in line 12, and the subject "streetlights" is separated from its verb "melts" in line 13. The lines should be read this way:
Through him, I / watch lambent streetlights / melt snow off their metal caps

2. *Imagery.* Look for important pictures or images in the poem. In "Muse," for example, there is a "snapshot" (photograph) of the little girl clinging to her father in lines 1–8, the description of the late-season storm that "hugs the seaboard" in line 16, and the attempt by the poet "to catch" the father's spirit in line 20.

3. *Transitions.* When reading prose you are aware of transitions, words that signal change or connection like "then" or "and." Transitions are used in poetry to divide the poem into different parts. Notice the function of transitions in "Muse"—"In this snapshot" refers to the image in lines 1–8, "Now" signals a transition to the present time in line 9, and "If I look quickly" in line 19 signals the beginning of the resolution of the poem.

4. *Emotion and Conflict.* Is there any emotion evoked by the poem? "Muse" is nostalgic, recalling a loving father and childhood, but there is also conflict. The poet wishes "to catch" her father, but as she tries "he fades" away. The conflict is resolved, however, because even though she can't "catch" her father, he serves to inspire her by reciting "snatches of poetry, stories / he once told, songs he never wrote / but thinks I could." Because the poet's father guides her poetry as her "Muse," her memory of him will always be alive.

Reading for Meaning

Read "Muse" once again and answer the following questions:

1. What is the meaning of the title? To whom does it refer?
2. What is happening in the "snapshot" (lines 1–8)?
3. How does time "stop to lie" (line 5)?
4. What does "Now" signal (line 9)?
5. With what is the changeableness of the weather contrasted throughout the poem?
6. How do the last four lines of the poem relate to the title?
7. In your own words, write a short summary of the poem.

Vocabulary in Context

Write down the definition of each of the italicized words below taken from the poem. Try to guess the meaning from the context. Use a dictionary only if you have to.

1. "or my *pinafore* starched and pressed,"
2. "watch *lambent* streelights / melt snow off their metal caps,"

Writing from Reading

For each of the following assignments, remember to consider your *subject, purpose,* and *audience.*

1. The little girl in the poem "whispers secrets" intended only for her father. Freewrite or brainstorm about what she might have told him, and then write a first and final draft of an essay.

2. First, brainstorm about your own childhood, listing memories important to you. Once you have completed your list, go back over it and select *one* memory to write more about. Prewrite only about that memory and then write a first and final draft of an essay.

3. Has time ever "stopped to lie" in some memory you have had—where a person or thing became exaggerated? For example, perhaps the grammar school you attended or a house you once lived in as a child was smaller than you remembered when you went back to visit it. Maybe the neighborhood bully wasn't quite so menacing as you once thought, or your first love not quite so dazzling. Pick one such instance and write about it.

4. Write a short poem about your own "muse," someone who has inspired you through words, deeds, or example. Don't worry about rhyme. Think back to one particular instance when your "muse" inspired you, and attempt to capture that image in your poem. Put your image in sentence form. How do you feel about that person *now*? Put those thoughts, too, in sentence form. Imitate how the writer of "Muse" makes a line break, often beginning a sentence at the end of one line and completing it in the next, as in "A classic / northeaster hugs the seaboard." Your first effort may be rough. If you're frustrated, put it away for a while and return to it. In that case even the effort will be a valuable learning experience.

REVISING POETRY

In Chapter 8 we studied a professional writer's process of revision (see pp. 105–17). We will now examine the revision process of the author of the poem we have been reading in this chapter, "Muse." Martha M. Vertreace is assistant professor of English and poet-in-residence at Kennedy-King College, Chicago. Her work has recently appeared in several publications, including *Midwest Quarterly, The Hampton-Sydney Poetry Review, College English,* and *Another Chicago Magazine.* Here is Vertreace in her own words:

> The question of where poetry—or a specific poem—comes from is one I am asked at every reading I do. Some people believe in an almost magical source of poetry, something I call the "Fluttering Muse" theory, the "Muses" being the Goddesses of poetry and art in Greek mythology. The poet gets quiet, prepares herself, perhaps through ritual chanting, to receive a message from the gods. Others believe that ideas come through merely mechanical means—word games, free writing, idea clusters.
>
> For me, the truth lies somewhere between those two poles. Certainly there is an element of chance—or luck—or inspiration—in terms of getting ideas. It is impossible to control what ideas come. Yet, there is an aspect to the getting of ideas that is mechanical as well. Poets are notorious word-hoarders; journals, personal letters, books, cereal boxes all provide ideas; all are grist for the poetic mill.

Certainly the major life events which affect everyone are favorite sources of ideas, as if by writing so often about such concerns, the poet can be reconciled with troublesome issues.

"Muse" is another of my numerous poems about my father, Walter Charles Vertreace, who died suddenly when I was sixteen. The poem began as snatches of lines that I thought of, fragments of memories which my father had passed on to me, the family photo album with its ghosts. There is a richness in this material, as any poet can attest. The danger inherent in it, however, is the temptation to descend into the maudlin, the too-sweetly sentimental.

Now let's examine the first draft of "Muse" side-by-side with the poet's own commentary.

First Draft

My father carries me on his back
my runny nose pressed against his cheek
as I whisper secrets I would tell only him;
his response, that silly, shy smile
In this snapshot, time stops to lie
as if smiles were ever that bright
or my pinafore so starched and pressed,
its ruffle airy.
Now he follows me, just beyond reach,
just at the corner of my eye, a shade
with no outline. If I look quickly,
if I try to catch him, he fades
as if by seeing I would return him
to the shadows he escaped to
twenty years past. Instead,
he whispers snatches of poetry,
stories he wants told, songs he never wrote
but thinks I can.

Poet's Commentary

I gathered together scraps of lines and images which I had collected, and formed the bare outlines of the poem. At this stage, I ignore such valid concerns as emphatic line breaks or finding the exact word, searching instead for what I am trying to say. Often the meaning of a poem comes clear only in the process of writing.

In this draft, the first eight lines suggest that our memories—our "snapshots"—blot out troublesome elements of the past. The rest of the poem looks at the source of inspiration—my father.

Martha's first draft here is her prewriting. She ignores line breaks or other surface concerns to get directly at the meaning. In your brainstorming or freewriting for poetry, perhaps even in your first draft, you just want to get started, to get something quickly down on paper on which to build later. So far there are two parts to the poem—the "snapshot" in lines 1–8 and her thinking of her father as an inspiration in the rest of the poem.

Drafts 2–4

Muse
My father carries me on his back
my runny nose pressed against his cheek
as I whisper secrets only for him;

Poet's Commentary

The idea of my father as a source of inspiration gave me the title "Muse." But I was not sure what I meant,

his response, that silly, shy grin
In this snapshot, time stops to lie
as if smiles were ever that bright
or my pinafore so starched and pressed,
its airy ruffle nearly over my head.
Now he follows me, just beyond reach
at the corner of my eye, a shade
with no outline. If I look quickly,
if I try to catch him, he fades
as if by seeing I would return him
to shadows he escaped to
twenty years past. Instead,
he whispers snatches of poetry, stories
he wants told, songs he never wrote
but thinks I can.

so in drafts 2, 3, and 4, I
worked only on cosmetic
changes—like line breaks
and word choice. When I
reached an impasse like
that, I go feed the cats, buy
coffee, read the paper,
watch a ball game, or do
anything else other than sit
at my desk trying to
squeeze out ideas. When I
return to the piece, I reread
the drafts to see if I can
recapture the original—
although elusive—impetus
for the poem.

Martha tells us that there were few changes between drafts 1 and 4 and that at this point she felt "blocked" in her writing. When this happens, she does what student writers should do, that is, put away her work and do something else for a while. This option, of course, is available only if you haven't got a pressing deadline. In writing, begin early and allow yourself time.

Drafts 5–7

Poet's Commentary

Muse
My father carries me on his back
my runny nose behind his ear
as I whisper secrets only for him;
his response, that silly, shy grin.
In this snapshot, time stops to lie
as if smiles were ever that bright
or my pinafore so starched and pressed,
its airy ruffle nearly over my head.
Now he follows me, just beyond reach
at the corner of my eye, a shade
with no outline. Through him, I
watch lambent streetlights
melt snow off their metal caps,
water dripping, then freezing
into fringe at night. A classic
northeaster hugs the seaboard.
Tidal Basin greys into anonymity,
ground too warm to hold late season
snow. If I look quickly, if I try
to catch him, he fades as if
by seeing I would return him
to shadows he escaped to
twenty years past. Instead, he

In drafts 5 through 7, I
linked references to my
father with natural
change—the weather.
Storms roar along the
Eastern seaboard where
I grew up and cause
much damage that people
simply come to expect. By
blending these disparate
images, I show that
memories of my father
provide a sense of home, a
rootedness in the face of
inevitable change. Thus,
he becomes the muse by
becoming the source of
poetry itself, the poetic
past, rich in material.
 Someone once said
that a poem is never
finished, merely abandoned.
The changes in this poem
represent an attempt to

continued

continued

Drafts 5–7	Poet's Commentary
recites snatches of poetry, stories he once told, songs he never wrote but thinks I could.	clarify the action of the central figure, my father as muse. Changing "whispers" to "recites" more fully defines the way he told the poetry, not as a mere utterance but as a declamation. By changing "wants" to "once," I show the muse to act less by his volition than by his very being. He does what he does because he must, not because he wants to. At this point, I abandon the poem.

Having studied the evolution of Martha's poem and her commentary on its development, we as student writers can learn several important things about our own process of writing. First, think about the hard work Martha put in—not only the seven drafts that we see but also the time she spent turning the words, phrases, and ideas around in her head. It is impossible to give you a full understanding of what a poet goes through, but Martha gives you an approximation, a peek at some of the more conscious elements of her process of writing and revising.

In Martha's commentary, note that she is not always sure where she is heading—until it comes out in the writing. Writing is an act of discovery, but you can get there only by writing, not merely by thinking about writing. She also explains in her commentary how the idea about her father as a source of inspiration led her to the title of the poem. Titles give student writers a central focus, a point of reference to work around. Martha reveals to us that her "Muse" is not only her father, but her own roots and the ideas and feelings they generate.

CHAPTER

—— **16** ——

Special Writing Tasks: Content Essay Exams and Exit Essay (Competency) Exams

CONTENT ESSAY EXAMS

Different writing situations call for different writing strategies. For the essay exam in a content class like biology, literature, or history, look over every question before you start, allowing some time for prewriting and proofreading. If you are given a choice of questions, choose quickly and don't look back. Do the questions you are sure of first, saving the more difficult ones for later.

Analyze the words in each question carefully. Does the question call for you to *discuss* (write about), *evaluate* (make a judgment), *enumerate* (make a list and explain), *explain* (to make clear) or, *compare*? Once you have analyzed what the question calls for, do some prewriting—a brainstorming list is probably the most useful in essay exams—on some scratch paper, the back of the answer sheet, or the back of the question sheet. Then do your writing with your prewriting list as a guide.

In essay questions it is important for you to get as much basic information down as possible right away, leaving details for later. *Take the essay question and turn it into a statement for your first sentence:*

1. What physical problems are caused by the use of steroids?

> The physical damage from steroids can be wide-ranging: heart problems, kidney failure, and even severe emotional problems.

2. What is the basic philosophy underlying Huxley's *Brave New World*.

> The basic philosophy of *Brave New World* is to preserve surface order in society at all costs, even by denying opportunity for further acquiring knowledge and sedating the population with drugs.

Teachers pressed for time may scan your paper quickly, so impress them immediately. Also, leave a few lines blank at the end of each answer so you can write more if you have extra time at the end of the exam.

Below are sample essay exam questions and answers from biology, literature, and history. As you read, notice how the answers give the content information first, reserving details for later.

1. *Biology.* What is genetic engineering?

> Genetic engineering means that scientists may be able to alter the gene code of future human beings, preserving only those characteristics judged as important and eliminating others. By removing from or adding to the human DNA structure, scientists can program people for the future. The hope is that science will be able to eradicate from our genes traits like disposition to cancer or other diseases. For example, scientists know that the gene for Huntington's disease, which causes madness in people of middle age and is hereditary, exists somewhere on the fourth chromosome. In the future, they hope to remove this gene from people.
>
> There is also danger in genetic engineering. Scientists have no idea what virus could be loosed into the atmosphere if an experiment goes wrong or what harm could be done to a human if a mistake is made in working with the DNA.

2. *Literature.* What is the theme of Golding's *Lord of the Flies*?

> The theme of the novel *Lord of the Flies* is that man is basically evil and needs the structures of society to keep him from reverting to savagery. When the boys have no adults to guide them, their real nature is exposed. They torture and kill each other and eventually destroy even their island home.
>
> Without adult supervision—parents, teachers, policemen—the boys in the novel kill Simon and Piggy, and try to kill Ralph. But they are only a reflection of the outside world, engaged in a nuclear war. At the end of the story, the boys still alive are rescued by the commander of a destroyer, himself out hunting other prey.

3. *History.* What were some of the results of the Vietnam War?

> For Vietnam the results of the war were control by the Viet Cong and the terrible loss of lives and considerable damage done to the environment from bombing and defoliants. For the U.S., the results of the war were a decline in morale and a new wariness about our government's involvement in foreign affairs.
>
> The Viet Cong regime rules Vietnam dictatorially, allowing very few personal liberties. Former U.S. sympathizers have been brutally punished,

causing desperate Vietnamese to flee the country as "boat people." Back home in the U.S., returning soldiers were not treated as the heroes of our previous wars. Because the war was seen as unjust and unwise, those who fought and suffered in it were treated with apathy or even hostility. Having barely survived the war itself, the soldiers found themselves fighting a new battle for self-respect at home.

EXIT ESSAY (COMPETENCY) EXAMS

Some college systems require students to take exit essay or competency tests for placement and for advancement to higher levels of English. All students take the same exam, which often gives two choices of topics. Because the exam demands *competency*, not perfection, you know that you can make mistakes and still pass the exam. The exams are usually graded by two or more different teachers, and your name is covered up, so that no reader knows whose paper it is.

This type of test requires a different approach from the content essay test, where course material is emphasized, and from your more emotional personal writing. The writing called for in the exit exam is more objective, and it helps to have a system of answering the exit essay question that can be used for almost any topic.

Because the exit essay is often a timed test, there is pressure on you to make your choice of topics and to get started right away. Choose your topic quickly and stay with your choice. But you should still use the writing process you have been taught. Begin with ten minutes of brainstorming, free writing, clustering, mapping, or outlining, and reserve the final few minutes for proofreading the finished paper. If you are worried about neatness (which does influence readers), do your prewriting on the back of the answer or the question sheet. It's in your favor, however, for your reader to see your prewriting because it proves you know and can use the writing process.

In responding to any exit essay question, try to use the following built-in system to organize your thoughts:

1. Think of the first paragraph as an introduction to the paper, in which you rephrase the question and end with your thesis.

2. In the middle paragraph, the body of your paper, develop the points that support your thesis, usually one main idea for each paragraph. Your strongest idea should be placed in the final middle paragraph. Each main or supporting idea is stated in the first sentence of each paragraph as the topic sentence. This is where your prewriting—especially a brainstorming list, or outline if you have time to write one—can be very helpful, each point or idea listed in order for you as you write your final draft. Also, use clear transitions, such as "first," "second," "another reason," and "finally" to help guide the reader.

3. In your final paragraph, the conclusion, repeat the thesis (you may wish to rephrase it) and summarize your ideas in the same order as in your

middle paragraphs. As you write this copy, think of it as the final copy, in which you can correct any errors simply by drawing a line through them because you may not have enough time to rewrite the whole paper.

Writing Practice

Below is a sample exit essay question. Do your prewriting, writing, and proofreading before looking at the following sample student answer.

Directions

You have fifty minutes to write an essay on the topic assigned below. Allow yourself time for planning, writing, and proofreading. Be as clear as you can in your essay. Remember also that correct sentence structure and grammar usage count toward your grade.

> It seems disastrous to me that kids waste so much time watching television. Our youth would be more serious about life, more intelligent, and better prepared for the future if TV were banned for everyone below 21.

Do you think this opinion is correct or not? Write your own views on this topic, using examples or supporting reasons.

[Beware of "either/or" questions which tempt you to take one extreme position or the other. In the question above, a compromise view of your own may make more sense than either extreme. If that is the case, explain the reasons for each position, and then choose for yourself a sensible middle view.]

Sample Student Paper

Prewriting.

15,000 hours of watching TV by high-school age
good shows—*Sesame Street, Electric Company, The Wonder Years, National Geographic Specials*
violence on TV—*Miami Vice,* Clint Eastwood and Rambo movies, even Saturday-morning cartoons like *Masters of the Universe*
TV used as babysitter for "latchkey" kids
time could be spent reading or playing outside
can kids tell fantasy from reality?
illiteracy
commercials show products many kids can't afford

Outline.

Thesis—Although some TV programs are valuable for adults, most TV for kids is a waste of time.
Reason 1. TV is used by many parents as a babysitter.
Reason 2. The enormous amount of violence on TV makes it hard for kids to distinguish fantasy from reality.

Reason 3. The 15,000 hours of TV watching a kid does by high school robs him or her of time that could be spent reading, studying, or playing sports.

Essay.

```
                Television: Drug for Kids


     TV has had an enormous impact on American life. For exam-
ple, news of political upheavals and disasters has been
brought to us within minutes, such as the assassinations of
our leaders like Kennedy and King and the impeachment of
President Nixon. For young kids, however, TV is largely a
waste of time.
     First, many parents use TV as an electronic babysitter
for ''latchkey'' kids and others. While both parents work,
the child is left with TV as his or her parent. And rather
than spend time reading and studying with their children,
many parents plug the kids into TV for doses of Miami Vice or
L. A. Law, not to mention the pornography on some cable sys-
tems. For every hour of worthwhile TV, like Sesame Street
and Electric Company for little kids and National Geographic
Specials for the older ones, kids sit dazed watching hours
of junk.
     Also, the large amount of violence on TV has made it dif-
ficult for kids to distinguish fantasy from reality. The
body count on one show of Miami Vice often numbers more than
a dozen. Even the Saturday cartoons such as Masters of the
Universe have become filled with murder and violence. The
VCR does its damage, too, with tapes of Clint Eastwood,
Rambo, and others.
     A final problem with TV for kids is that the 15,000 hours
they watch by high-school age could have been better used.
Instead of reading books, doing their homework, and studying,
kids spend all those hours stuck on the TV. These kids could
be improving themselves physically and socially by playing
outside in sports or in other healthy activities. Watching
TV should be severely restricted for everyone under 18.
     Watching TV should not be a major pastime for kids. Par-
ents abuse TV by making TV babysit their children. Also, the
violence on TV gives children an unreal sense of the world.
Finally, TV steals from kids' time for reading, studying, and
playing. Let's wipe out the couch potato syndrome by se-
verely curtailing kids' time in front of the tube.
```

CHAPTER
— 17 —

Business Writing: The Application and the Resume

Some of the most important writing you ever do may be a letter of application for a job and a resume. In this kind of writing, you want to present yourself in the best possible light: you want to be neat, courteous, and forceful. This chapter helps you to prepare good letters of application and resumes.

THE APPLICATION

When you apply for a job, your application letter and your resume *stand for you*. Few prospective employers will even grant you an interview unless they are first impressed by your application and resume.

Your application letter, sometimes called a "cover letter," usually accompanies your resume. Employers will usually hire only those applicants who write excellent letters and resumes. Here is a good sample letter of application:

(Date of letter)
June 19, 1989

(Inside address—person to whom letter is sent)
Mr. James Trabert
Director of Personnel
IBM Company
820 North Michigan Avenue
New York, NY 10023

(Greeting followed by colon)
Dear Mr. Trabert:

(The first paragraph tells why you are writing)
I am applying for the position of computer programmer advertised in the New York Times. I have been interested in IBM since I started my college studies, and I feel I have the qualifications and experience necessary for the job.

(The second paragraph gives highlights of your resume.)
As you can see from my resume, I graduated with honors from Iona College with a B.S. in Computer Science. In addition to my academic record, I received favorable reviews of my part-time work as computer programmer at Kodak Corporation.

(The third paragraph requests an interview.)
Enclosed please find my resume. May I have an interview with you at your earliest convenience?

(Closing—leave space for signature.)
Sincerely,

John B. Costello

John B. Costello

Notice that the letter is clear, short, and business-like. Also, there are no abbreviations in such a formal letter, except for the Post Office designations of states, like NY and IL. Because the appearance of a letter is important, leave lots of space between each part.

Although the basic form of the application letter can remain the same, the inside address will, of course, change every time you write to a new prospective employer. The resume, however, should be updated at least every few years when you have acquired more training and experience.

Checklist for the Letter of Application

1. Do I have the date in the upper right-hand corner?

2. On the left-hand side, do I have the full name, title, and address of the person to whom I am writing? (*Never send a letter without knowing the correct spelling of the person's name.*)

3. Do I have the greeting followed by a colon? (*If you are writing to a woman, use "Ms." if you don't know her marital status.*)

4. Does paragraph 1 tell *why* I am writing?

5. Does paragraph 2 give the main points of my resume?

6. Does paragraph 3 politely request an interview at the convenience of the prospective employer?

7. Do I have a closing which allows space for my signature?

8. Is my letter properly spaced, leaving a lot of space between sections?

THE RESUME

There are different formats for the resume, particularly as you get older and receive more education and job experience. Some formats emphasize your schooling or job record, whichever is stronger.

Try to keep your resume to one page for quicker reading, and include references with complete addresses and telephone numbers—listing them makes less work for the potential employer. One simple warning here: always check with people before you use them as references. Ask your reference if he or she would assume that task and if he or she would give you a favorable recommendation. An unfavorable letter of recommendation could sabotage you for years. Never use people about whom you are doubtful.

This sample resume follows a clear format:

(*Personal data centered at top.*)
John B. Costello
1113 Marine Drive
Brooklyn, NY 12871
(201) 738-9871

(*List schooling, beginning with most recent and working backwards.*)
Education
1989 B.S. Computer Science, with Honors, Iona College
1985 Graduated with Honors, Brooklyn High School

(Give a brief job history, again starting with the present and going backwards in time.)
```
Employment
1986-1988 Computer programmer, Kodak Corporation,
Brooklyn, NY
1985-1986 Cashier, Bank of Brooklyn
```

(Give full business address and phone number of at least three references, preferably a mix of college teachers and work supervisors.)
```
References
Dr. John Ablan, Professor of Computer Engineering, Iona
College, 715 North Avenue, New Rochelle, NY 10801
Phone (202) 238-1120

John Meyer, Director of Computer Programming, Kodak
Corporation, 201 West Furillo, Brooklyn, NY (10023)
Phone (201) 779-4738

Ursula Jones, Director of Personnel, Kodak Corporation,
201 West Furillo, Brooklyn, NY (10023)
Phone (201) 779-4756
```

Checklist for Resume

1. Do I have my personal information centered at the top?
2. Is my education listed in reverse chronological order, listing any honors or special awards?
3. Is my job history also listed in reverse chronological order, and do I include titles or brief job descriptions?
4. Do I list references from my employment and schooling, giving full names, titles, addresses, and phone numbers?

Copyrights and Acknowledgments

INDEX